"*Agent-Based Modelling for Criminological Theory Testing and Development* allows insights into social problems that are not possible using conventional methodologies. This volume brings together some of the best criminological minds working on agent-based modelling right now. As such, this manuscript is destined to help shape the field for years to come."

–Prof. Michael Townsley, Head of School of Criminology and Criminal Justice, Griffith University

"*Agent-Based Modelling for Criminological Theory Testing and Development* is a powerful tool and framework for testing and developing criminological theories. This book covers the simulation of crime patterns and the roles of different agents that influence crime patterns, contributed by the leading scholars in the field of crime simulation. It is a must-read for students, scholars and professionals who are interested in the formulation and what-if analysis of criminological theories."

–Prof. Lin Liu, Department of Geography, University of Cincinnati

Agent-Based Modelling for Criminological Theory Testing and Development

Agent-Based Modelling for Criminological Theory Testing and Development addresses the question whether and how we can use simulation methods in order to test criminological theories, and if they fail to be corroborated, how we can use simulation to mend and further develop theories.

It is by no means immediately obvious how results being observed in an artificial environment have any relevance for what is going on in the real world. By using the concept of a "stylized fact," the contributors bridge the gap between artificial and real world. With backgrounds in criminology or artificial intelligence (AI), these contributors present agent-based model studies that test aspects of various theories, including crime pattern theory, guardianship in action theory, near repeat theory, routine activity theory, and general deterrence theory. All six simulation models presented have been specially developed for the book. Contributors have specified the theory, identified stylized facts, developed an agent-based simulation model, let it run, and interpreted whether the chosen stylized fact is occurring in their model, and what we should conclude from congruence or incongruence between simulation and expectations based on the theory under scrutiny. The final chapter discusses what can be learnt from these six enterprises.

The book will be of great interest to scholars of criminology (in particular, computational criminologists and theoretical criminologists) and AI (with an emphasis on AI for generative social processes), and more widely researchers in social science in general. It will also be valuable for master's courses in quantitative criminology.

Charlotte Gerritsen is an assistant professor at VU University Amsterdam, Department of Computer Science.

Henk Elffers is a senior researcher at the Netherlands Institute for the Study of Crime and Law Enforcement (NSCR) Amsterdam, and professor emeritus at the Department of Criminal Law and Criminology, VU University Amsterdam.

Crime Science Series

Crime science is a new way of thinking about and responding to the problem of crime in society. The distinctive nature of crime science is captured in the name.

First, crime science is about crime. Instead of the usual focus in criminology on the characteristics of the criminal offender, crime science is concerned with the characteristics of the criminal event. The analysis shifts from the distant causes of criminality – biological makeup, upbringing, social disadvantage, and the like – to the near causes of crime. Crime scientists are interested in why, where, when, and how particular crimes occur. They examine trends and patterns in crime in order to devise immediate and practical strategies to disrupt these patterns.

Second, crime science is about science. Many traditional responses to crime control are unsystematic, reactive, and populist, too often based on untested assumptions about what works. In contrast crime science advocates an evidence-based, problem-solving approach to crime control. Adopting the scientific method, crime scientists collect data on crime, generate hypotheses about observed crime trends, devise interventions to respond to crime problems, and test the adequacy of those interventions.

Crime science is utilitarian in its orientation and multidisciplinary in its foundations. Crime scientists actively engage with front-line criminal justice practitioners to reduce crime by making it more difficult for individuals to offend, and making it more likely that they will be detected if they do offend. To achieve these objectives, crime science draws on disciplines from both the social and physical sciences, including criminology, sociology, psychology, geography, economics, architecture, industrial design, epidemiology, computer science, mathematics, engineering, and biology.

Edited by Richard Wortley, UCL

Agent-Based Modelling for Criminological Theory Testing and Development
Edited by Charlotte Gerritsen and Henk Elffers

For more information about this series, please visit: https://www.routledge.com/criminology/series/CSCIS

Agent-Based Modelling for Criminological Theory Testing and Development

Edited by Charlotte Gerritsen
and Henk Elffers

LONDON AND NEW YORK

First published 2021
by Routledge
2 Park Square, Milton Park, Abingdon, Oxon OX14 4RN

and by Routledge
52 Vanderbilt Avenue, New York, NY 10017

Routledge is an imprint of the Taylor & Francis Group, an informa business

© 2021 selection and editorial matter, Charlotte Gerritsen and
Henk Elffers; individual chapters, the contributors

The right of Charlotte Gerritsen and Henk Elffers to be identified
as the authors of the editorial material, and of the authors for their
individual chapters, has been asserted by them in accordance with sections
77 and 78 of the Copyright, Designs and Patents Act 1988.

All rights reserved. No part of this book may be reprinted or reproduced or utilised
in any form or by any electronic, mechanical, or other means, now known or
hereafter invented, including photocopying and recording, or in any information
storage or retrieval system, without permission in writing from the publishers.

Trademark notice: Product or corporate names may be trademarks or registered trademarks,
and are used only for identification and explanation without intent to infringe.

British Library Cataloguing-in-Publication Data
A catalogue record for this book is available from the British Library

Library of Congress Cataloging-in-Publication Data
A catalog record has been requested for this book

ISBN: 978-0-367-22852-1 (hbk)
ISBN: 978-0-367-52407-4 (pbk)
ISBN: 978-0-429-27717-7 (ebk)

Typeset in Times New Roman
by Newgen Publishing UK

Contents

List of contributors ix
Acknowledgments xii

1 Agent-based modeling for criminological theory testing and development 1
CHARLOTTE GERRITSEN AND HENK ELFFERS

2 Generating crime generators 13
TOBY DAVIES AND DANIEL BIRKS

3 Using agent-based models to investigate the presence of edge effects around crime generators and attractors 45
VERITY TETHER, NICK MALLESON, WOUTER STEENBEEK, AND DANIEL BIRKS

4 Examining guardianship against theft 71
ELIZABETH R. GROFF AND JENNIFER BADHAM

5 A simulation study into the generation of near repeat victimizations 104
WOUTER STEENBEEK AND HENK ELFFERS

6 Creating a temporal pattern for street robberies using ABM and data from a small city in South East Brazil 146
ERIC ARAÚJO AND CHARLOTTE GERRITSEN

7 Corruption and the shadow of the future: a generalization of an ABM with repeated interactions 167
NICK VAN DOORMAAL, STIJN RUITER, AND ANDREW M. LEMIEUX

8 Agent-based modeling for testing and developing theories: what did we learn? 187
HENK ELFFERS, CHARLOTTE GERRITSEN, AND DANIEL BIRKS

Index 197

Full program codes available

Full program codes of all agent-based models used in this book as well as some supplementary files are available through the following link: https://osf.io/5vhks/

Contributors

Eric Araújo holds an adjunct professor position and is head of the Behavioural Informatics Laboratory (BILbo) at the Federal University of Lavras, Brazil. Araújo also holds a PhD with the thesis title of "Contagious: Modeling the spread of behaviours, perceptions and emotions in social networks." His research involves using agent-based modeling to address topics such as social contagion in networks, crime prevention for public safety, and cognitive models for panic and emergency situations.

Jennifer Badham is a visiting researcher with the Centre for Research in Social Simulation at the University of Surrey, UK. Dr. Badham's research uses computational methods to understand the ways in which individual behavior, social structure, and social phenomena mutually influence and constrain each other. Other research interests include models and the modeling process as tools for interdisciplinary communication and engagement in social policy.

Daniel Birks is associate professor of Quantitative Policing and Crime Data Analytics ay the School of Law, University of Leeds, UK, and a turing fellow at the Alan Turing Institute, the UK's National Institute for Data Science and artificial intelligence. He holds degrees in artificial intelligence, computer science, cognitive science, and criminology. His research interests are broadly based in the fields of environmental criminology, crime analysis, and computational methods.

Toby Davies is a lecturer in the Department of Security and Crime Science at University College London (UCL), UK. His background is in mathematics, and his research is concerned with the application of quantitative methods to the modeling and analysis of crime. He has particular interest in the spatiotemporal characteristics of crime, and the modeling of these towards the end goal of crime prediction. In addition, his research involves the application of network science in the context of crime, particularly in relation to the role of urban form in shaping patterns of crime.

Nick van Doormaal, MSc, is a PhD candidate at the Netherlands Institute for the Study of Crime and Law Enforcement (NSCR) and at the Department of Sociology of Utrecht University. His PhD research focuses on wildlife crime, site security, and law enforcement operations in protected areas.

Henk Elffers is a senior researcher at the Netherlands Institute for the Study of Crime and Law Enforcement (NSCR) Amsterdam, and professor emeritus at the Department of Criminal Law and Criminology, VU University Amsterdam. He is interested in a rational choice approach to criminal decision making in a spatial context.

Charlotte Gerritsen is an assistant professor at VU University Amsterdam, Department of Computer Science. Her research is located at the intersection of artificial intelligence and the social sciences. She aims to enrich agent-based models with knowledge of human behavior (with an emphasis on deviant behavior) in order to make these models more realistic. This allows her to use these models to understand, prevent, and predict (deviant) behavior.

Elizabeth R. Groff is a professor in the Department of Criminal Justice at Temple University, Philadelphia, PA, USA, where she is also associated faculty in the Center for Security and Crime Science. Dr. Groff applies theory and various methodologies (geographic, experimental, and agent-based modeling) to the study of crime-related issues. She also emphasizes evidence creation to improve police practice. Her recent research has examined the impacts of changes in crime policy and police practice on prosecution. Other research interests include geographic criminology, police practices, and the use of technology in policing. She is a fellow of the Academy of Experimental Criminology.

Andrew M. Lemieux is a researcher at the Netherlands Institute for the Study of Crime and Law Enforcement (NSCR). His work revolves around the collection and use of data for wildlife protection, with an emphasis on problem solving and situational crime prevention.

Nick Malleson is a professor of Spatial Science at the University of Leeds, UK. He has a PhD in geography and undergraduate degrees in computer science (BSc) and multidisciplinary informatics (MSc). Most of his research focuses on the development of agent-based models aimed at understanding and explaining social phenomena. He has particular interests in simulations of crime patterns, in models that can be used to describe the flows of people around cities, and in how "big data," agent-based modeling, and smart-cities initiatives can be used to better understand the daily dynamics of cities and reduce the impacts of phenomena such as pollution or crime.

Stijn Ruiter, PhD, is a senior researcher at the Netherlands Institute for the Study of Crime and Law Enforcement (NSCR) and professor at the Department of Sociology of Utrecht University. His main research interests include the study of spatiotemporal patterns in crime and offender decision making in both offline and online environments.

Wouter Steenbeek is a senior researcher at the Netherlands Institute for the Study of Crime and Law Enforcement (NSCR). Most of his research focuses on spatiotemporal crime patterns and explaining these patterns as a function of the characteristics of places and how offenders, targets, and guardians use their spatial environment over daily and weekly time cycles. Other research interests include neighborhood processes of disorder and crime and quantitative methods.

Verity Tether is a postgraduate researcher at the University of Leeds, UK, based in Leeds Institute for Data Analytics. She has a background in geography, and her PhD research examines geographic patterns of crime around facilities, specifically focusing on traditional crime generators and crime attractors.

Acknowledgments

For the preparation of this book, all authors have participated in two dedicated workshops in Oud-Poelgeest, Oegstgeest, the Netherlands, in 2018 and 2019. We are grateful to the Netherlands Institute for the Study of Crime and Law Enforcement (NSCR), Amsterdam, and to the Department of Artificial Intelligence, VU University Amsterdam, for their financial support to these workshops.

We would like to thank all contributors to this volume for the fruitful discussions during, between, and after those workshops, mutually helping us all in developing initial research ideas into chapters fulfilling the requirements set by the group as a whole. Next to that, we are grateful for their assistance in the peer review process of the chapters.

We would also like to thank the external reviewers, whose blind reviews have helped the authors to improve their chapters, in order to reach scientific excellence: Martin Andresen, Vasco Furtado, Nicola Lettieri, Martin Neumann, Amy Thornton, and an anonymous reviewer. Thank you!

1 Agent-based modeling for criminological theory testing and development

Charlotte Gerritsen and Henk Elffers

Introduction

Within the field of criminology, research is typically conducted using well-established methods. Information is gathered by extracting insights from existing law enforcement data, conducting field research and interviews, through the use of vignette studies, or by performing controlled experiments. The outcomes of this research are most often analyzed manually or by the use of statistical methods. While these types of research have all proven successful, they do not cover the entire field of possibilities. What if data sets become too large to study by hand? Or if the number of relevant concepts increases and the possible interactions grow beyond limits? Such data cannot be analyzed in the traditional manner. While the experimental method is a crafty approach for research, sometimes real-life experiments are impossible; for instance, in cases where we would like to experiment with alternatives to the present legal system of law enforcement. It is not possible to treat people in a way that the law prohibits, but it would be very useful to explore what the results of such alternative measures, now contra legem, would be. This is where innovative research methods come into play. New methods are being developed every day with an emphasis on computational data science analysis.

One research method that can extend the possibilities of the current spectrum of research is called *agent-based modeling* (ABM). This method, which is often used to perform dynamical social simulations, can be used to test what implications certain strategies with respect to crime might have before these strategies actually become part of daily practice (Brantingham & Brantingham, 2004; Gerritsen & Klein, 2014; Gerritsen, 2015; Gerritsen & Elffers, 2016). As well as testing informal theories in a formal manner, ABM may also be used to make predictions. In the next section we will go into the method of ABM in more depth.

Agent-based modeling

ABM is a computational method that enables the user to create, analyze, and experiment with models composed of *agents* (for a detailed explanation of the modeling and simulation cycle, see Gerritsen, 2015). Here, agents are autonomous entities that interact with each other and with their environment in some artificial simulated world (Gilbert, 2008). A model is a representation of an object, system, or idea other than that of the entity itself, according to Shannon (1975). In a model the most important concepts of the relevant real-world system are described, as well as the relationships between them. The subject of the model may be very complex and often not all concepts or relationships between the concepts are fully known. This means that it is usually not possible to describe all aspects and relations completely and unambiguously. Hence, a model is typically a simplification of reality and is not presumed to be a complete representation. When drawing conclusions based on the model it is important to realize that the model is the outcome of some assumptions and decisions made by the developer. So it might not represent reality as you know it.

Once a model has been developed one thing to do with it is to imitate the dynamics of a process over time, which is called *simulation*. Doing so, a simulation model helps to clarify the interaction between different aspects in order to accurately study a model. The output of the simulation model can be evaluated by comparing it to real-world situations. If there is a mismatch then something is wrong, either with the model or with the underlying theory.

Constructing a model of a real-world process has a number of advantages. First of all, it can be less expensive, less time consuming, and more feasible to perform experiments using a model than in the real world. Besides that there are some more profound advantages. Using a model makes it possible to study a process that cannot be studied directly – for example, processes that occur inside the human brain, e.g., cognitive processes. Although a lot is known about cognitive processes, it is not always trivial to get insight into mechanisms that are going on. Another example is when a researcher wants to study processes that occur over long time periods, so long that repeated observations are difficult or impossible.

Models also have great potential when you want to study a process that does not yet exist in real life. An example is the impact of installing safety measures in a public location. To determine where and how much equipment needs to be installed it is useful to test the effect in advance by using hypothetical situations.

In these examples the researcher may get more insight into the process under investigation although the model may not be identical to the real-world process.

Agent-based modeling in criminological research

A nice introduction of the use of ABM in environmental criminology has been given in Birks (2018). Reasons for building agent-based models may differ, from practical predictions to theory development. When focusing on practical predictions, authors want to relate real-world data directly to their simulation model, for example for studying crime displacement in existing cities (e.g. Liu et al., 2005), with a goal to make actual predictions, e.g., on how the crime pattern would change if a certain bridge was closed for traffic. Theory-oriented scientists may deliberately abstract from empirical information, and use their simulation environment as an analytical tool for researching the consequences of theoretical assumptions, within a given or newly proposed theory (e.g., Bosse & Gerritsen, 2008). In this second perspective, researchers and policy makers use simulations as formalized thought experiments, to shed more light on the process under investigation. In this line of thinking, simulation is used as a method for investigating the structure of a theory, though it is of course possible, and to be hoped for, that the resulting insights may, sooner or later, be helpful in developing and improving existing policies (e.g., for surveillance) (Elffers & Van Baal, 2008). Some authors take an intermediate position (e.g. Bosse et al., 2010; Malleson & Brantingham, 2009) in which they initially build their simulation model to study the structure of a phenomenon, but they define their basic concepts in such a way that it can be connected to empirical information, if that becomes available.

So while more and more researchers within the criminological domain find their way to the use of ABM, with lots of beautiful research as a result (e.g., Birks, 2017; Groff et al., 2018; Liu & Eck, 2008; Malleson & Evans, 2013), ABM is currently mainly used for applied research. The field of testing and developing theories is still highly underdeveloped, with only a few publications illustrating the potential (e.g. Birks et al., 2012; Birks & Elffers, 2014). In the present volume all authors focus on this niche, highlighting the use of ABM for criminological theory testing and theory development.

In the next sections we will first discuss theory testing, and then enlarge the field towards theory development.

Criminological theory testing

How exactly can ABM help theory testing? Within empirical sciences the standard way of theory testing is the empirical cycle:

1. *Formulate a theory* covering a certain field.
2. *Derive expectations* from that theory: if the theory holds, what will be the case in such-and-such circumstances?
3. *Design* and *execute* a study that *observes* what is actually occurring in the specified circumstances.
4. *Compare* the observations with the expectations. If they are congruent, the theory is *corroborated*; if they are incompatible, the theory is *rejected*.
5. Then:
    a. If a theory is corroborated, we can always go back to *step 2* in order to test the theory *again* in a *different* set of circumstances.
    b. If a theory has been *rejected*, we have to go back to *step 1* in the cycle, and formulate an *adapted* version of the theory, or indeed replace

the original one with a completely *new* one. With the adapted or new theory we can go through the cycle again.

We like to stress that, in a strict sense, theory testing comprises the first four steps of the cycle. Step 5a is in fact testing the same theory all over again, which presumably is most fruitful by deriving expectations in step 2 for a different set of circumstances. Step 5b, however, may be seen as theory development, informed by the results of a test performed in steps 1–4.

Deriving expectations

Deriving expectations from a theory is not always easy, due to the complexity of the theory and the complexity of the "circumstances" in which the results of that theory are expected to materialize.

ABM is useful when the complexity of theoretically founded expectations defies our analytical shrewdness. This is often the case when the theory is formulated on the level of actions of individual agents, while these actions are governed by the state of the world in its totality (i.e., the combination of the states of all other agents), which then is the aggregated result of all actions, aggregated over all agents. It is exactly this aggregation over sometimes many interacting agents that constitutes the complexity of the enterprise.

Let us present an example: imagine a criminal decision-making theory (within the routine activity paradigm) that claims: *potential offenders aim to victimize only attractive targets and do so only when they will not be seen by passers-by (guardians)*.

Following the empirical cycle discussed above, let us try to derive expectations from that theory, in the special case of offenders aiming at home burglary. We try to establish what spatial distribution of burglaries we may expect according to the theory. First of all, we have to be more explicit on the content of the theory, in order to make progress (*specification of formulated theory*). In its present form, it is too gross to be able to derive what actions offenders take and how they exactly react to guardians. (Notice that such specification of a formulated theory is just as necessary when we try to test the theory by methods other than by ABM.) In our example, a possible specification of the theory may be as follows. Imagine a prospective burglar walking down a street, looking for an opportunity to burgle an attractive target; if the target he meets is not surpassing a minimum attraction threshold, he moves on to the next possible target, but as soon as he finds a target that surpasses a minimal threshold of attraction value, he looks around to check whether somebody might see him. If he perceives somebody in that street closer than a given distance, he decides not to burgle the given attractive house, as he is afraid of being seen by such a guardian. If, however, there is no guardian available within the given distance, he continues and burgles the selected target. We then need to be more explicit on the whereabouts of the guardians, e.g., like this: let people pass through the streets at a given pace, starting at arbitrary points, and at each crossroad taking an arbitrary direction.

Though the original theory was rather simple, the still rather straightforward specification makes the situation already pretty complicated; indeed, we think it is already prohibitively difficult to derive what spatial burglary pattern we may expect. That pattern will be dependent on the number of active burglars, how they move through space, their preference for attractive targets, the distribution of attraction values over space, the number of passers-by, their movement patterns, and most complexifying, on the dynamics of how burglars and guardians meet in the presence of attractive targets. We challenge the reader to bring forward an analytical solution to the question of what spatial pattern will be produced by the (specified) theory.

Many theories about human behavior meet the same difficulty, viz. that deriving exact expectations in given circumstances is very hard and often impossible. It is here that ABM simulation comes in handy. In fact, our specification above is already almost enough to construct an agent-based model, with offender agents and guardian agents, moving around on a street network of our choice, where the streets have houses (house agents) of various attraction levels. Indeed, such ABMs, in rather more complex situations, have been published (e.g., Birks & Davies, 2017; Bosse et al., 2010). Running such an ABM will indeed produce a spatial pattern, and given that the ABM has a number of non-deterministic processes on board, repeatedly running the model will provide us with a distribution of expected spatial patterns. Moreover, these results can be parameterized by some of the parameters of the specified theory, such as the minimal attraction level, the distance at which guardians are a threat, the number of offenders and guardians, the pace of guardians, the distribution of attraction values, and so on. All in all, using an ABM is a very powerful approach to deriving expectations from a theory, not analytically but constructively. As a side remark, building an ABM as an expression of a theory is also very helpful in the specification phase: how do we specify how the various agents react in various circumstances? Sometimes the theory is already explicit, but quite often we need to make a choice, which comes down to further specification of a theory. The necessity to be explicit on how agents behave, as a function of the state of other agents, helps in identifying where a theory needs specification.

Observation on what actually occurs in given circumstances

We have argued that ABM methodology can help in mastering the second step of the empirical cycle, producing expectations. Indeed, this is ABM's strong point. But what about the third step, the observation phase, which is constituted by doing an empirical study and producing an empirical realization of the theory? Here we meet the weak point of ABM for theory testing. The observation stage should produce empirical results in the *same circumstances* that were present when the expectations were derived. But circumstances used in ABMs are generally of a highly abstract type, and reality, in which the empirical study can be situated, is not abstract, but real. For example, the study of Bosse et al. (2010), cited above, has an ABM in which burglar agents move over a chessboard, and guardians (police officer agents in this case) too. (This study was not a theory-testing study, but investigated, given routine activity theory, which police surveillance strategies were more or less effective in curbing crime.) We cannot observe "real behavior" of "real burglars" and "real police offers" on a chessboard. They, obviously, live and act in the real world. So, does the whole ABM approach to theory testing then run aground? We may have a fine set of expectations, but if we cannot produce empirical data in the same circumstances, the whole framework of the empirical cycle falls apart. Notice that, likewise, studies not using simulation methods may have problems in finding real-world circumstances that fit to the situation for which the expectations had been derived.

Stylized reality approach

The solution to this awkward situation has been found in the idea of comparing the expectations with what may be called "stylized reality." In many a field in criminology, criminologists have found empirical regularities. Take, as an example, gender differences in criminal involvement. All over the world, for almost all types of crime, it has been observed that a higher proportion of males are involved in such crimes than the corresponding proportion of females. While the exact figures may (and do) differ in various countries and for various crime types, it is an empirical regularity that more men than women are involved in crime. Such a rather sweeping statement is called a *"stylized fact"*; it has "stylized away" the differences between empirical findings in various circumstances, and concentrates on the common characteristics. As an example, if we use ABM for testing a theory on crime involvement, we would demand that expectations generated by ABMs for that theory produce expectations that display a gender gap in involvement too. The logic behind this change in approach is this: ABM shows that such-and-such expectations are the consequences in certain circumstances. We cannot find these exact circumstances in reality, but we can show that in *all* circumstances already investigated, certain regularities, realizations of stylized facts, have been observed. We maintain therefore that in *all* circumstances such stylized facts will occur, hence also in the hypothetical, not researched, real circumstances parallel to those of the ABM, had it been possible to construct such circumstances in reality. Therefore, we interpret (step 4 of the empirical cycle) an eventual absence of the stylized facts in the results produced by the simulation as an argument to reject the theory under scrutiny, while the existence of the stylized facts in the ABM results is counted as a corroboration of the theory. Indeed, the logic is flawed in principle: that a phenomenon has been observed in many cases does not imply that it will occur in all cases. We hope

ABM for theory testing and development 7

nevertheless that the reasoning is powerful enough to support or reject for many instances of theory testing.

Notice that this way of reasoning, which we may call the "*stylized empirical cycle,*" stands or falls with the stature of the stylized facts. If a reader rejects the claim of an author that a given statement about the state of the world deserves the status of a stylized fact, she will by implication not follow that author's claims about rejecting or corroborating the theory under scrutiny.

Therefore, in the context of ABM for theory testing, researchers should be very clear about which stylized facts they have recognized, and argue why they consider that these "facts" deserve the label of stylized facts.

In our previous example of burglars' decision making, most environmental criminologists would list as one of generally recognized stylized facts that hot spots of victimization should emerge.

The null model

Usually, an ABM is built in the form of a number of rules that specify for each agent for each moment in time what action that agent takes, as a function of a whole set of characteristics, both in terms of attributes of that agent itself and in terms of attributes of other agents. In most ABMs nowadays quite a multitude of such rules are built in; that is exactly the strong point of ABMs. In the example above, on burglars targeting houses under scrutiny of guardians, there are rules on how burglar agents determine attraction values of targets, how they make an inventory of guardian agents as close by or far off, rules on how they move after a burglary and after declining an opportunity. There is a rule on how an attraction value changes after a target has been victimized. There are rules on guardians' movements. Moreover there are initial conditions, say on the distribution of attraction values over targets, and threshold values over burglar agents. Let us assume that the ABM produces outcomes (i.e., the expectations derived by simulation from the specified theory) that indeed conform with the stylized facts as had been put forward. We interpret this as support for the theory, but if we are satisfied with such a rather indiscriminate statement, we lose detail. Which of the ABM rules, meant as embodying parts of the theory, are actually responsible for producing the stylized fact-conforming outcomes? And which ones are superfluous? We can investigate that by trying to identify a *null model* that does *not* replicate stylized facts, i.e., we have a variety of the model in which parameters are specified such that we in fact disengage a rule (Birks et al., 2012). In the example, e.g., we can put off the attraction value mechanism by specifying that a burglar agent *always* engages a target agent, irrespective of the latter's attraction value (of course only when no guardian is present). Are stylized facts still reproduced, viz. that hot spots emerge? Then the attraction value mechanism seems not to be necessary, at least not in the given specification of the theory, and when other rules are operating. But if no hot spots emerge any more (although they had indeed been reproduced in the full model), we may interpret such as that differential thresholds for attraction values are necessary, in the given model specification and with other rules operative. By turning various rules on and off, one by one or in sets, we can get a much more detailed picture with respect to a particular stylized fact. It is here that we already touch on the idea of theory development, as we get insight into the finer details of a previously rather gross version of a theory.

We propose that in order for an ABM exercise to contribute to theory testing, it should conform to the following set of demands:

1. A clear criminological theory is specified.
2. A clear ABM mechanism is constructed, and it is shown which components of the theory are reflected in which rules or initial conditions.
3. A clear stylized fact or set of stylized facts is specified, and it is argued that they find ample support in the relevant community of criminologists.
4. In order to derive expectations from the theory through the ABM, a clear plan is specified about under what parameter settings the ABM should run and produce results. Then these results are produced, and an adequate descriptive presentation of them is given.
5. A clear statement is formulated whether or not stylized facts are reproduced by the simulated theoretical expectation.
6. The procedure of turning on and off various rules is executed in order to get insight into which components of the theory are necessary or superfluous.

An ABM study that conforms with these six requirements does indeed deserve the name of an *ABM for criminological theory testing.*

ABM for criminological theory development

It would be an overstatement that all or most criminological research is testing theories. In fact, many published articles have more the characteristics of theory *development*. Authors may already at the outset of the article be convinced that the theory under scrutiny is not good enough for describing what occurs in reality. This may be the case because earlier publications have already pointed out such flaws in the standard theory. In a community of scholars who have great confidence in a theory, this usually does not lead to an immediate outright rejection of that theory. Bruinsma (2016) even maintains that this is, regrettably, almost never the case. Instead, researchers set out to improve the theory, thus rescuing the most important parts of it, while making repairs such that the flaws are mended (Lakatos, 1974). Now ABM methodology is, par excellence, helpful here, as theory development is served through the sixth point above, which we may call "comparative parameter space exploration." By investigating which combination of rules and parameter settings do and do not produce stylized facts, authors get insight into where and how "patches" should be attached to the dearly held theory. After all, exploration of the parameter space (sixth point) is rather more a theory *development* than a theory-*testing* exercise.

In our burglary example above, let us – for the sake of argument – assume that the stylized fact of hot spots is indeed reproduced when burglars' threshold values have a small standard deviation, but does not appear when burglars have a very large spread in threshold values. Researchers may then start to wonder how to understand this, within the context of the given theory, and may – if they are creative enough – suggest an adaptation to the theory that covers these new observations. Of course, they then should reiterate the whole empirical cycle with their newly formulated "improved theory," and put it to the rigorous test as formulated in steps 1–6. Again, exploring the parameter space as is proposed in step 6 is exactly where ABM is extremely useful and helpful, as it is easier to study new parameter settings in a simulated world than in the real world. Perhaps we may say that the two strong points of ABM for theory testing and theory development are its suitability for deriving what to expect in specified circumstances and its capability for exploring what results turn up under various, maybe even unusual, parameter settings.

Summing up, we argue that the simulation approach is a promising methodology for both testing and developing criminological theory, in the vein of the empirical cycle. Whereas the strong point in simulation is its capability for deriving expectations from a given complex theory, its weak point is the comparison of expectations with observed outcomes in the real world. In order to make that possible, we have introduced the concept of stylized facts, empirical regularities found in all or nearly all studies in a given field. Our whole approach is critically dependent on the existence of stylized facts. Can we indeed isolate in a given field such regularities? What do we have to stylize away, i.e., how can we abstract from differences and concentrate on likenesses? Do actual implementations of ABM simulation work indeed verify what we expect: corroborating or rejecting criminological theories? And, if the latter is occurring, can we than use simulation methodology in order to adapt and develop theory? The purpose of our book is to present a number of ABM studies in order to find out whether our hopes that ABMs are indeed fruitful for testing and developing theory are realistic.

What to expect? Outline of the book

After the present introductory Chapter 1, six teams of authors each present an ABM constructed to test and/or develop a criminological theory according to the method outlined above. They produce a number of examples in which ABM proves to be a key method to test and develop criminological theories.

Five chapters look into the movements of offenders and guardians around space. They are addressing claims proposed by crime pattern theory, in a wide sense, crime pattern theory perhaps being the most influential theory about the spatial aspects of offender decision making (Brantingham &

Brantingham, 1993, 2008). One chapter researches corruption between multiple law enforcers.

Chapter 2 (Davies and Birks, "*Generating crime generators*") tests a central part of crime pattern theory, viz. the role of crime generators. The authors construct a general framework of offender agents and guardian agents, all of them moving around their daily business over an abstract street network, with houses that may or may not be targeted by offenders. All agents have a set of personal activity nodes and, moreover, share with others a number of so-called *shared activity nodes*. These shared activity nodes are proposed as a representation of crime generators. The crime they model is interpersonal victimization. Davies and Birks investigate in detail whether and how the number of shared activity nodes, as well as their intensity (i.e., their level of "sharedness") has an impact on the occurrence of interpersonal victimization. Their chapter contributes to our understanding of the concept of a crime generator, and shows that crime generators indeed have a role to play in generating stylized crime patterns, but also points to new developments and issues to be investigated in more depth.

Chapter 3 (Tether, Malleson, Steenbeek, and Birks, "*Using agent-based models to investigate the presence of edge effects around crime generators and attractors*") is also looking into the movements of offender agents in an abstract space, in which "edges" have been constructed between areas where generators were located and areas where this was not the case, and the same for attractors. While the existing crime pattern theory on edge effects suggests that crime would concentrate around edges, the simulation did not produce this at all; in fact crime seemed to shy away from edges. In that sense, crime pattern theory is rejected, and Tether and colleagues, in the vein of theory development, suggest how the theory needs adaptation.

Chapter 4 (Groff and Badham, "*Examining guardianship against theft*") also proposes an ABM with offenders and guardians as agents, who move around, during their routines which vary over the week, among potential targets. Targets have varying attractiveness levels for being victimized. In the tradition of Reynald's theory of "guardianship in action," guardians may be passers-by or may reside inside a possible target. While Groff and Badham's results are, for the greater part, in accordance with theoretical expectations, the authors also outline a number of possibilities to use their ABM for further research into guardianship–offender interaction. In addition, they discuss what light their ABM sheds on the old but unresolved question of whether more people means more crime (due to more possible targets) or less crime (due to more guardians).

Chapter 5 (Steenbeek and Elffers, "*A simulation study into the generation of near repeat victimizations*") addresses the stylized fact of near repeat victimization, the often observed increase of risk for targets around a previous victimization, for some time period. They attempt to sort out three explanations for this phenomenon: changing awareness spaces, boosting of target attractiveness around a victimization, and the occurrence of runs (spates) of crimes. The first one does not generate near repeats, but the second and third do, independently of each other, where the run mechanism seems to be stronger than the boost mechanism.

Chapter 6 (Araújo and Gerritsen, "*Creating a temporal pattern for street robberies using ABM and data from a small city in South East Brazil*") attempts to model street robbery, guided by routine activity theory. Its ABM has offenders and citizens as agents, who move through the city of Lavras, Brazil. Offenders are, in accordance with routine activity theory, fitted out with a motivational strength and, in accordance with crime pattern theory, with an awareness of opportunities. Araújo and Gerritsen look into the temporal distribution of offenses over the hours of the day, comparing the simulated distribution not only with stylized facts but also with real data from the city studied. They show that the simulation corroborates the theories proposed.

Chapter 7 (Van Doormaal, Ruiter, and Lemieux, "*Corruption and the shadow of the future: a generalization of an ABM with repeated interactions*") tests a generalization of Hammond's (agent-based) theory on corruption prevalence and looks into under what conditions a society will switch from a low corruption state into a high corruption state, or vice versa, under a dynamic scheme of repeated interactions between cooperating, possibly corrupt, individuals. They showed that, different from Hammond's one-shot results, a switch did not always occur in a repeated interaction case. On the basis of their results, Van Doormaal and colleagues suggest in which direction theory should be developed.

Many chapters share an interest in testing environmental criminology theories, such as crime pattern theory. In order to make it possible for the reader to study each chapter on its own, all authors give a short introduction to the theoretical concepts in this line of thought.

Computer codes that have produced the results presented in the chapters are available through the following link: https://osf.io/5vhks/. Some authors use NetLogo; others prefer to program their ABMs in R. For many chapters, , the code has been checked by some of the other authors.

In the concluding chapter we sum up our findings and discuss the potential of ABM for criminological theory testing and theory development, as it emerges from the various chapters.

References

Birks, D. (2017). Simulating crime event decision making: agent-based social simulations in criminology. In: W. Bernasco, J.-L. van Gelder, & H. Elffers (eds.), *The Oxford Handbook of Offender Decision Making*. New York: Oxford University Press, pp. 541–566.

Birks, D. (2018). Computer simulations: agent-focused environmental criminology. In: G.J.N. Bruinsma & S.D. Johnson (eds.), *The Oxford Handbook of Environmental Criminology*. New York: Oxford University Press, pp. 311–339.

Birks, D., & Davies, T. (2017). Street network structure and crime risk: an agent-based investigation of the encounter and enclosure hypotheses. *Criminology*, 55(4):900.

Birks, D., & H. Elffers (2014). Agent-based assessments of criminological theory. In: G. Bruinsma & D. Weisburd (eds.), *Encyclopedia of Criminology and Criminal Justice*. New York: Springer, pp. 19–32.

Birks, D., Townsley, M., & Stewart, A. (2012). Generative explanations of crime: using simulation to test criminological theory. *Criminology*, 50(1):221–254.

Bosse, T., & Gerritsen, C. (2008). Agent-based simulation of the spatial dynamics of crime: on the interplay between offenders, hot spots and reputation. *Proceedings of the Seventh International Joint Conference on Autonomous Agents and Multi-Agent Systems* (AAMAS'08), 1129–1136.

Bosse, T., Elffers, H., & Gerritsen, C. (2010). Simulating the dynamical interaction of offenders, targets and guardians. *Crime Patterns and Analysis*, 3(1):51–66.

Brantingham, P.L. & Brantingham, P.J. (1993). Nodes, paths and edges: considerations on the complexity of crime and the physical environment. *Journal of Environmental Psychology*, 13:3–28.

Brantingham, P.L., & Brantingham, P.J. (2004). Computer simulation as a tool for environmental criminologists. *Security Journal*, 17(1):21–30.

Brantingham, P., & Brantingham, P. (2008). Crime pattern theory. In: R. Wortley & L. Mazerolle (eds.), *Environmental Criminology and Crime Analysis, Crime Science*. London: Routledge, pp. 78–93.

Bruinsma, G.J.N. (2016). Proliferation of criminological theories in an era of fragmentation. *European Journal of Criminology*, 13(6):659–676.

Elffers, H., & Van Baal, P. (2008). Realistic spatial backcloth is not that important in agent based simulation research. An illustration from simulating perceptual deterrence. In: L. Liu & J. Eck (eds.), *Artificial Crime Analysis Systems: Using Computer Simulations and Geographic Information Systems*. Hershey, PA: Information Science Reference, pp. 19–34.

Gerritsen, C. (2015). Agent-based modelling as a research tool for criminological research. *Crime Science*, 4:2, DOI 10.1186/s40163-014-0014-1.

Gerritsen, C., & Elffers, H. (2016). Investigating prevention by simulation methods. In: B. LeClerc & E.U. Savona (eds.), *Crime Prevention in the 21st Century*. New York: Springer, pp. 235–244.

Gerritsen, C., & Klein, M. (2014). Dynamical simulation in criminology. In: G. Bruinsma, & D. Weisburd (eds.), *Encyclopedia of Criminology and Criminal Justice*. New York: Springer, pp. 1220–1231.

Gilbert, N. (2008). *Agent-Based Models*. Thousand Oaks, CA: Sage.

Groff, E.R., Johnson, S.D., & Thornton, A. (2018). State of the art in agent-based modeling of urban crime: an overview. *Journal of Quantitative Criminology*, 35(1), 155–193.

Lakatos, I. (1974). Falsification and the methodology of scientific research programmes. In: I. Lakatos & A. Musgrave (eds.), *Criticism and the Growth of Knowledge*. London: Cambridge University Press, pp. 91–196.

Liu, L., & Eck, J. (2008). *Artificial Crime Analysis Systems: Using Computer Simulations and Geographic Information Systems*. Hershey, PA: Information Science Reference.

Liu, L., Wang, X., Eck, J., & Liang, J. (2005). Simulating crime events and crime patterns in a RA/CA model. In: F. Wang (ed.), *Geographic Information Systems and Crime Analysis*. Reading, PA: Idea Publishing, pp. 197–213.

Malleson, N., & Brantingham, P.L. (2009). Prototype burglary simulations for crime reduction and forecasting. *Crime Patterns and Analysis*, 2(1), 47–66.

Malleson, N., & Evans, A. (2013). Agent-based models to predict crime at places. In: G. Bruinsma & D. Weisburd (eds.), *Encyclopedia of Criminology and Criminal Justice*. New York: Springer, pp. 41–48.

Shannon, R.E. (1975). *Systems Simulation: The Art and Science*. Englewood Cliffs, NJ: Prentice-Hall.

2 Generating crime generators

Toby Davies and Daniel Birks

Introduction

That crime concentrates in space is a fundamental result within environmental criminology, having been demonstrated across a range of spatial scales (e.g. Steenbeek & Weisburd, 2015). As well as having important practical implications, such concentration invites theoretical explanation, and several behavioural principles have been advanced as a means of rationalising these patterns. Prominent among these are those based on the routine activities perspective (Cohen & Felson, 1979), which focuses on understanding the conditions under which the actors required for a crime to occur – offender, target and guardian – converge in space (and time). An important extension of this is crime pattern theory (Brantingham & Brantingham, 1981, 1995b), which proposes that the distribution of such convergences is strongly governed by the spatial structure of individuals' daily lives – the places that they habitually visit – and, by extension, the structure of the 'urban backcloth' more generally.

The focus on routinely visited places within these theories naturally invites consideration of how such effects might vary from location to location. In particular, the simple observation that some places host many more interactions than others – because they feature in the routine activities of many more people, for example – implies that they may experience elevated levels of crime. Such locations have been stylised as 'crime generators' and 'crime attractors' within theoretical arguments (Brantingham & Brantingham, 1995a), and their distinctive criminal character has indeed been demonstrated in empirical studies (e.g. Groff & Lockwood, 2014).

The conditions under which such phenomena emerge, however, are not precisely defined. Most immediately, it is not clear *how many* interactions must occur at a location in order for it to constitute, for example, a crime generator: the simple notion of high activity encompasses a wide range of circumstances. Furthermore, such volumes of interaction can arise in a number of ways: a place might be visited regularly by a small subset of people, or be an occasional stop for a much larger population (with many possibilities in between). Importantly, understanding these dynamics represents a considerable empirical challenge: while it may be feasible to measure the number of people present in a location at particular times, it is not known, for example, whether it is the only place that is visited by those people, or one of many. In general, it is not clear 'how shared' a location must be in order for generator-like crime concentrations to arise (and indeed whether such 'sharedness' is causally sufficient).

Furthermore, while the influence of shared locations is typically only considered in their immediate spatial vicinity, this is only one aspect of what is predicted by theory. The extent to which activity patterns are shaped by such locations extends much further, with potential consequences for both the overall volume of crime and its spatial distribution within the broader environment. It has been shown, for example, that the directionality of offender journeys-to-crime (i.e. between homes and crime locations) is consistent with their orientation towards likely activity nodes (Frank et al., 2012). Such directional patterns, when aggregated, are also seen to form 'ridges' – abrupt changes in orientation – which correspond to key arterial pathways, often coinciding with routes between key activity centres (Song et al., 2013). Furthermore, the presence of attractors interacts with other morphologies of crime: the concentration of offences near land use boundaries – referred to as 'edges' – is more pronounced when an activity centre is present nearby (Song et al., 2017). Together, these suggest that activity nodes can exert influence on the patterning of crime far beyond their immediate vicinity.

Again, such effects represent an empirical challenge, due to the difficulty of measuring the extent of activities associated with a particular location. In general, for example, it is not possible to identify incidents that might occur away from a location but be attributable to it because the victim was en route to (or from) that location at the time of the offence. In most empirical research, likely activity nodes are identified *a priori*, and the question examined is whether crime patterns are consistent with their location; although such findings are meaningful, they are primarily correlational, since the behaviours and events in question cannot be directly attributed to the activity node.

In the context of these challenges, agent-based modelling (ABM) provides a promising approach: not only does it allow theoretical constructs to be encoded and manipulated without limit, but it also facilitates analyses of their implications at a much finer granularity (and much higher level of information) than would be possible in a real-world context. In the present context, it allows different variations of the mechanisms of crime pattern theory to be realised in a precise manner: we can control the extent to which activity nodes are shared between individuals, and explore the consequences of these variations for the occurrence of crime. Importantly, these consequences can be explored in such a way that effects are directly attributable to particular activity nodes, which is not possible in traditional empirical study. Acknowledging ABM's ability to address different but complementary questions regarding the causal sufficiency – not necessity – of theoretical accounts (see Birks et al., 2012, Johnson & Groff, 2014), in this chapter we employ the approach with two primary aims: (1) to assess the degree to which the mechanisms proposed by crime pattern theory are sufficient to produce localised concentrations of crime (i.e. generator-like phenomena); and (2) to explore the impacts of these theoretical mechanisms at higher spatial scales – in particular at street segment and environment-wide levels.

Theoretical background

Crime pattern theory is broad in scope, and seeks to rationalise the occurrence of crime at multiple scales and in terms of multiple influential factors. An important principle throughout the theory is that the patterning of crime can be explained, to some extent, by the way that the daily activities of individuals intersect and overlap. The theory proposes that individuals' routine activities are centred around a small number of 'activity nodes', at which they spend most of their time and between which they move at regular intervals. These nodes, and the paths between them, form 'activity spaces', and it is proposed that it is where these activity spaces intersect with criminal opportunities that crime will occur. Although this in itself does not imply that crime will concentrate, the fact that some activity nodes are shared between many people – transport hubs or entertainment districts, for example – means that some locations will be in the activity spaces of more people than others, and therefore give rise to more opportunities for crime in their vicinity. Crime pattern theory identifies two archetypes amongst such locations: crime generators, at which crime occurs simply because of the large volume of interactions, and crime attractors, which specifically attract offenders because of the criminal opportunities there (Brantingham & Brantingham, 1995a). Of course, the relationship between volumes of interactions and the occurrence of crime is not straightforward, and depends on the particular characteristics of both the actors and the places: large crowds may lead to no crime, while a place can act as a generator for one offender only. Nevertheless, all else equal, greater levels of interaction will in general be associated with higher levels of crime.

Before proceeding further, we should note that our scope here is restricted to crime events associated with shared activity nodes (SANs), but not occurring within the nodes themselves (e.g. within buildings or facilities). Although crime pattern theory is indeed applicable at micro-scales – nodes themselves can contain micro-versions of activity spaces, paths and generators – for reasons of simplicity we consider only one scale here. In addition, we consider crime within nodes to be a fundamentally different phenomenon to that occurring elsewhere; both building design and place management (see, for example, Madensen & Eck, 2012) raise particular complexities. In this work, our focus is on criminal opportunities arising from the movements of potential offenders, victims and crime preventers within the urban backcloth.

Of the two archetypal cases, crime generators represent the more expedient example from the perspective of theory testing. Since they require no purposive behaviour on the part of criminals, modelling the hypothesised behaviour requires less complexity and fewer assumptions (i.e. 'moving parts'). As such, examining the circumstance under which such locations emerge is a convenient means to test the extent to which crime risk can derive purely from the volume of potential victim–offender convergences at (or associated with) a place. Empirical evidence suggests that this is indeed the case: several studies have demonstrated that levels of crime in the vicinity of such activity nodes are higher than those elsewhere (Groff & Lockwood, 2014). Examples of the kinds of locations that have been examined in this way include subway stations (McCord & Ratcliffe, 2009), parks (Groff & McCord, 2012), bars (Bernasco & Block, 2011) and public housing communities (Haberman et al., 2013).

Open questions

Such studies, however, have a number of limitations with respect to the level of theoretical insight or precision they offer. The first of these is in the criteria by which such locations are identified: while the locations examined are indeed hubs of activity in some sense, there may still be large variation in the number of individuals that frequent them. This raises the question of how 'shared' a location must be in order to have this character (i.e. how many people must frequent it), and whether increasing intersection necessarily corresponds to higher crime. Conversely, it might also be asked whether a location being within the activity spaces of many individuals is necessarily a guarantee of higher crime. Ultimately, the question is under what conditions an SAN constitutes a crime generator.

A second problem is the sense in which effects are attributed to particular locations. Studies of the generator effect typically examine offending within some (arbitrary) radius of the location in question, under the assumption that crimes in this region can be ascribed to the location in some sense. Even if this is indeed the case, however, the activity associated with the location will certainly not be limited to such an immediate vicinity: people must travel to and from these locations from elsewhere. A stadium, for example, attracts visitors from a wide catchment area, and the journeys to and from it would not occur if it did not exist. Since – in line with crime pattern theory – journeys involve interactions with potential targets for crime (either individuals or properties), it is important to account for these effects when considering the impact of an activity node. By this argument, it is possible that effects associated with a facility can be manifested some distance away; that an activity node can have 'upstream' effects, and indeed 'generate' crime elsewhere. Research has shown that offender behaviours consistent with attraction towards likely activity nodes can form 'ridges' of crime occurrence far removed from the nodes themselves (Song et al., 2013). Although some studies have attempted to attribute crimes to particular crime attractors (Frank et al., 2010), this relies on assumptions about the journey to crime and directionality; in general, the activity spaces of offenders and victims – aside from the locations of the crimes themselves – are unknown.

Similarly, one issue that is rarely considered in the analysis of crime generators is their 'net' effect on crime; that is, whether the effect of such a location increases (or decreases) crime at the macro-level. Since generators experience risk because they draw activity, it is possible that they result in corresponding decreases elsewhere, in places where activity levels are consequently lower. The question is essentially one of displacement, or rather 'placement' (Barr & Pease, 1990): if a crime generator is introduced, does it just draw crime from elsewhere, or does it have a supplementary effect? Clearly this is not a simple question from a behavioural perspective and relates to the substitutability of activity nodes; routine activities are not zero-sum. Nevertheless, studies of crime generators rarely consider their overall effect – whether a city in which activity nodes overlap to a greater extent is safer than one where they do not. Indeed, to do so would be extremely challenging, given fundamental difficulties in establishing the relevant counterfactual (i.e. the level of crime in the absence of the facility); as outlined by Nagin and Sampson (2019), the ability to construct such counterfactual worlds is a distinct strength of ABM.

One reason why non-linear effects might be anticipated at crime generators – why crime volumes might not simply scale with volumes of people – is guardianship. The ability of 'capable guardians' to negate potentially criminal interactions is one of the central considerations in routine activity theory (Felson, 1995; Hollis et al., 2013), and may be particularly apposite at crime generators, at which particular types of guardian, such as 'place managers', may be present (Madensen & Eck, 2012). Although the activity patterns of guardians have rarely been considered, SANs should, as well as hosting more offender–target interactions, also theoretically provide a greater supply of potential guardians, who may either intervene during criminal acts or deter them prior to commission (see Reynald, 2011). Since such actors are more likely to be present at SANs, it might be expected that crimes are more likely to be prevented there. Somewhat counter-intuitively, this may mean that, even though generators themselves experience elevated levels of crime, their effect at the macro-level is a reductive one. Even if there is no net effect on the number of potentially criminal interactions, crime may still reduce if the interactions occur in locations where they are more likely to be prevented. Again, such an effect would be impossible to examine empirically: guardianship, by its nature, is manifested as the absence, rather than presence, of an event, and thus cannot be measured directly.

The present study

While the questions outlined above are broad in scope, our fundamental focus here is on theory testing. Specifically, we are concerned with the question of whether elements of crime pattern theory – in particular, those relating to the overlaps and intersections of individual activity spaces – are capable of producing localised concentrations of crime as manifested as 'crime generators'. This is a question of generative sufficiency, in line with the theme of this volume.

In fact, however, we adopt a variation of this approach here, for two reasons. The first is that, we argue, a binary test of these theoretical mechanisms would be reductive, and not especially meaningful. It seems trivial that the absence of overlap between activity spaces will not produce concentrations, while the other extreme – perfect alignment – will be guaranteed to do so. Although this comparison of extremes is facile, it seems clear from the preceding section that the real question is one of degree: *how much* overlap is sufficient and/or necessary?

This question of sufficiency or necessity is itself, however, our second issue. The recipe for theory testing on which this volume is based stipulates that testing should be done with respect to 'stylised facts' – generalised regularities which models ought to produce in order to reflect the real world. In this respect, however, we have also found the present context to be problematic. Although many studies on this topic exist, there is no identifiable consensus with respect to exactly what constitutes a crime generator; in particular, how pronounced the local concentration of crime must be.

The most common metric employed to quantify the concentration of crime around particular places is the Location Quotient (LQ), first introduced by Brantingham and Brantingham (1995a). In simple terms, this compares the concentration of crime (per area) within a buffer region around the places in question with the concentration of crime elsewhere, expressing this as a ratio. Formally, for some defined radius r, it is defined as:

$$LQ = \frac{c_v/a_v}{c_e/a_e}$$

where c_v is the number of crimes occurring within r of one of the study locations, a_v is the total area within r of one of the study locations, c_e is the count of crime elsewhere and a_e is the total area elsewhere. A ratio greater than 1 therefore indicates that crime is more concentrated around the study locations than it is elsewhere, and vice versa for a ratio less than 1.

Although the LQ is not without shortcomings (see McCord & Ratcliffe, 2009), it does provide a robust measure of concentration, and can be interpreted straightforwardly. However, what it does lack is an accompanying statistical approach for establishing the significance or magnitude of any concentration effect. Although the former can be addressed by calculating a null distribution based on randomly selected locations within the study area (Groff & McCord, 2012), the question of effect size remains: what level of concentration constitutes a crime generator? Previous work has largely followed

Rengert, Ratcliffe, and Chakravorty (2005) in taking 2 as the threshold value, but this is essentially arbitrary and may not reflect real-world perceptions. In the present context, this issue is complicated further by the fact that we are not concerned with crime occurring within the activity nodes themselves (which was included in the previous studies); this means that any values we calculate are likely to be conservative.

Establishing an LQ threshold for real-world crime generators is, we believe, beyond the scope of this chapter; this does, however, leave us without an explicit stylised fact for the purpose of theory testing. Rather than select an arbitrary value for this purpose – which, we believe, would be counter-productive – we instead depart slightly from the intended recipe and take a more exploratory approach. In the analysis that follows, we examine the effects of variations to the hypothesised mechanisms in a number of terms, and at a number of scales: in terms of local concentration, in terms of spatial distribution and at global level. While we believe the findings are instructive in themselves, this leaves open the possibility that they can be interpreted subsequently with respect to any given (specific) definition of a crime generator.

In the following sections, we first present our model, reviewing the theoretical principles on which it is based and outlining the refinements that we introduce here for the first time. After this we set out the experiments we conduct using the model, present their results at both micro and macro spatial levels, and conclude by discussing implications for theory.

Method

As remarked above, several aspects of the above formulation highlight the limitations (or impossibility) of a traditional empirical approach. Most immediately, these relate to the infeasibility of manipulating the key factors involved in an experimental way: activity nodes cannot be added or removed, and individuals' routine activities cannot be altered exogenously. More fundamentally, several crucial aspects simply cannot be observed, including guardianship events and the routes that victims were taking at the point of victimisation. In this context, ABM offers a well-suited alternative. As is well-established, ABM allows for almost unlimited manipulation of behaviours and environmental conditions, which means that theorised mechanisms can be implemented to varying degrees, allowing their ability to reproduce observed phenomena to be iteratively established. In addition to this, the exact circumstances leading to each event – the behaviours and perceptions of the actors involved – can be observed, in a way that would not be possible in a real-world setting.

In the investigation that follows, we employ a modified version of a core behavioural model previously introduced by Birks, Townsley, and Stewart (2012, 2014) and subsequently extended by Birks and Davies (2017). The model encodes key propositions of environmental theories of crime, including crime pattern theory, and previous research has shown that it is capable of reproducing well-established empirical features of crime, including its spatial concentration, repeat victimisation and 'journey to crime' distance decay effects. While the model has previously been applied to both property and interpersonal crime, in this version, we focus on interpersonal victimisation, since it involves activity patterns of both victim and offender and thus corresponds strongly to the notions of encounter-based crime that we are concerned with here (though, to be clear, the principles should also apply to property crime). We also introduce a number of behavioural modifications to the model – outlined in the following section – with the current research question in mind. Most immediately, we introduce a more sophisticated routine activity structure for agents: the notion of SANs was absent from previous versions and is crucial in the current context.

The model

As discussed above, the model presented here seeks to simulate the occurrence of interpersonal crime interactions. We define interpersonal crime interactions as those that occur when an offender agent encounters one or more civilian agents – each going about their routine activities – and either victimises them, resulting in a crime, or is prevented from doing so by the presence of another agent acting as a capable guardian.

Drawing on the model framework described in Birks and Davies (2017), we instantiate a population of offenders and civilian agents who perceive, reason and act on an abstract block-based street network. Following the discussion above, in particular we are interested in examining the impacts of changes to routine activity structures on crime risk – and in turn, the implications of these findings for existing theoretical depictions of crime generators provided within the broader literature. As usual, our model operationalises a series of fundamental assumptions that are specifically derived from the theoretical frameworks we seek to explore.

1. Individuals undertake routinised, spatially structured activities via the street network that primarily originate from home (Golledge & Spector, 1978) and involve visiting a series of routine activity locations that represent significant locations such as places of work, socialising venues or the homes of friends/family (Brantingham & Brantingham, 1981). The extent to which these activity locations are shared with others varies, from those shared with – at most – relatively few people (e.g. home) to those frequented by many (e.g. shopping malls, train stations and schools).
2. In order for a crime to occur, a motivated offender must converge with a suitable target in the absence of capable guardians (Cohen & Felson, 1979). For interpersonal victimisation, the offender and target in question will be individuals.
3. When such convergences occur, the likelihood of victimisation occurring is the result of three factors: (1) the current motivation of the offender;

(2) the suitability of the potential target (which varies across targets; see Cornish & Clarke, 1986); and (3) the presence or absence at the location of convergence of other individuals who may act as informal guardians, preventing victimisation (Reynald, 2011).

Model component specification

Having introduced our model and set out the theoretical propositions it seeks to operationalise, we now specify the model's primary components, detailing our synthetic environment, the agents that inhabit it and the conditions under which it is used to enact a series of simulation experiments.

Model environment

As in Birks and Davies (2017), our agents interact with one another on an abstract network that is built to provide a rudimentary representation of a block-based street network. The network is made up of three key elements: street segments, intersections and location nodes. Adapting our previous approach, and as illustrated in Figure 2.1 via a smaller example, this environment is instantiated in the following sequence of steps:

1. We begin each simulation by creating a uniform grid of 15 × 15 intersections, with neighbouring intersections connected by street segments (Figure 2.1a).
2. Along each street segment, five location nodes are created (Figure 2.1b) – each of these represents a discrete location in the environment, and properties are created at each of these (Figure 2.1c). Collectively this approach generates 2100 location nodes – 14 ×15 = 210 vertical street segments and 210 horizontal street segments, with each hosting five location nodes.
3. For each of the 2100 properties, an occupant agent is instantiated (Figure 2.1d). This occupant can be a citizen agent (with $p = 0.95$) or an offender agent (with $p = 0.05$), thus generating a population of approximately 1995 citizen agents and 105 offender agents.
4. Depending upon the experimental configuration of the model, each of these agents is allocated a collection of routine activity locations, some of which are shared between multiple agents (see below). Each of these locations is a single location node.

Agents

The environment discussed above is populated by two types of agent: offenders and civilians. We now describe the key characteristics and behaviours that define these agents – some of which are shared by both types of agents, and some of which are specific to each type.

22 *Toby Davies and Daniel Birks*

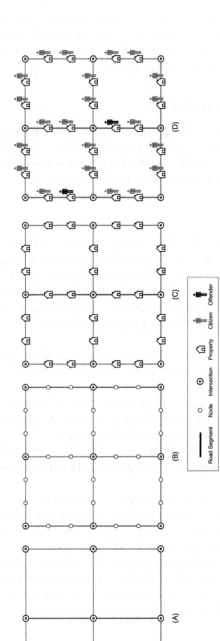

Figure 2.1 Construction of simulation environment: (A) instantiation of underlying grid; (B) addition of location nodes; (C) creation of properties; and (D) instantiation of agents.

General agent characteristics

HOME LOCATION

All agents (offenders and non-offenders) are allocated a home location in the form of a location node in the environment. The home location is the location node at which agents are instantiated (see step 3 above). It is from here that they begin the simulation and to where they periodically return during their routine activities.

PERSONAL ACTIVITY NODES

In addition to their home location, all agents are allocated four additional location nodes, chosen randomly from the model environment, to act as their routine activity space. As in our previous work, these are intended to represent a place of work, home of friends/family etc.

SHARED ACTIVITY NODES

In the model presented in this chapter we also implement the notion of SANs – our primary environmental feature of interest. To do this, we first create a number of such nodes, again selected at random from the set of all location nodes. For each agent, each of these SANs is added to the agent's routine activity space according to a defined probability, p(shared). For example, a value of p(shared) = 0.2 means that each SAN has a 20% chance of appearing in the activity space of any given agent. In our simulations, we vary both the number of SANs and p(shared).

ROUTINE ACTIVITY NODES

An agent's set of routine activity nodes is the union of their sets of personal activity nodes and shared activity nodes, outlined above.

Offender agent characteristics

MOTIVATION

The likelihood of victimisation depends on whether an offender is motivated to offend. As in our previous research, and with a focus on exploring the impacts of our primary constructs of interest – namely, configurations of routine activity nodes – we hold offender motivation static over time and across all offender agents, such that p(motivated) = 0.005.

Non-offender agent characteristics

SUITABILITY

To model interpersonal victimisation, where agents are the potential targets of offenders, we follow our previous approach of representing the attractiveness of each target using a single variable. This value – p(suitable) – represents the probability that an offender will find the target in question suitable for victimisation, and is intended to reflect the risk, reward and effort associated with victimising a target. At simulation initialisation, each citizen agent is assigned a value of p(suitable) drawn from a uniform distribution over the interval [0, 1].

Agent behaviours

We now outline the key agent behaviours that characterise the perception, reasoning and actions of our simulated agents. For the most part, these mirror the behaviours applied in our previous work (beginning in Birks, Townsley, & Stewart, 2012, 2014 and more recently in Birks & Davies, 2017). While a description of all of these model components is briefly rehearsed here, interested readers may wish to consult previous publications where greater detail is provided regarding the underlying rationale of some modelling choices. In a number of places we have also modified previous, or added new, functionality in response to our evolving ideas and those of our colleagues and peers (including many of the authors featured in this volume). More detail is provided in relation to these aspects to ensure it is clear how the model presented here differs from those previously used.

Routine movements – offender and non-offender agents

In our model, the routine activities of agents are structured around activity nodes, with agents travelling between them via the street network. As discussed above, at simulation initialisation all agents are allocated a home location, four personal activity nodes and, in some cases, one or more SANs – collectively, these make up an agent's routine activity space. The agent navigation behaviour allows agents to both select and traverse between the nodes in this activity space.[1]

Mirroring Birks and Davies (2017), in traversing the street network, with each simulation cycle an agent is able to move from one location node or intersection to the next adjacent location node or intersection. Thus, in our environment, where each street segment contains five location nodes, it takes an agent six cycles to traverse a street segment.

Conversely, departing somewhat from Birks and Davies (2017), the model presented in this chapter presents a new destination selection behaviour which (1) incorporates the notion of a trip schedule in order to better approximate the temporal structuring of routine activities; and (2) defines a series of transition probabilities that identify how agents select their next destination.

Trip scheduling

In our previous models (Birks et al., 2012, 2014; Birks & Davies, 2017) we have taken a relatively abstract approach to representing the timing of agent activities, with agents continually travelling between routine activity locations. One consequence of this is that there was large variation in the number of trips carried out by agents, since those whose journeys were shorter could complete more trips in the same number of cycles. This called into question whether agent lifetimes were genuinely equivalent: if a trip represents a fundamental unit of activity, then all agents should carry out a similar number over the course of the simulation. Here we adopt a new trip-scheduling functionality which seeks to better reflect the temporal structure of real-world routine activities, while also minimising the computational burdens associated with doing so.

We define a trip as the travel from one (routine or shared) activity node to another. Our new trip-scheduling approach reflects the periodic nature of real-world routine activities, along with the fact that there are certain times when concentrations of travel behaviour manifest: the commute to and from work (i.e. 'rush hour') is an obvious example. In addition, it seeks to ensure that across any given simulation the number of these trips undertaken by each agent is equivalent,[2] thus avoiding the need to control for the number of trips taken by an agent in reconciling their victimisation risk (as we do in Birks & Davies, 2017). A direct implication of this approach is that the lifetime of a simulation is now defined in terms of the total number of trips (rather than cycles, as before).

In implementing this new approach, we make necessary assumptions about the number of potential trip choices an agent might make in a single 'simulated day' – here we arbitrarily assume five (noting that future models might more formally explore heterogeneity in trip frequency across agents). The scheduling of trips and their subsequent simulation then runs according to the following logic:

1. At the start of each 'trip' each agent selects a new destination from their routine activity nodes.
2. Each agent plans a route to reach that destination via the shortest path on the street network,[3] and calculates the number of cycles required.
3. The model collects all trip lengths (in cycles) and identifies the longest trip across all agents. This will be used as the trip duration for this trip window.
4. All agents randomly select a departure time such that they will arrive at their destination on, or prior to, the final cycle of the trip window. Note that, for the agent with the farthest distance to travel, this will require immediate departure.
5. The simulation begins and agents depart at their selected departure time.
6. When the cycle count reaches the maximum duration of the trip window, and thus all agents are now at their destination, the trip count increments and the procedure repeats.

We can envisage this logic with a three-agent (A, B, C) example, as depicted in Figure 2.2. Agent A selects a destination that is 17 moves away from their

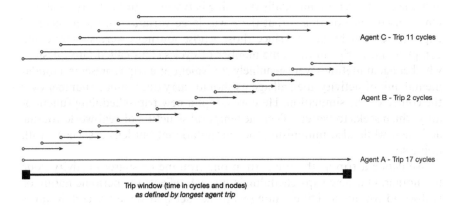

Figure 2.2 Illustration of trip-scheduling mechanism, showing possible departure times and travel times for three example agents.

current location; agent B – 2 moves; and agent C – 11. The trip window is thus identified as 17 cycles, since this is the maximum time required by any agent. All agents now select a departure time – agent A must depart at cycle 0, agent B can select at random any departure time between cycle 0 and 15 (as they require two cycles to reach their destination) and agent C can depart at any time between cycle 0 and 6 (as they require 11).

The reason for this approach – rather than simply having all agents depart simultaneously – is to avoid introducing potential bias due to variable trip length. If all agents began simultaneously, all agents would be in transition immediately, leading to a high number of interactions (especially so for SANs, from which many agents would be departing); on the other hand, later cycles would see only those agents with the longest journey lengths still active, in a very sparsely populated environment. The purpose of our scheduling routine is to avoid this and ensure that the distribution of interactions is as close to the 'mean field' as possible.

A final implication of this approach is that the model need not simulate any period of time when all agents are simply stationary and not interacting with one another. This significantly reduces model runtimes.

Transition probabilities

Following the notion of the 'simulated day' introduced by the trip-scheduling approach discussed above, we also modify our routine movements behaviour with the aim of better reflecting how trip choices are made throughout a day. We do this by creating a series of transition probabilities which determine the locations agents will choose to visit that is dependent on both their current location and the current trip 'time'. Table 2.1 depicts these probabilities. In particular, Table 2.1 shows that agents begin each simulated day at their home

Table 2.1 Transition probabilities governing the routine movements of agents. Offending (offender agents only)

Current location	Trip number	Probability – remain at current location	Probability – return home	Probability – navigate to routine / shared activity node
Home	1–4	$p = 0.2$	NA	$p = 0.8$
Routine / shared activity node	1–4	$p = 0.4$	$p = 0.2$	$p = 0.4$
Any node	5	NA	$P = 1$	NA

location and then either remain at home (with $p = 0.2$) or travel to another routine activity node or SAN (with $p = 0.8$), with the particular destination selected at random. Once at another node, they remain where they are (with $p = 0.4$), return home (with $p = 0.2$) or move to another randomly chosen routine activity node or SAN (with $p = 0.4$). At trip 5 each agent returns home (or stays there). Whilst largely arbitrary, the selection of these transition probabilities is motivated by a desire to provide a rudimentary abstraction of spatially structured activities within a given day (Golledge & Spector, 1978), such that agents begin the simulated day at home and return there at the end of each day, and may navigate between, or stay at, routine activity nodes during that time.

Offending – offender agents only

When an offender agent encounters another agent during their routine movements, it assesses whether to victimise them. Following our previous models, for each simulation cycle after an offender agent has moved it then assesses whether a potential target is present at its current location. If multiple potential targets exist then the one with the greatest value of the suitability characteristic (see above) is selected. The decision to offend against this target is then made probabilistically, drawing on a behavioural calculus which incorporates: (1) the offender's motivation; and (2) the suitability of the target. Specifically, the probability of commission at a location s and time t is given by:

$$p(\text{commission})_{(s,t)} = p(\text{motivated}) \times p(\text{attractive})_{(s,t)}$$

Note that offender agents can both move and attempt victimisation (assuming a potential target is present) within a single simulation cycle. Thus, an attempt or successful commission of an offence by an agent does not take any additional cycles. Additionally, for parsimony's sake, successful commission of a crime has no effect on the subsequent navigation behaviour of offender or victim agents; that is, they continue with their routines as normal.

Guardianship – offender and citizen agents

We also simulate informal guardianship, such that the presence of one or more agents (other than offender and target) at the commission of crime may dissuade or interrupt the offender and thereby prevent crime from occurring. Following Birks and Davies (2017), each agent present at the point at which an offender decides to victimise a target (according to the calculus above) has an independent probability, p(guard), of preventing the occurrence of crime. In the model presented in this chapter, we fix p(guard) = 0.2 for all agents in all contexts (again noting that future model revisions might include context-dependent aspects of guardianship capability, as explored in Birks & Davies, 2017).

Simulation experiments

In line with our aim to examine varying realisations of crime pattern theory, with respect to the overlap of activity spaces, we run the model across a range of experimental conditions, measuring outcomes at a range of scales. Our two key independent variables relate to the number of SANs present in any given environment, and the degree to which they are shared by the population of agents that inhabit it. To this end, we explore the impacts of instantiating the model with 0 (our control configuration), 1, 5 and 10 SANs. We explore the degree to which these locations are shared by our simulated population by varying the probability that each SAN will feature in a given agent's routine activity space. Three values of p(shared) are examined: 1 (our control condition, where all SANs feature in the activity spaces of all agents), 0.2 and 0.1. These choices are made to ensure a form of equivalency across conditions: since the expected number of SANs for each agent is the product of their number and their probability, several of the conditions (e.g. 5*0.2 and 10*0.1) are matched in this sense.

Following the schedule discussed above generates the equivalent of a 4 ×3 experimental design, consisting of 12 unique model configurations. Due to the non-deterministic nature of our model, for each of these configurations we run 100 simulation replications, resulting in 1200 unique primary simulation runs. Each simulation is run for 100 trips – the equivalent of 20 simulated days following our new trip-scheduling implementation.

Seeding the environmental setup

To maximise the robustness of our experimental design, we utilise a seeded simulation initialisation procedure, which permits control of model environment and population initial conditions across experimental conditions. This means that, for each of the 100 replications, the environment used for each experimental configuration is identical in all respects other than the presence of SANs: the factors held constant include the home and personal activity

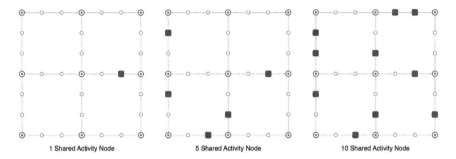

Figure 2.3 Example of the placement of shared activity nodes in successive model conditions, in which additional nodes are added cumulatively.

node locations of each agent, and their individual characteristics (e.g. attractiveness). This approach is equivalent to replicating our experiment in 100 unique study areas.

With respect to SANs, we can also ensure that the changes across conditions are cumulative, such that nodes are added sequentially, rather than re-instantiated at each stage. For example, for each replication, the SANs used for the $n = 5$ condition include the node already used for the $n = 1$ condition, plus four additional nodes (randomly chosen), rather than an independent selection of five new nodes.[4] This is to ensure that changes between successive conditions (i.e. those due to the additional nodes) can be meaningfully understood in spatial terms. Figure 2.3 depicts this.

Results

In this section, we will examine the outputs generated by our array of simulations, examining their consistency with theory and their wider characteristics.

Existence of crime generators

In a previous section, we introduced the LQ as a measure of crime concentration around particular locations. Here, we proceed to examine the LQ values for the SANs in our simulations. In Figure 2.4, we show values for two different radii: 1 and 2. For this analysis, distance is measured in terms of street segment separation: a radius of 1, for example, includes the segments containing the nodes and all immediately adjacent segments.

The plots show several notable features. Most immediately, LQ values are greater than 1 across all conditions, suggesting that there is indeed an elevated concentration of crime in the vicinity of the SANs. However, the LQ values for low probabilities of inclusion are fairly low, indicating that the elevation

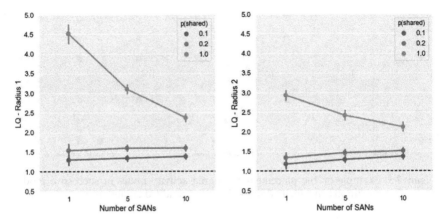

Figure 2.4 Mean Location Quotient (LQ) values across experimental configurations, calculated on the basis of radii (a) 1 and (b) 2. Error bars represent 95% confidence intervals. SANs, shared activity nodes.

is much less pronounced in these cases. This is, of course, unsurprising: assuming that the high LQ values derive from the extent to which activity nodes are shared, any decrease in p(shared) from 1 simply dilutes the effect.

The results for p(shared) = 1 show a decrease in LQ as the number of SANs is increased. Although at first sight this suggests that the effect is weaker, in fact it is to be expected. In order for the LQ values to be equal, each additional SAN would have to generate an equal volume of crime in its vicinity, but clearly this cannot be the case: the presence of SANs is not additive, and each additional one draws activity away from its predecessors. Nevertheless, it is instructive to see this pattern illustrated: if too many locations are shared between individuals, then none can be a focus for crime.

One final observation worth making is the comparison between results that are equivalent in terms of the expected number of SANs per agent. For example, in each of the configurations ($n = 1$, $p = 1$), ($n = 5$, $p = 0.2$) and ($n = 10$, $p = 0.1$), each agent's activity space will contain one SAN on average, but the results are markedly different: LQ values are higher when the SAN is the same for all agents, rather than one of several. This implies that the effect is not simply a function of how *many* shared nodes each agent has, but the extent to which they coincide.

Spatial patterns

Having identified that crime is indeed concentrated in the vicinity of SANs, we move on to consider its more general distribution. In particular, we are interested in whether such activity nodes can cause crime levels to either increase or decrease in places other than those in the immediate vicinity of the nodes themselves. The rationale for this is that the movement patterns that can be attributed to a given node extend much further than its immediate vicinity, since individuals must travel to it from elsewhere.

Given the focus on travel patterns, it is natural to examine this issue in terms of properties of the street network: the street network is the substrate on which travel occurs, and a primary driver of variation in activity patterns. Metrics defined at the street segment level can act as proxy measures for these activity levels, providing a means to operationalise concepts from crime pattern theory.

In previous work concerned explicitly with the effect of street network structure on crime (Birks & Davies, 2017), we used the metric *betweenness* as a measure of a street segment's likely level of usage during routine activities. Betweenness was originally developed in the field of social network analysis (Freeman, 1977) as a measure of 'brokerage', but has subsequently found wider use in network analysis, and that of street networks in particular. Its basic principle is fairly simple: it measures how frequently each street segment is used in travel through the network, assuming that one journey occurs between all possible origins and destinations, travelling via the shortest path. Although these assumptions are simplistic, it nevertheless provides a first-order estimate of likely use, and has been shown to be positively associated with offending in both real-world (Davies & Johnson, 2014) and simulation studies (Birks & Davies, 2017).

In Figure 2.5, we show the spatial distribution of betweenness for the network studied here, and its correlation with victimisation. Since the network we are working with for this study is fully connected, betweenness is relatively uninformative: it simply reflects the 'centre of gravity' of the network, since

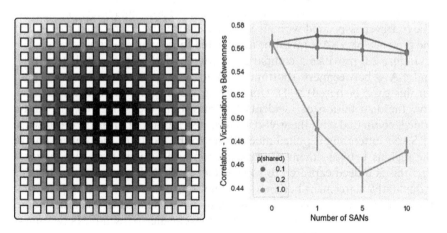

Figure 2.5 (a) Betweenness values per street segment for the network used for the model, and (b) mean correlations between victimisation counts and betweenness across experimental configurations. Error bars represent 95% confidence intervals. SANs, shared activity nodes.

more journeys will naturally flow through this. However, the correlation with victimisation counts is somewhat revealing. The fact that the correlation is decreased when SANs are added is because they bias activity patterns towards them: all locations are no longer equal, so activity is no longer just a function of geographical centrality.

In fact, the converse rationale can also explain the subsequent increase in correlation when the number of SANs increases to 10. Since the placement of SANs is uniformly random, and agents move between them, the addition of further locations will bring the distribution of activity closer to that of the original setup; to see this, consider the extreme case in which every location is an SAN. As the number increases, therefore, betweenness will become an ever-better predictor of activity, and therefore victimisation.

Although these findings do not in themselves correspond to substantive changes in the spatial distribution – and are only seen in the relatively extreme regimes of p(shared) = 1 – they are illuminating with respect to underlying behaviour. In particular, the above reasoning highlights a shortcoming of betweenness – for which it is also criticised in real-world studies – which is that it does not account for the fact that some locations act as the origins and destinations for many more trips than others. This is precisely the case for the SANs introduced here, and the reason for the decreasing predictive value of betweenness (likely to be even more pronounced for non-uniform networks). Although this is difficult to account for in real-world studies, the ABM framework offers additional possibilities in this respect.

To estimate activity patterns associated with SANs, we introduce a modified version of betweenness, referred to as 'SAN betweenness'. The modification here is simple: rather than considering trips between all pairs of locations when calculating betweenness, we consider only those trips which begin/end at a SAN. The values derived therefore reflect the estimated usage of segments due to travel associated with an SAN. Of course, it is along such routes that the presence of a SAN might be anticipated to influence victimisation.

Figure 2.6 provides a comparison between victimisation levels (top row) and SAN betweenness (bottom row) for one particular simulation run (in this case, p(shared) = 1). Considering victimisation first, it can be seen how the distribution of incidents becomes more focused as the SANs are added: compared with the well-dispersed distribution of crime in the absence of SANs, offending is pulled much closer to the locations themselves, and to the regions between them. Comparing top and bottom rows also suggests that this is indeed captured to some extent by SAN betweenness, as there is a qualitative agreement between the regions where crime is taking place and those where SAN-related activity is taking place. Related to an earlier point, however, it can be seen how SAN betweenness begins to resemble betweenness itself as the number of SANs increases.

Examining this more systematically, Figure 2.7 shows the correlation between victimisation and SAN betweenness across all experimental configurations. As anticipated, SAN betweenness becomes an increasingly

Generating crime generators 33

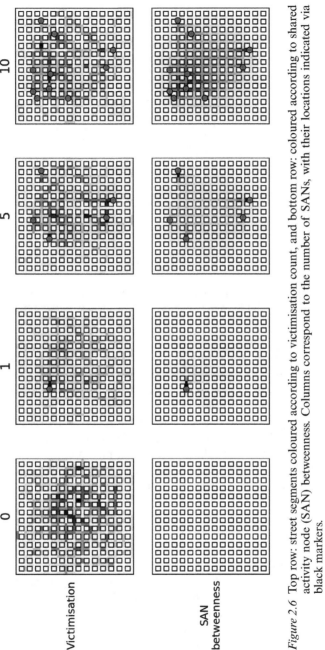

Figure 2.6 Top row: street segments coloured according to victimisation count, and bottom row: coloured according to shared activity node (SAN) betweenness. Columns correspond to the number of SANs, with their locations indicated via black markers.

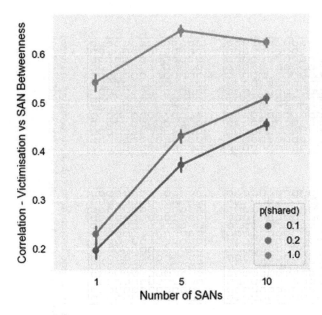

Figure 2.7 Mean correlation values between victimisation count and shared activity node (SAN) betweenness across experimental configurations. Error bars represent 95% confidence intervals.

good predictor of victimisation as the number of SANs increases, reflecting the greater degree of structure within agents' routine activities. Again, the effect is moderated by p(shared), since this dilutes the extent to which the sharing, and therefore overlap, occurs. However, it is notable that, for $p = 1$, the relationship begins to plateau when the number of SANs reaches its maximum value, while it continues to increase for lower values. When $p = 1$, the influence of the SANs immediately reaches its maximum level, since all agents share all SANs, and increasing the number simply distributes this. For lower values of p, though, increasing the number of SANs means that more agents will overlap.

Aggregate volume

Having examined the spatial distribution of offences associated with SANs, we now move on to consider their effects at the aggregate level. Although it is clear that SANs influence the spatial distribution of crime, it is not clear whether their net effect is positive or negative.

In Figure 2.8, we show the count of (a) victimisation and (b) prevention events across our experimental conditions. These reveal particularly interesting behaviour. The most immediate observation is that the addition of additional SANs causes a reduction in crime, with the number of

Generating crime generators 35

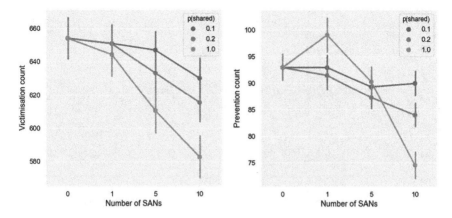

Figure 2.8 Counts of (a) victimisation, and (b) prevention events across experimental configurations. Error bars represent 95% confidence intervals. SANs, shared activity nodes.

victimisations falling consistently across conditions. As has been the case with other analyses, this behaviour is moderated by p(shared), but a similar story is evident across conditions. This behaviour is perhaps surprising, since it might have been anticipated that the additional overlap in activity spaces would lead to greater victimisation.

One possible explanation for this effect concerns guardianship: it may be the case that the addition of SANs leads to reductions in crime because potential criminal interactions (i.e. instances where an offender would otherwise victimise a target) are more likely to be interrupted. However, Figure 2.8b shows that this is not the case, with the number of 'prevention' events also decreasing in almost all cases. In fact this can be seen directly, by plotting the number of crime interactions – the sum of actual and prevented crimes, which would be the number of crimes if guardianship was absent – directly. This is shown in Figure 2.9, along with the prevention rate (the proportion of crime interactions that are prevented).

From this it is clear that the reduction in victimisation is not caused by guardianship: although the prevention rate fluctuates somewhat, the reduction would happen even in the absence of guardianship. This effect is difficult to rationalise, since it would have been expected that increased 'sharedness' would lead to more offender–target convergences, and therefore more victimisations. We can gain some further insight into the source of variation by examining victimisation rates separately according to whether the victim was en route to an SAN at the time of victimisation, or one of their other activity nodes. This is shown in Figure 2.10, and the rates are calculated on a 'per trip' basis; in other words, they represent the probability of being victimised on a given trip.

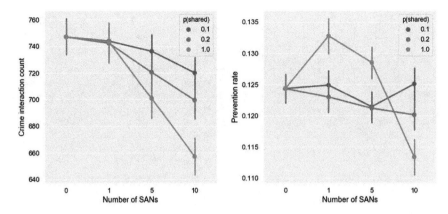

Figure 2.9 (a) Count of potential crime interactions, and (b) prevention rate per interaction, across experimental configurations. Error bars represent 95% confidence intervals. SANs, shared activity nodes.

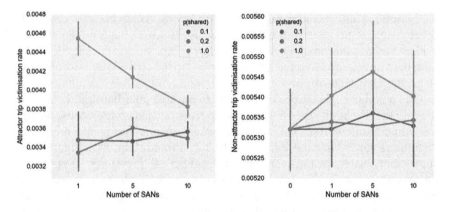

Figure 2.10 Per-trip victimisation rates for (a) trips to shared activity nodes (SANs), and (b) all other trips. Error bars represent 95% confidence intervals.

These tell something of a story with respect to victimisation. While the victimisation rate for non-SANs remains broadly constant (certainly within margin of error), the rate for trips to SANs decreases as more SANs are added. In addition, the victimisation rate is lower overall for SAN trips. Importantly, these rates are calculated on the basis of 'potential crime interactions', which means they reflect the situation in the absence of guardianship.

Taken as a whole, these results imply that: (1) trips to SANs are safer than other trips; and (2) trips to SANs become safer as the number of SANs increases. These being true, the overall results stand to reason: as the number of SANs increases, the proportion of trips involving SANs increases, and so the number of crime interactions decreases. The question, therefore, is why this should be the case.

Possible explanations can be identified by considering the criminal mechanism within the model. For each victim–target convergence, whether a crime takes place depends on only two factors: (1) the motivation of the offender (which is fixed), and (2) the attractiveness of the target (which is random). Since these could not generate systematic variation in the number of crimes, this leaves only one explanation for our main results: that the differences were due to variations in the number of convergences.

Although further investigation will be required to conclusively establish exactly which mechanisms (or combination thereof) are responsible for these outcomes, a likely explanation concerns the nature of trips across the various conditions. In the absence of SANs, movement is essentially random, with each agent travelling between their own idiosyncratic set of activity nodes. The upshot of this is likely to be a 'melee' effect in the centre of the environment, with random interactions happening as agents cross the world (somewhat analogous to Brownian motion).

The introduction of SANs, rather than compounding these interactions, may in fact reduce them by adding structure to agents' activity spaces. By attracting some proportion of activity to a particular location (in a highly structured way), the SAN in fact removes agents from the mix of random interactions, and its associated threat. Although agents will still be victimised as they travel to these locations, the risk is less than it would be due to random encounters, and the ordered nature of movement means that interactions occur in a structured way. The addition of further SANs simply serves to 'partition' routine activities even more, with routine activity spaces more tightly focused.

Discussion

The notion of the 'crime generator' is one of the foremost ideas within crime pattern theory, and one which exemplifies its key principles. The idea that some locations experience disproportionate levels of crime as a result of the fact that they bring together individuals – and therefore criminal opportunities – not only offers an explanation for why crime concentrates in such locations, but also why the locations of such facilities shape crime patterns at the macro-level. However, while inherently plausible, the crime generator hypothesis is more often than not post-hoc in nature, and the ability to test its specific mechanisms is hindered by a variety of logistical and ethical constraints.

The fundamental idea at the heart of the crime generator hypothesis is that some activity nodes are shared by many people, and therefore play host to a large number of interactions between potential offenders and victims. This is a broad statement, however, and the term 'shared by many people' in particular is imprecise. Not only is it unclear how many people must share a node for the effect to arise, but overlaps in activity can take many different forms: a situation in which individuals exclusively visit one local shopping mall is different to one in which they rotate between all malls in a city, for example. Even though the numbers of people present at the nodes themselves might be equivalent, the implications are much wider: people must travel to these locations from elsewhere, and they therefore give rise to interactions far beyond their immediate spatial vicinity. Since individuals' routine activity spaces cannot typically be observed – less still, manipulated – these issues are typically inaccessible to traditional empirical study.

In the context of these limitations, this chapter has presented a computational agent-based model formalising crime pattern theory's crime generator hypothesis. The model is concerned with interpersonal victimisation, and seeks to emulate the activity patterns and consequent interactions of virtual potential offenders, victims and guardians. Using this model, we have conducted a series of controlled simulation experiments devised to examine the impacts of activity node sharing on interpersonal victimisation risk at local, street and global levels. In doing so, we have tested the causal sufficiency of mechanisms put forward by theory in explaining empirical regularities of crime – the core premise around which this volume is motivated. Building on our primary findings we have then utilised our model to explore the wider implications predicted by the crime generator hypothesis at scales that are inaccessible to empirical methods.

Our findings demonstrate a number of things. First, at the local level, the presence of SANs does indeed give rise to localised concentrations of crime. This primary observation occurred across all experimental conditions, including manipulations to both the number of SANs within an environment, and the proportion of the simulated population that share those nodes. In simple terms, this indicates that mechanisms consistent with crime pattern theory's depiction of a crime generator do indeed produce localised hotspots of crime that can be directly attributed to the sharing of activity nodes. Though this finding may seem obvious, the attribution is critical: in an equivalent empirical investigation, only the volumes of people at these locations could be measured, and a counterfactual (i.e. how many crimes would occur in the absence of the shared node) would be essentially impossible to establish.

While sensible, however, these results do highlight a point of caution for the study. Although crime concentrates locally in all configurations, the level of clustering is relatively low in several cases, and so the question arises of whether these locations constitute generators in a meaningful sense. As far as we are aware, there is no consensus within the literature with respect to how pronounced such a concentration must be, and it is therefore difficult to identify specific criteria within the model. In fact, this highlights an issue which can arise with the use of stylised facts as criteria for model validation: if the stylised fact is not sufficiently precise, then the bar for theoretical sufficiency can be set too low.

To be clear, the issue here is not with the use of stylised facts, but rather a challenge for criminology more generally. To continue the previous analogy, the bar for model validation can only be set higher if such a bar exists; in many cases, the degree to which phenomena have been characterised in empirical work remains relatively vague, to the extent that they are not sufficiently well defined to discriminate between model outputs. Exceptions to this, whereby specific ranges of real-world values are identified – as in the 'law of crime concentration' (Weisburd, 2015), for example – provide more discriminating criteria, and further empirical efforts of this type can only strengthen ABM.

Nevertheless, we should also remember that our model only seeks to simulate crime events that occur outside the nodes themselves, and not those that occur within them. Since such events would usually be included in real-world examinations of crime generators, aligning our results with empirical observations may be difficult. This, we would argue, is a strength of our approach, allowing us to separate effects which due to limitations of crime data are often difficult to disentangle in real-world settings.

Moving on to consider how SANs influence the level and distribution of crime at the street level, outcomes of our experiments demonstrate that the presence of SANs also causes crime to concentrate on streets beyond their immediate vicinity. In this case, our ability to identify both victimisation and guardianship events that can be directly attributed to the presence of an SAN is a clear example of measurement that would not be possible in an empirical setting.

Our examinations of such effects show that these distributions of crime are systematic in nature and largely predictable in street network terms, aligning with anticipated routes that exist between SANs. To quantify these patterns, we have introduced the notion of *SAN betweenness* – a measure of the degree to which street segments are likely to feature in 'popular' journeys (i.e. those that either begin or end at SANs). This implies that the distribution of crimes attributable to SANs can be reconciled with the journeys that individuals are likely to take to reach them. Beyond this study, SAN betweenness may provide a useful metric when considering real-world distributions of offending, since it addresses the simplistic assumption in regular betweenness that an equal number of journeys begin at all locations. Of course, it has been used here in an abstract context, and so its use in varying real-world settings will need exploration.

Finally, when examining the impact of SANs at the environment level, our results demonstrate what appears to be a counter-intuitive outcome: that increasing the number of SANs in an environment reduces overall crime risk. Deconstructing this seemingly protective effect of SANs, analyses indicate that overall reductions are primarily due to the decreased risk to individuals during travel directly associated with SANs: the more activity nodes are shared, the less likely an individual is to be victimised when travelling to one. Although the precise reasons for this require further investigation, the nature of our model means that it must result from a decrease in the number of offender–victim interactions. We propose that this results from the greater 'orderliness' of activities imposed by the presence of SANs: in comparison with the 'chaotic' patterns of movements which occur when activities are unstructured – leading to many 'random' collisions – movement towards SANs resembles flocking, with agents following common routes in the same direction.

Taken collectively, the results of our experiments paint an interesting picture regarding the role SANs may play in influencing spatial crime risk. In formalising crime pattern theory's depiction of crime generators, our model predicts that, as a population's activities become more ordered, greater levels of inequality in victimisation are observed, yet on average environments become safer. These two findings are not inconsistent, and may have real-world relevance: while an activity node might generate crime locally, it is perfectly possible that it also 'draws' crime from elsewhere, for a net reduction. The latter effect is clearly much more difficult to test empirically, but our results suggest that such a 'placement' (Barr & Pease, 1990) effect would be an interesting topic for real-world study. As mentioned previously, the directionality of offender journeys has been shown to be consistent with the notion that SANs exert a 'pull' effect over a wide radius (Frank et al., 2012; Song et al., 2017); their 'net' effect, however, has not yet been studied.

At the same time, it should be remembered that the model with which these experiments are undertaken represents a formalisation of a collection of theoretical frameworks. The extent to which its results are immediately transferable to real-world settings is not clear; this is not, though, our primary goal. Agent-based work elsewhere has begun to integrate fine-grained (i.e. event-level) real-world data, both for initialisation and validation (Nguyen et al., 2019). In line with the theme of this volume, however, our aim is different: while our overarching ambition is clearly to identify those theories that are a true reflection of real-world phenomena, here we seek to assess the explanatory capacity of those theories with respect to high-level, generic phenomena – our stylised facts.

In this regard then, we believe our model clearly highlights the utility of ABM not only for theory testing but also refinement. While we have demonstrated that the depiction of crime generators put forward by theory can indeed produce the general phenomenon it purports to explain, we have also shown a number of other effects which result from these same propositions – one of which does not feature in the theoretical literature that underpins our model (and would be hard to predict without a model of some kind). Estimating the degree to which this finding can accurately be reconciled with what is known about empirical distributions of crime will require further research – computational, empirical and perhaps theoretical.

At the same time, our approach is clearly not without weakness. Above all, it is simply a model, and is therefore only valid to the extent that its underlying propositions are. While, for reasons of parsimony, we have sought to carry out the most pathological test of the crime generator hypothesis that we can, it is undeniable that choices made in the modelling process always mask substantial complexity in the real world. In order to further test the validity of the hypothesis, its robustness to these factors would have to be examined. Such tests could examine the impact of varying a range of model assumptions and parameters, such as the size of the street network, the ratio of offender to non-offender agents and the transition probabilities associated with agent trip selection, to name but a few.

A particularly important example in the present study is our implementation of routine activities, and the sharing of activity nodes. It is clear that this is a simplification of reality – for one thing, there are almost no activity nodes in the real world that are *not* shared – and so it is possible that our findings in relation to these may better reflect the abstract nature of our model than what would occur in reality. Furthermore, as made clear in the chapter, here we do not consider crime occurring within activity nodes; only that which is external to them. With these caveats in mind, one would certainly require much more research (both empirical and computational) before proposing that policy makers tender to build more shopping malls and transport hubs in the expectation that crime will be reduced. As empirical understanding of activity spaces improves (e.g. via mobility sensing), this will provide a more solid grounding for this aspect.

Moving forwards, we propose a number of potential avenues for future research. First, our experiments have purposely not explored the impact of the location of SANs – the placement of which is uniformly random in our work. While we have sought to keep the model as simple as possible, in real-world settings, just as crime is concentrated, so are SANs – in central business districts, nightlife areas and transport hubs, to name but a few. Future experiments could be run to examine the impact of varying spatial configurations of SANs.

Similarly, our models have simulated the impact of SANs that exist within a largely abstract street network – in the hope of having the best chance of understanding their role in crime risk divided from that of the street network (see Elffers & van Baal, 2008). Nevertheless, our previous research has demonstrated that changes in the connectedness of street networks can materially influence the distribution of interactions between potential offenders, victims and guardians (Birks & Davies, 2017). Consequently, experiments examining the impacts of SANs in different environments would also further test the validity of the model. As well as these, numerous other possibilities for further refinement can be identified, with respect to the structure of offender routines and mobility in particular.

The opening chapter of this volume well argues that ABM may offer criminology and criminal justice scholars new insights into the validity of theory and – importantly – formalised means to evaluate proposed causal pathways that link individual behaviours to observed patterns of crime. It is our hope that, if nothing else, we have generated (!) some interest and debate in this endeavour.

Notes

1 Although, in reality, individuals also travel to other locations besides their routine activity nodes, such trips (which would be largely unstructured) are omitted here for parsimony.
2 Note that a 'trip' can sometimes involve remaining at the current location, so the number of actual journeys may not be exactly equal; however, this difference is not systematic, as it was in previous models.
3 Where multiple shortest paths of an equal length exist between an agent's current location and destination, one is selected at random for that particular trip.
4 To be clear, the SAN locations vary across each of our 100 replications; the cumulative process relates only to successive experimental conditions within the same replication.

References

Barr, R., & Pease, K. (1990). Crime Placement, Displacement, and Deflection. *Crime and Justice*, *12*, 277–318. https://doi.org/10.2307/1147441

Bernasco, W., & Block, R. (2011). Robberies in Chicago: A Block-Level Analysis of the Influence of Crime Generators, Crime Attractors, and Offender Anchor Points. *Journal of Research in Crime and Delinquency*, *48*(1), 33–57. https://doi.org/10.1177/0022427810384135

Birks, D., & Davies, T. (2017). Street Network Structure and Crime Risk: An Agent-Based Investigation of the Encounter and Enclosure Hypotheses. *Criminology*, *55*(4), 900–937. https://doi.org/10.1111/1745-9125.12163

Birks, D., Townsley, M., & Stewart, A. (2012). Generative Explanations of Crime: Using Simulation to Test Criminological Theory. *Criminology*, *50*(1), 221–254. https://doi.org/10.1111/j.1745-9125.2011.00258.x

Birks, D., Townsley, M., & Stewart, A. (2014). Emergent Regularities of Interpersonal Victimization: An Agent-Based Investigation. *Journal of Research in Crime and Delinquency*, *51*(1), 119–140. https://doi.org/10.1177/0022427813487353

Brantingham, P. J., & Brantingham, P. L. (1981). Notes on the Geometry of Crime. In P. J. Brantingham & P. L. Brantingham (eds.), *Environmental Criminology*. Beverly Hills, CA: Sage, pp. 27–54.

Brantingham, P. L., & Brantingham, P. J. (1995a). Location Quotients and Crime Hotspots in the City. In C. Block, M. Dabdoub & S. Fregly (eds.), *Crime Analysis Through Computer Mapping*. Washington, DC: Police Executive Research Forum, pp. 129–149.

Brantingham, P. L., & Brantingham, P. J. (1995b). Criminality of Place. *European Journal on Criminal Policy and Research*, *3*(3), 5–26. https://doi.org/10.1007/BF02242925

Cohen, L. E., & Felson, M. (1979). Social Change and Crime Rate Trends: A Routine Activity Approach. *American Sociological Review*, *44*(4), 588–608. https://doi.org/10.2307/2094589

Cornish, D. B., & Clarke, R. V. G. (1986). *The Reasoning Criminal: Rational Choice Perspectives on Offending*. The Hague: Springer Verlag.

Davies, T., & Johnson, S. D. (2014). Examining the Relationship Between Road Structure and Burglary Risk Via Quantitative Network Analysis. *Journal of Quantitative Criminology*, *31*(3), 481–507. https://doi.org/10.1007/s10940-014-9235-4

Elffers, H., & van Baal, P. (2008). Realistic Spatial Backcloth is Not That Important in Agent Based Simulation Research: An Illustration From Simulating Perceptual Deterrence. In L. Liu & J. Eck (eds.), *Artificial Crime Analysis Systems: Using Computer Simulations and Geographic Information Systems*. Hershey, PA: IGI Global, pp. 19–24.

Felson, M. (1995). Those Who Discourage Crime. In J. E. Eck & D. Weisburd (eds.), *Crime and Place* (Vol. 4). Monsey, NY: Criminal Justice Press, pp. 53–66.

Frank, R., Dabbaghian, V., Reid, A., Singh, S., Cinnamon, J., & Brantingham, P. (2010). Power of Criminal Attractors: Modeling the Pull of Activity Nodes. *Journal of Artificial Societies and Social Simulation*, *14*(1), 6.

Frank, R., Andresen, M. A., & Brantingham, P. L. (2012). Criminal Directionality and the Structure of Urban Form. *Journal of Environmental Psychology*, *32*(1), 37–42. https://doi.org/10.1016/j.jenvp.2011.09.004

Freeman, L. C. (1977). A Set of Measures of Centrality Based on Betweenness. *Sociometry*, *40*(1), 35–41. https://doi.org/10.2307/3033543

Golledge, R. G., & Spector, A. N. (1978). Comprehending the Urban Environment: Theory and Practice. *Geographical Analysis*, *10*(4), 403–426. https://doi.org/10.1111/j.1538-4632.1978.tb00667.x

Groff, E. R., & Lockwood, B. (2014). Criminogenic Facilities and Crime across Street Segments in Philadelphia: Uncovering Evidence about the Spatial Extent of Facility Influence. *Journal of Research in Crime and Delinquency*, *51*(3), 277–314. https://doi.org/10.1177/0022427813512494

Groff, E., & McCord, E. S. (2012). The Role of Neighborhood Parks as Crime Generators. *Security Journal*, *25*(1), 1–24. https://doi.org/10.1057/sj.2011.1

Haberman, C. P., Groff, E. R., & Taylor, R. B. (2013). The Variable Impacts of Public Housing Community Proximity on Nearby Street Robberies. *Journal of Research in Crime and Delinquency*, *50*(2), 163–188. https://doi.org/10.1177/0022427811426335

Hollis, M. E., Felson, M., & Welsh, B. C. (2013). The Capable Guardian in Routine Activities Theory: A Theoretical and Conceptual Reappraisal. *Crime Prevention and Community Safety*, *15*(1), 65–79. https://doi.org/10.1057/cpcs.2012.14

Johnson, S. D., & Groff, E. R. (2014). Strengthening theoretical testing in criminology using agent-based modeling. Journal of Research in Crime and Delinquency, 51(4), 509–525.

Madensen, T. D., & Eck, J. E. (2012). Crime Places and Place Management. In F. T. Cullen & P. Wilcox (eds.), *The Oxford Handbook of Criminological Theory*. New York: Oxford University Press pp. 554–578. https://doi.org/10.1093/oxfordhb/9780199747238.013.0029

McCord, E. S., & Ratcliffe, J. H. (2009). Intensity Value Analysis and the Criminogenic Effects of Land Use Features on Local Crime Patterns. *Crime Patterns and Analysis*, *2*(1), 17–30.

Nagin, D. S., & Sampson, R. J. (2019). The Real Gold Standard: Measuring Counterfactual Worlds That Matter Most to Social Science and Policy. *Annual Review of Criminology*, *2*(1), null. https://doi.org/10.1146/annurev-criminol-011518-024838

Nguyen, V. T., Brantingham, P. L., & Fetecau, R. C. (2019). *A Crime Aggregation Model on Street Networks (CAMOSNet)*. https://summit.sfu.ca/item/18913

Rengert, G. F., Ratcliffe, J. H., & Chakravorty, S. (2005). *Policing Illegal Drug Markets: Geographic Approaches to Crime Reduction*. Monsey, NY: Criminal Justice Press.

Reynald, D. M. (2011). Factors Associated with the Guardianship of Places: Assessing the Relative Importance of the Spatio-Physical and Sociodemographic Contexts in Generating Opportunities for Capable Guardianship. *Journal of Research in Crime and Delinquency*, *48*(1), 110–142. https://doi.org/10.1177/0022427810384138

Song, J., Andresen, M. A., Brantingham, P. L., & Spicer, V. (2017). Crime on the Edges: Patterns of Crime and Land Use Change. *Cartography and Geographic Information Science*, *44*(1), 51–61.

Song, J., Spicer, V., Brantingham, P., & Frank, R. (2013). Crime Ridges: Exploring the Relationship between Crime Attractors and Offender Movement. *2013 European Intelligence and Security Informatics Conference*, 75–82. https://doi.org/10.1109/EISIC.2013.18 https://doi.org/10.1080/15230406.2015.1089188

Steenbeek, W., & Weisburd, D. (2015). Where the Action is in Crime? An Examination of Variability of Crime Across Different Spatial Units in The Hague, 2001–2009. *Journal of Quantitative Criminology*, *32*(3), 449–469. https://doi.org/10.1007/s10940-015-9276-3

Weisburd, D. (2015). The Law of Crime Concentration and the Criminology of Place. *Criminology*, *53*, 133–157.

3 Using agent-based models to investigate the presence of edge effects around crime generators and attractors

Verity Tether, Nick Malleson, Wouter Steenbeek, and Daniel Birks

Introduction

The understanding that crime is found clustered in geographic space is well established in criminological literature (Herbert and Hyde, 1985), following centuries of investigation into the relationship between crime and space (Ratcliffe and Breen, 2011). Analysis of these clusters has led to the identification of different causal mechanisms underpinning their locations, and the consequential classification of two different types of crime clusters: crime generators and crime attractors (Brantingham and Brantingham, 1995). Crime generators are places in a city which are used by a large number of people for activities unrelated to crime (Clarke and Eck, 2003), thus creating a number of criminal opportunities for opportunistic offenders. Examples of crime generators include railway stations (Kurland et al., 2014) and parks (Groff and McCord, 2012). The large number of offences experienced here are primarily due to the high concentration of people (Clarke and Eck, 2005), and consequently the crime problem can be exacerbated by increased use of the space (Clarke and Eck, 2003). Crime attractors, on the other hand, are areas of the city that lure motivated offenders with the potential for criminal opportunity, and are exemplified by areas infamous for illegal activities. Crime problems here are aggravated by the growing reputation of the area (Clarke and Eck, 2005), and as a result, crime attractors are considered to be the result of offenders' experiences and networks (Brantingham and Brantingham, 2008). Examples of crime attractors include red-light districts (Brantingham and Brantingham, 1995, 2008; Clarke and Eck, 2003, 2005) and drug markets (Brantingham and Brantingham, 1995). Both crime generators and crime attractors can range in size from individual buildings to a small area of a city (Bernasco and Block, 2011; Houser et al., 2019).

Another well-established concept in the investigation of crime concentration is that of the effect of edges on crime patterns. Initially conceptualised as the "border-zone hypothesis" by Brantingham and Brantingham (1975), this has identified that boundaries between areas, whether physical or perceived, experience more crime events than internal zones. Several explanations of this phenomenon have been proposed, including the frequent and legitimate presence of strangers in these areas (Brantingham and Brantingham, 1993), the absence of formal guardianship here (Kim and Hipp, 2018) and the ability to exit the area quickly after committing a crime (Herbert and Hyde, 1985; Kim and Hipp, 2018). The effect of edges has been examined at a variety of scales, including a macro-level study of the city by Shawn and McKay (1942, cited by Rengert et al., 2012) and a meso-level investigation of communities by Rengert et al. (2012).

Whilst much research, detailed later, has been undertaken to investigate crime patterns around criminogenic facilities, very few pieces of work have specifically examined the relationship between crime generators and attractors and their edges. Moreover, those studies which have examined this have not examined the boundaries of the generator or attractor *itself*. Instead, Song et al. (2017), for example, considered the impact of crime generators and attractors on edge effects, comparing edge effects in areas within 500 metres of a generator/attractor with those further away. Likewise, Kim and Hipp (2018) studied the impact of the proximity to highways and parks, among other city features, on crime rates, examining these features as the boundaries themselves, rather than a criminogenic facility.

Not only has the relationship between these topics been seldom studied, there has been little theoretical investigation into the mechanism of how crime generators and attractors could lead to the emergence of edge effects. Indeed, Kim and Hipp (2018) stress the need to examine the mechanisms behind edge effects on offending, and Song et al. (2013) highlight that further research into edges is vital to theoretical understanding of areas which experience many crime events. More generally, Weisburd (2015) has stressed the need for theory development in studies investigating crime at very small geographic units – the so-called *geography of place*.

The present research

Consequently, this work aims to investigate the emergence of edge effects around crime generators and attractors, in order to test whether these theoretical concepts can be considered in conjunction with each other. Agent-based models of crime generators and attractors shall be created to identify the potential presence of edge effects around these spaces, exploring whether the mechanisms underpinning crime generators and attractors do, or do not, lead to the occurrence of increased crime events at their boundaries. Abstract environments shall be used, as seen elsewhere in computational criminology (such as in Birks et al., 2012, 2014), allowing these theoretical concepts to be investigated without the additional complexity of a real geographic space.

Not only does this work fill the aforementioned literature gap on testing of these concepts, but there are also a number of strengths of using agent-based models to theoretically test this relationship, over empirical analysis. Song et al. (2017), for example, identified limitations in defining an edge and finding appropriate data for analysis, but the abstract nature of these models means that the complexities of this definition, as discussed later in this chapter, are avoided. Moreover, empirical research into crime generators and attractors is not without methodological limitations (Kurland et al., 2014). As noted by Ratcliffe (2012b), for example, in their investigation on violence around bars, Homel and Clark (1994) did not specify the precise area "around" the bar which they would be studying.

Whilst that is a limitation of that specific project, there are also more general challenges encountered when undertaking research into crime generators and attractors; Holloway and McNulty (2003, p. 206), for example, following their investigation into crime patterns around public housing projects, note that "project-to-project differences" can lead to different patterns around the sites. Although Holloway and McNulty did not specify these sites as crime generators or attractors, this point is also pertinent to this area of research as well. However, this has been mitigated for this research; by creating an abstract environment for the theoretical testing, the differences between individual crime generator and attractor sites can be reduced. Furthermore, when investigating the impact of criminogenic sites on their vicinities, Ratcliffe (2012b) identified problems with the often-used empirical method of concentric buffers, such as the confounding effect of clustering of bars in space. When this is the case, it is challenging to identify which crimes can be attributed to which bars, rendering identification of the effects of each site difficult. The use of agent-based models, however, allows a single crime generator or attractor to be present in a space, eliminating this potential problem.

Despite these strengths of agent-based modelling, it is also important to consider the limits of using this methodology for this theory testing. Groff (2007), for example, highlights that agent-based models do not empirically test a theory, but examine the extent to which it is possible. Moreover, Crooks et al. (2008) stress that theories cannot be confirmed, only falsified. As a result, testing of this theory should not stop if edge effects are identified, and this work should act rather as a basis for further research.

The following chapter is separated into four main sections. Firstly, a literature review will provide a more in-depth introduction into crime generators and attractors, as well as edge effects and crime distribution around these facilities. After this, the methodology shall discuss the model specifications and stylised facts used in this work. Results and discussion follow, ending with a conclusion.

Literature review

Crime generators and attractors

The concept of crime generators and crime attractors is underpinned by ideas from both crime pattern theory (Brantingham and Brantingham, 1981), which posits that an offence occurs when offenders' "activity space" meets a criminal opportunity (Brantingham and Brantingham, 2008), and routine activity theory (Cohen and Felson, 1979), which proposes that a crime will occur where and when there is a convergence of a motivated offender, a potential victim and the absence of a guardian. As a result, crime generators and attractors are not considered to be part of one theory over the other, and the theoretical explanations of this phenomenon are instead used interchangeably. Despite this potential ambiguity, and the aforementioned methodological limitations in studying these spaces empirically, this concept has nevertheless been widely accepted in environmental criminology (Kurland et al., 2014).

Although few studies have attempted to quantify the differences between crime generators and attractors (Newton et al., 2014), some authors have acknowledged ways in which they could be distinguished. Bowers (2014), for example, suggested that these different spaces are likely to experience different types of crimes. Crime generators, she claims, could be more likely to see high frequencies of property crimes, as opposed to crime attractors, which could experience more violent crimes. Clarke and Eck (2003, 2005), on the other hand, contend that these facilities can be distinguished based on their crime rates; although both types of spaces would experience high counts of crime, crime generators would see low crime rates, as there is a large number of potential targets. Conversely, crime attractors would have far higher crime rates, as there are relatively fewer targets available. Ratcliffe (2012a) offers a further distinction, suggesting that crime attractors diffuse crime into their vicinities, whereas crime generators do not have this effect.

Since the introduction of the crime generators and attractors idea in 1995 (Brantingham and Brantingham, 1995), it has not been without criticism. A number of authors have, for example, questioned the existence of two discrete types of clusters. Clarke and Eck (2003, 2005), for instance, suggested the existence of a third: crime enablers. These, they claimed, are spaces where crimes occur due to poor management practices, which lead to minimal regulation of criminal behaviour (Clarke and Eck, 2003, 2005). A location can become a crime enabler rapidly, such as by the removal of a car park attendant (Clarke and Eck, 2005), or slowly, if place management gradually deteriorates (Clarke and Eck, 2005). Crime enablers have, however, been excluded from this research, which is focusing on the two cluster types initially conceptualised by Brantingham and Brantingham (1995).

Moreover, the distinct nature of generators and attractors as separate entities has also been challenged (Brantingham and Brantingham, 1993, 1995; Frank et al., 2011; Kurland et al., 2014). Irvin-Erickson and La Vigne (2015), for example, in their study of transit stations, stress that a transit hub can be identified as both a generator and an attractor, concluding that time of day is central to which cluster type it can be considered to be. Moreover, Clarke and Eck (2003, 2005) suggested that a facility can transition between each of these types of cluster. An example of a shopping area is given by Clarke and Eck (2003, 2005); a shopping centre is traditionally considered to be a crime generator (Brantingham and Brantingham, 1995), but as more people visit the centre, the opportunity for crime increases, potentially attracting new offenders, and consequently rendering it a crime attractor.

Edge effects

As previously stated, the idea of edge effects, underpinned by concepts from crime pattern theory (Rengert et al., 2012), claims that more crime occurs in the space between two adjacent, yet dissimilar, areas than in the internal zones (Brantingham and Brantingham, 1975). These edges are considered to be the boundaries between two different areas of a city, where the change between these two spaces is sufficiently clear to be discernible (Brantingham and Brantingham, 1993). Whilst this can be a physical boundary, such as a railway or a lake, it can also be a conceptual boundary between two areas (Brantingham and Brantingham, 1975). As a result, these edges can be either well defined or subtle (Song et al., 2013, 2017). As this work is exploring an abstract space, the edges examined here represent any form of boundary. This was considered the most appropriate for this testing, as it is impossible to discount one form or the other from investigation into crime generators and attractors. Whilst, for example, it is possible that crime attractors could primarily be bounded by conceptual edges, due to their largely unofficial and undefined nature, crime generators, on the other hand, may see more defined borders; spaces like parks (given as an example of a crime generator by Groff and McCord, 2012), shopping precincts (Brantingham and Brantingham, 1995) or high schools (Kurland et al., 2014) can have more clearly delimited boundaries than areas such as drug markets, as an example of an attractor (Brantingham and Brantingham, 1995).

Although the effect of crime clustering at edges has been investigated relatively less than that between crime and other environmental features (Kim and Hipp, 2018), a number of studies have found empirical evidence for edge effects. The first work investigating this phenomenon was that of Brantingham and Brantingham (1975), which was motivated by concepts from both criminological and sociological literature, both of which pointed to increased crime at area boundaries. Applying this theory to the city of Tallahassee, Florida, they identified higher burglary rates in blocks which bordered edges, which they defined using demographic data. Similar patterns have also been found in work by researchers such as Kim and Hipp (2018), who examined crime at both physical and conceptual edges in Southern California, USA; Song et al. (2013), who identified 64% higher crime in conceptual edge areas compared to interior areas in Burnaby, Canada; and Song et al. (2017), who found increased evidence for edge effects near crime generators in parts of Metro Vancouver, Canada. Despite this, however, an investigation by Herbert and Hyde (1985, p. 265) in Swansea, UK, found "discernible but inconsistent" evidence for edge effects, leading to the suggestion that it may not be appropriate to apply this concept to all contexts (Herbert and Hyde, 1985).

Crime distribution around crime generators and attractors

Crime generators and attractors tend to be investigated as criminogenic facilities, with minimal consideration of the space in which they are located (Boessen and Hipp, 2018). Additionally, as highlighted by Bowers (2014), there has previously been little distinction between crimes that occur within the crime generator and attractor, and those in their vicinity, despite Brantingham and Brantingham's (1995, p. 13) claim that many of the crimes which occur at facilities such as crime generators "in fact occur at the edges of the high activity location". It seems logical, therefore, that the immediate environment of these spaces is intrinsically connected to the facility itself (Ratcliffe, 2012a), and consequently ought to be considered collectively.

However, the consequences of crime generators and attractors on crime in their surroundings have not been found to be consistent. Some researchers propose that crime generators and attractors would lead to more crime in their vicinity. Ratcliffe (2012a), for example, in his study of crime around locations which sell alcohol, identified that crime clustered within 330 feet of these facilities. Additionally, it has been suggested that offenders commit crime whilst *en route* to a generator or attractor (Bernasco and Block, 2011; Bowers, 2014; Frank et al., 2011). Given that one of the explanations proposed for edge effects is the frequent presence of strangers in these areas, it seems likely that this could lead to increased criminal activity in the areas bordering crime generators and attractors. This suggestion has been countered, however, with the possibility that, in some situations, the social ties associated with the facility would lead to increased guardianship by residents, thus reducing crime in this surrounding zone (Boessen and Hipp, 2018). Moreover, Ratcliffe (2012a) has suggested that crime generators and attractors could lead to different crime patterns in their vicinity; that attractors may transmit crime into areas nearby, but that generators would not cause this spreading.

Evidently, the relationship between these spaces and their surrounding neighbouring areas is complex. However, the majority of work investigating their wider effects has identified higher volumes of crimes in areas which are in close proximity to these facilities. Bernasco and Block (2011), for example, found that blocks in Chicago which contain a crime generator or attractor have the highest robbery count, those adjacent have fewer and those which are further away have fewer still – so-called *distance decay*. Further studies which identified this pattern around a variety of facilities include Groff and Lockwood (2014) and Furr-Holden et al. (2016). Other researchers have discovered this trend around a particular kind of facility, such as Fagan and Davies's (2000, cited by Bowers, 2014) investigation of violent crime around public housing projects and Roncek and LoBosco's (1983, cited by Ratcliffe, 2012b) study of offences in the vicinity of high schools. The impact of drinking establishments on crime has also been found to replicate this pattern in a number of pieces of work, including that of Groff (2011), Kumar and Waylor

Investigating edge effects 51

(2003) and Ratcliffe (2012a). Indeed, Ratcliffe (2012a, p. 115) highlights that high density for violent crime tends to cluster around alcohol establishments, and "declines rapidly" as one moves further from these facilities.

Other pieces of research have, however, found evidence which contradicts this pattern. Holloway and McNulty (2003), for example, examined the impact of public housing on crime in Atlanta, and identified that, whilst some of these projects exhibit this pattern, others show either less pronounced effects, or none at all, stressing the variability around different facilities. Moreover, Griffiths and Tita (2009) found no evidence of distance decay of homicide around public housing in Los Angeles, and Boessen and Hipp (2018) found that blocks near to parks generally experience less crime than those further away.

Consequently, it is a combination of this complexity, lack of theoretical investigation and the aforementioned limitations to empirical analysis which drives this theory testing. As stressed by Boessen and Hipp (2018), improved understanding of the context of crime generators, and thus also attractors, is needed, in order that we are able to better comprehend the wider effects of these facilities on crime patterns.

Methodology

The model presented in this chapter was created using NetLogo, a program which has been used in previous criminological research (such as Weisburd et al., 2017 and Collins et al., 2017). NetLogo consists of a two-dimensional grid of cells called "patches", and mobile agents, referred to as "turtles". In this model, only one type of agent is represented – offenders. Three different model configurations were created – a traditional crime generator and a traditional crime attractor, in both of which offender movement was underpinned by theory, alongside a control model in which movement was random. The latter was used to assess the impact of the crime generator and attractor on the base case.

This section shall provide detail of the specification of these models, as well as the stylised facts used to assess their results.

Model specification

Environments

As previously stated, the environments modelled here were all abstract representations of reality, in order to reduce the additional complexity of a real-world geography (Elffers and van Baal, 2008). The environment was designed as a torus, to prevent the clustering of agents within the centre of the model.

Features which remained consistent across all three model environments are as follows.

Criminal opportunity

Upon initialization, each patch in the environment was allocated a value in the range [1,100], representing the potential for criminal activity, where the higher value signifies more opportunity. Higher opportunity is represented on Figure 3.1 with a lighter-coloured patch. This value was integral to the mechanism which leads to crime being committed, which is discussed later.

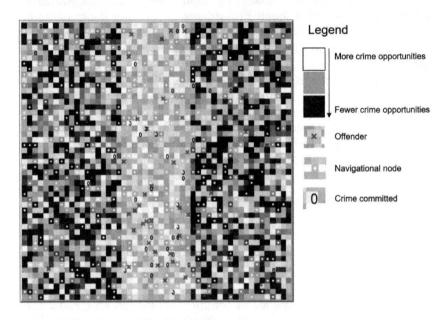

Figure 3.1 Model environment example.

Although crime type can be separated into property crime and interpersonal crime, the concept of "crime" in this model represents either of these forms. Given that crime generators and attractors are likely to experience different types of offences (Bowers, 2014), and that the environments modelled here are abstract, this was considered to be more appropriate than selecting one crime type over the other. By not including the additional complexity of victim behaviour, the model is better able to highlight the core mechanisms that influence the patterns of crime around generators and attractors.

A brief summary of each model environment is as follows.

Control model

The control model represents an environment with no specific crime generator or attractor, suggesting evenly distributed criminal opportunities, with minimal clustering. In this model, the criminal opportunity was randomly allocated across the environment, within the range [1,100].

Generator model

Within the generator model, a central band of the environment represented the generator area, as demonstrated in Figure 3.1. This strip was used to represent this space, rather than a square area, to simplify the analysis of results. Using a circular central area, rather than a strip, would not influence the conclusions drawn. All patches here had a random criminal opportunity value in the range [50,100], compared with those outside to the space, which had random values in the range [1,100]

Attractor model

The attractor model used the same central band as the generator model to demarcate the attractor area, as demonstrated in Figure 3.1, with the same range of opportunity values. The difference between the two areas was in how they influence the behaviour of agents, as discussed below.

Navigational nodes

As seen in other agent-based models in criminology, such as Birks et al. (2012, 2014) and Groff (2007), a set of navigational nodes was created to represent transport intersections. This network of nodes, which were randomly distributed across the environment, was used by agents to navigate the space.

As proposed by routine activities theory, each agent was allocated a set of "routine nodes" in the models, as well as a home node, where they started the simulations. These nodes represented those places visited more frequently, such as work and shopping facilities (Frank et al., 2011), and were consequently visited more often than nodes which were not considered routine. In the control and attractor models, 10% of all nodes were randomly allocated to each offender upon initialisation as their routine nodes. This value was chosen arbitrarily, as no literature could be found which was able to improve the estimate of how many places a person routinely visits. In the generator model, aligned with the theoretical mechanisms underpinning these spaces, all navigational nodes located within the generator space also formed part of the offenders' routine nodes, as well as the random 10%. As the latter were randomly allocated, some could be located within the generator area. This could lead to the agents having varying numbers of routine nodes between runs; if an offender's randomly selected 10% fell inside the generator area, they had fewer routine nodes in the outside space than an offender whose random routine nodes were all outside the generator. The number of routine nodes, however, does not significantly impact agents' movement, and is not as important as their location; it is the central clustering which is fundamental to the generator mechanism. The distribution of these nodes, as well as the home node, is demonstrated in Figures 3.2 and 3.3 – examples of the generator and attractor environment respectively.

54 *Verity Tether et al.*

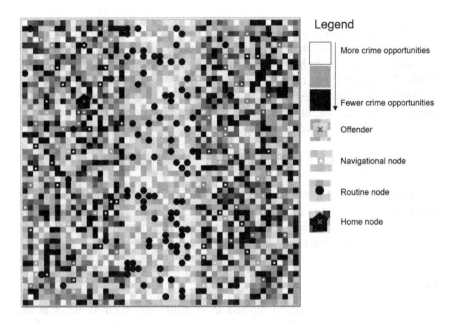

Figure 3.2 Generator model environment example.

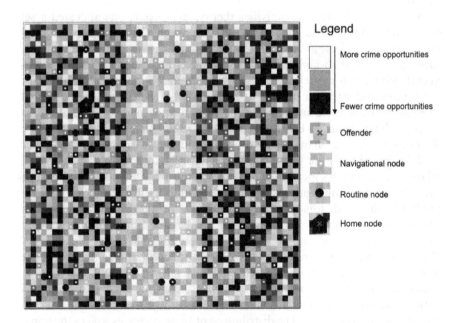

Figure 3.3 Attractor model environment example.

Agent specification and behaviour

In these models, each agent had a value representing their motivation to commit a crime, which was in the range [1,100]. Upon initialisation, all offenders were allocated a random value for this variable. The motivation variable fluctuated with each step of the model, either increasing or decreasing each offender's motivation, creating some offenders who were more motivated to commit a crime than others. This variable was limited to the range [0,100]. Committing a crime reduced this motivation variable by 10%, representing satiety. A more specific value could not be identified in a literature search.

In all environments, the offenders moved around the environment via the navigational nodes. To move, the agents randomly selected a node to be their destination, moved towards it via the shortest path between the nodes until it was reached, then selected a different destination node. The model user is able to select the frequency with which the destination node is a routine node. In the model runs which created the results discussed in this chapter, every node visited was a routine node, in order to most accurately represent routine activities theory. However, if the user desires more random navigation of the environment, this is also possible.

In the control and generator models, the destination was either any random node or a routine node, as selected by the model user. When an offender selected a routine node as their destination, there was a 60% likelihood of selecting the home node over any other routine node, in order to represent increased time spent at home. If the offender was already at their home node and must select another routine node, they selected one at random. This is demonstrated in a flowchart in Figure 3.4. In the attractor model, however, this behaviour was over-ridden when the motivation of an offender crossed the threshold of 75. Once this value had been reached, the offender selected a destination node within the attractor area, modelling the theoretical "luring" of the offenders to the space. When this variable was under 75, the movement was the same as that of the control and generator environments. This threshold was selected arbitrarily as a more precise value was not found in a literature search.

The likelihood that a crime will be committed in a specific location (x,y) at a specific time (t) is a product of the probabilities that a suitably motivated offender is in an area with suitably high opportunity. It is calculated as follows, with λ representing a scaling value, as discussed later:

$$p(commit)_{(x,y,t)} = p(motivation)_{(x,y,t)} * p(opportunity)_{(x,y,t)} * \lambda \qquad (3.1)$$

Whilst there could be some merit in incorporating a temporal element to this model, such as agents spending longer at home than at other nodes, this has not been included here. Given that agents do not interact, and

56 *Verity Tether et al.*

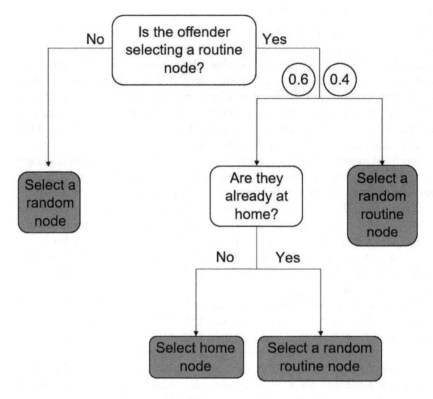

Figure 3.4 Offender movement flowchart.

consequently do not need to be synchronised, it was deemed unnecessary for this model. This would, however, be an interesting addition for a later version of this research.

Simulation experiments

As the model is stochastic, a number of separate simulations were executed for each experiment. Each simulation was run for each environment 1,000 times, lasting 3,000 iterations each. There were 250 navigational nodes in each environment, and 50 offenders. The random seed was set to a constant value upon initialisation, to ensure that the same layout of (randomly distributed) criminal opportunity and navigational nodes would be tested under each scenario, allowing for more direct comparisons between the results of each environment. Once the environment had been initialised, the random seed was given a new (random) value, so that each simulation would produce different results.

Analysis methods

After the model had been executed 1,000 times for each environment, the total count of crimes per patch was exported from NetLogo. To visualise the distribution of crime within the generator or attractor spaces, relative to the areas surrounding them, two different methods were utilised: scatter plots and choropleth maps. Prior to this, however, boxplots were created to examine variance between the model runs.

Scatter plots

In order to graphically display the crime distribution on a scatter plot, transects for each step along the *x*-axis were created. The average number of crimes along each transect was then counted, demonstrated graphically in Figure 3.5. This enabled the creation of a scatter plot for each environment, showing the number of crimes which occurred by each step across the *x*-axis. It is expected that the control area model would create a scatter plot which is fairly uniform across the environment, but the generator and attractor

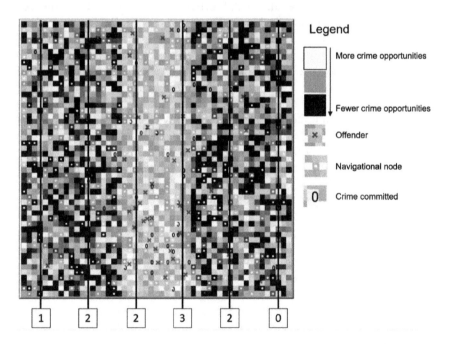

Figure 3.5 Transect example. By counting the number of crimes which are committed along each transect (showed in the box below each), the total number per step along the *x*-axis is obtained. This can then be converted into a scatter plot.

environments would both see increased crime within their boundaries, signifying the clustering of crimes in the generator or attractor space. The areas of interest in this work, however, are the edges of these spaces, and whether these areas experience more crime than the interior.

Choropleth maps

Whilst the strength in the scatter plots lies in their ability to simplify the data, clearly demonstrating the trend along the x-axis, this could mask any patterns which occur along these transects. As a result, the average number of crimes per patch was calculated for each environment, and then converted into a raster grid, to enable a clear visualisation of the crime patterns across the whole environment in the form of a choropleth map.

Stylised facts

In order to validate the results, they shall be compared with a stylised fact; that of crime concentration. It is well known that the spatial distribution of crime is neither random nor uniform, instead concentrating in space and time (Farrell, 2015; Frank et al., 2012; Wortley and Mazerolle, 2008). Indeed, Kinney et al. (2008) stress that the distribution of crime follows a power law: that crime is intensely concentrated in some locations, and tapers away to few crimes in others. Although crime concentration has been identified at a range of spatial scales (Johnson, 2010), this work concerns microgeographic spaces, and is thus examining what Weisburd (2015) termed the *law of crime concentration at place*.

Research into crime at microgeographic places began in the late 1980s (Weisburd, 2015), with the term *criminology of place* being coined in 1989 by Sherman et al. (Weisburd, 2015). Since then, interest in this field has grown, and a number of studies have identified clustering at this small spatial scale (see Weisburd (2015) for a detailed review on this subject).

Because studies of crime concentration have developed in a somewhat piecemeal manner, it has been highlighted that some concepts and terms can be imprecise (Farrell, 2015). Despite this, it is considered appropriate as stylised reality for this work. Not only is empirical evidence identifying it consistently found (Johnson, 2010), but Weisburd (2015) identified sufficient evidence to liken the clustering of crime at micro-places to a physical law, identifying that crime concentration consistently remains within a limited bandwidth. Moreover, Weisburd (2015, p. 135) suggests that crime concentration at place is "[p]erhaps the first and most important empirical observation in the criminology of place".

As a result, in order to corroborate the theory examined here, spatial concentration of crime must be identified by the results of the model, with both the generator and attractor models leading to the creation of crime clusters. However, as stressed by Crooks et al. (2008), validity of a model should not be considered in binary terms. Accordingly, presence of crime concentration will not automatically validate these models, rather suggesting a strong degree of validity.

Sensitivity testing

In order to test whether various settings and variables within the model were appropriate, sensitivity testing was undertaken. When specific tests were run, settings were adjusted, and run 100 times for each environment, for 3,000 iterations each. The sensitivity testing of this model focused on three primary parameters within the code.

Scaling value

Within the equation to calculate the probability of committing crime, Equation 3.1, a scaling value, λ, is used to uniformly reduce how frequently crimes are committed. A number of different scaling values were tested, in 0.01 increments between 0.01 and 0.09, as well as having no scaling value, in order to examine its impact on the crime patterns. It was identified that all values, including not using a scaling value at all, produced the same patterns in their outputs, and thus the specific value used is not of note. As a result, 0.05 was selected as this value, in order to make offences fairly infrequent, as the higher the number of crimes committed, the more computationally expensive it was to run the model.

Motivation variable

In order to assess the appropriateness of the motivation variable, tests were undertaken to explore its value upon initialisation. Giving all offenders the same value upon initialisation was found to lead to the same patterns as giving them a random value. As a result, the latter was selected, as it is more realistic, reflecting the population's varying propensity to commit crime (Brantingham and Brantingham, 1981).

Another feature examined was the effect of offending on the agents' motivation; whether it should reduce following an offence. The patterns for the control and generator models remained the same in either scenario, but those of the crime attractor became more similar to those seen from the generator model, which shall be discussed shortly. It was considered that the reduction of motivation following an offence is more realistic, and was consequently included in the code.

Number of navigational nodes

Given that a large number of navigational nodes would be more computationally expensive than a small number, tests were run to identify a suitable value for this variable. The use of a smaller number of nodes (50) led to wider variance in model results, whereas a larger number (500) led to more reliable results. Consequently, an intermediate value (250) was selected.

Results

In order to examine variance between each model run, boxplots were made of the results of all three environments, by transect. As many of the patches did not have a crime committed on them, the large number of zeros in the data was suppressing meaningful patterns. As a result, any zero value was removed. Figures 3.6–3.8 are the resultant boxplots, and demonstrate that, although a few outliers occurred, the majority of the model runs experienced relatively little variance.

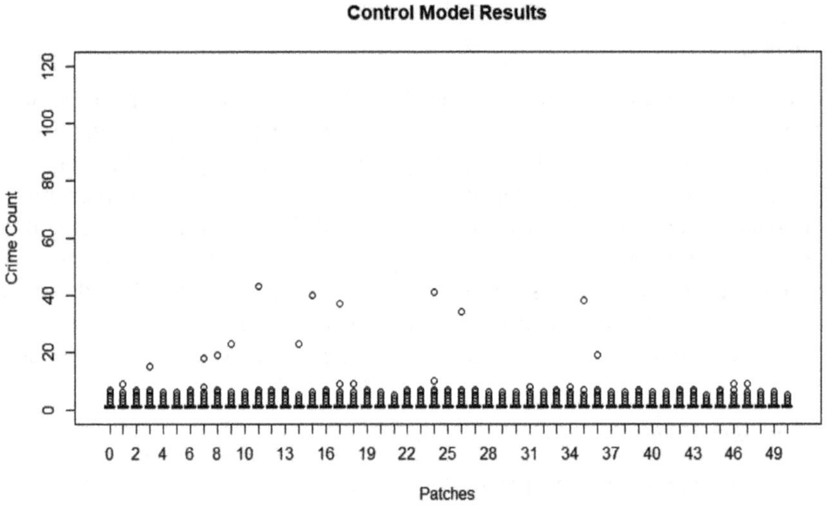

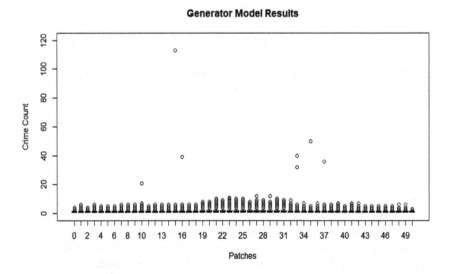

Figure 3.6 Control model boxplot.

Figure 3.7 Generator model boxplot.

Investigating edge effects 61

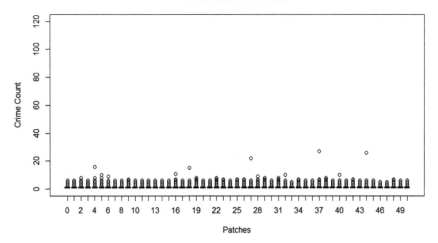

Figure 3.8 Attractor model boxplot.

Control area

Figure 3.9 presents the results of the model runs for the control area, showing the average crime count per transect of the environment. These results demonstrate, as expected, a fairly even distribution of crime across the environment with no noticeable clusters. There are, on average, around 0.27 crimes per patch across each transect, but this increases slightly to 0.285 in the centre, and declines slightly at the left- and right-most edges of the environment to

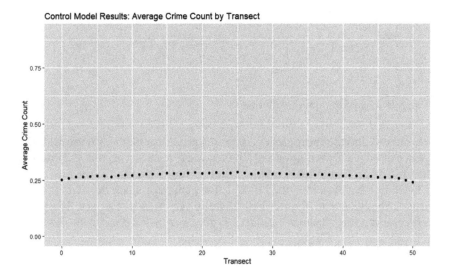

Figure 3.9 Control model scatter plot.

62 Verity Tether et al.

0.25 and 0.24 respectively. Due to this small range of values, the choropleth map of these results has not been included here.

As no clusters are evident here, these results indicate that any clustering identified by the generator and attractor models is solely the result of the mechanisms which underpin them.

Crime generator

The results of the model runs for the generator model identify a vast increase in crime within the generator space. As one can see from Figure 3.10, the scatter plot for the generator model, offending increases drastically once one enters the generator. On both sides of the boundary of the area, 0.31 crimes are committed per patch, which almost doubles to 0.59 crimes in the adjacent transects. The crime count then increases steadily, reaching its peak in the centre of the space, where 0.86 crimes are committed per patch.

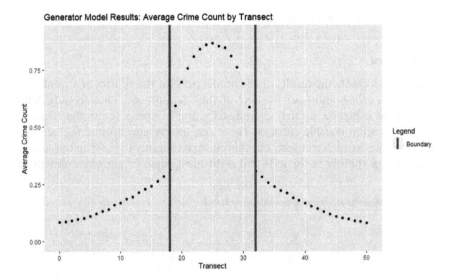

Figure 3.10 Generator model scatter plot.

From this and the choropleth map for the generator model, Figure 3.11, the absence of edge effects is apparent. In fact, the reverse is true, that the internal edges of the generator space see the lowest amount of crime in the area.

The crime patterns identified outside the generator space are also of note. Particularly evident in Figure 3.10, there is very steady distance decay. On average, offending declines by 0.013 crimes per patch as one moves each

Investigating edge effects 63

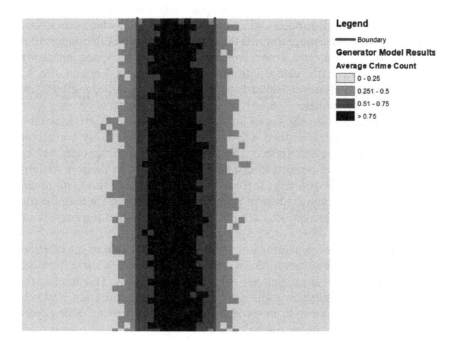

Figure 3.11 Generator model choropleth map.

transect away from the generator space. This distance decay, combined with the steady increase of crime towards the centre of the generator space, suggests that the presence of a crime generator in an area could lead to stark clustering of crime.

In order to corroborate or reject this finding, these results must be compared with the aforementioned stylised reality – that of crime concentration. Crime concentration is evident in both graphs for this model, consequently suggesting that the results identified here are valid; that edge effects are not present around the crime generator. However, as previously discussed, the need to consider validity in non-binary terms is relevant here. Whilst this suggests that the results of this work are valid, and that there is no potential relationship between edge effects and crime generators, additional research is needed in order to corroborate this further.

Crime attractor

As displayed in Figure 3.12, the scatter graph of the attractor model results overlaid on to the generator results, this simulation also identified an increase in crime occurrence within the attractor space, albeit to a lesser extent than those of the generator model. Unlike the crime generator, which sees a vast increase in crime occurrence towards the centre of the space, offending within the crime attractor occurs at a more consistent rate across the space, increasing only slightly towards the centre – from 0.405 at the internal boundaries, to 0.44 in the centre. However, similarly to the crime generator, edge effects are not present in this model.

In the space outside the crime attractor, similar patterns are identified to those of the control model, where offending remains fairly consistent across the external space. Indeed, this space even sees comparable values to the control area: around 0.25 crimes per patch. Whilst there is a slight decline evident in the transects furthest from the attractor, this is minimal. This decline is, however, evident in Figure 3.13, the choropleth map for the attractor model, where one can see noticeably less crime in the corners of the environments.

Although the crime generator saw crime almost double from the external to internal spaces, the attractor model does not identify such a harsh increase, instead increasing by approximately 0.15 crimes per patch. This model still does, however, reproduce the stylised reality of crime concentration, and validate the model. As a result, no potential relationship between edge effects and crime attractors can be concluded.

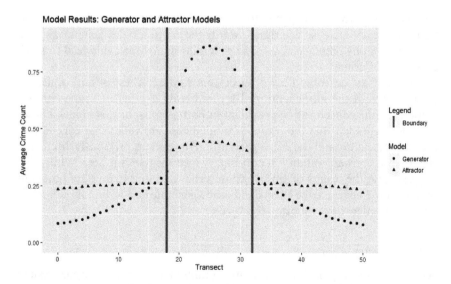

Figure 3.12 Generator and attractor model results.

Investigating edge effects 65

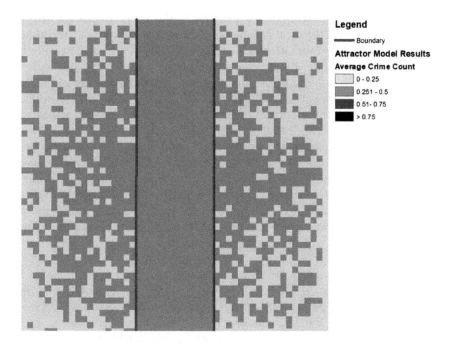

Figure 3.13 Attractor model choropleth map.

Discussion

The aim of this work was to use agent-based models to identify whether edge effects, in the form of increased crime around the edges of a space, occur around crime generators or crime attractors. However, neither the generator nor attractor model suggested that offending spikes on their edges. In fact, the edges of these spaces saw less crime than the centres, as offending increased with each step towards the centre of both of these areas. As a result, following validation of the models through stylised reality, this theory testing has suggested that, in this instance, the mechanisms underpinning crime generators and crime attractors alone do not lead to the emergence of edge effects around these spaces. If empirical evidence can also be found for this, it could have implications for policy, as it suggests that the internal areas of these facilities could require more guardianship than the edges.

However, it is not merely offences around the edges of these spaces which are interesting here. These models identified differing crime patterns for each type of space, both internally and externally. Inside the generator, for example, offending was found to increase steadily towards the centre of the space, where it reached its peak. Given that theory dictates that the majority of the crime problem experienced at generator locations is caused by more people using the space (Clarke and Eck, 2003), this suggests that the centre of the generator was the most heavily travelled area of the model. The inside of the attractor, however, saw far less variation, despite also increasing a little towards the centre. Indeed, the frequency of crime occurrence within the attractor area is fairly stable across the space. Moreover, the extent to which crime increases at the boundary of these spaces also differs; whilst offending almost doubles when one enters the generator space, the increase at the boundary of the crime attractor is less pronounced.

Furthermore, despite the fact that work on crime generators and attractors has rarely examined the vicinity of the facility under scrutiny (Boessen and Hipp, 2018), the patterns identified outside these spaces are also of note, as they suggest clear differences outside the generator and attractor. Whilst the model for the crime attractor found that offending outside this space is fairly uniform, with minimal fluctuation, that for the crime generator identified the clear existence of distance decay occurring in this area. As previously highlighted, a number of projects have identified the presence of distance decay around facilities (see, for example, Bernasco and Block, 2011; Bowers, 2014; Furr-Holden et al., 2016; Groff, 2011; Groff and Lockwood, 2014; Holloway and McNulty, 2003; Kumar and Waylor, 2003; Ratcliffe, 2012a), and thus this finding is in line with previous empirical investigations.

Could these patterns be used to quantify real-world generators and attractors? As previously stated, little work has been undertaken attempting to find ways to classify these spaces (Newton et al., 2014). However, the results of this analysis suggest that the spatial crime patterns in their vicinity, as well as those within the crime generator and attractor spaces themselves, are highly different. As a result, for example, the presence of clearly defined distance decay around a facility could suggest that it is a crime generator, rather than a crime attractor. Furthermore, these patterns could also suggest that an area which has many crime generators could see greater clustering of crime than an area with many crime attractors.

Moreover, these results appear to refute Ratcliffe's (2012a) suggestion that crime attractors radiate crime into their surroundings, whereas crime generators have no contagious effect. However, given that the focus of Ratcliffe's work was not on the distinction between these spaces, but their influence on their vicinity, the underlying mechanisms examined here were not tested. This again suggests that these mechanisms need to be explored further, in order to improve our understanding of them in a variety of settings.

However, this work is not without limitations, the most notable being the lack of testing for statistical significance. In an attempt to mitigate this, hot spot analysis, in the form of Getis-Ord Gi* analysis, was conducted using a GIS to identify areas which saw statistically significant crime hot spots. However, because this software was unable to identify the environment as a torus and thus the algorithm presumed a boundary around it, the patterns identified at the edges were incorrect. Future work would benefit from the application of tests to identify statistical significance.

Conclusions

Whilst this work aimed to investigate crime patterns on the edges of crime generators and attractors, the results across the whole environment were notable, identifying clear differences in the spatial distribution of crime both inside and outside these spaces.

This discovery could have broad practical implications, as well as contributing to theory development. If it is possible to identify whether a space is a crime generator or attractor, policing strategies planned for the area could be tailored to the mechanisms which are leading to offences occurring there. In order to develop this idea, further empirical analysis on crime generators and attractors is required to examine whether the theoretical presence of this pattern matches that identified empirically.

References

Bernasco, W., Block, R., 2011. Robberies in Chicago: a block-level analysis of the influence of crime generators, crime attractors, and offender anchor points. J. Res. Crime Delinquency 48, 33–57. https://doi.org/10.1177/0022427810384135

Birks, D., Townsley, M., Stewart, A., 2012. Generative explanations of crime: using simulation to test criminological theory. Criminology 50, 221–254. https://doi.org/10.1111/j.1745-9125.2011.00258.x

Birks, D., Townsley, M., Stewart, A., 2014. Emergent regularities of interpersonal victimization: an agent-based investigation. J. Res. Crime Delinquency 51, 119–140. https://doi.org/10.1177/0022427813487353

Boessen, A., Hipp, J.R., 2018. Parks as crime inhibitors or generators: examining parks and the role of their nearby context. Soc. Sci. Res. 76, 186–201. https://doi.org/10.1016/j.ssresearch.2018.08.008

Bowers, K., 2014. Risky facilities: crime radiators or crime absorbers? A comparison of internal and external levels of theft. J. Quant. Criminol. 30, 389–414. https://doi.org/10.1007/s10940-013-9208-z

Brantingham, P.J., Brantingham, P.L., 1975. The spatial patterning of burglary. Howard J. Crim. Justice 14, 11–23. https://doi.org/10.1111/j.1468-2311.1975.tb00297.x

Brantingham, P.L., Brantingham, P.J., 1981. Mobility, notoriety, and crime – a study in the crime patterns of urban nodal points. J. Environ. Syst. 11, 89–99. https://doi.org/10.2190/dthj-ernn-hvcv-6k5t

Brantingham, P.L., Brantingham, P.J., 1993. – Nodes, paths and edges: considerations on the complexity of crime and the physical environment. J. Environ. Psychol. 13, 3–28.

Brantingham, P., Brantingham, P., 1995. Criminality of place: crime attractors and crime generators. Eur. J. Crim. Policy Res. 3, 5–26.

Brantingham, P., Brantingham, P., 2008. Crime pattern theory, in: Wortley, R., Mazerolle, L. (eds.), *Environmental Criminology and Crime Analysis*. Willan Publishing, Devon, pp. 78–93.

Clarke, R., Eck, J., 2003. *Become a Problem Solving Crime Analyst in 55 Small Steps*. London: Jill Dando Institute of Crime Science.

Clarke, R., Eck, J., 2005. *Crime Analysis for Problem Solvers in 60 Small Steps*. Washington, DC: Center for Problem Oriented Policing.

Cohen, L., Felson, M., 1979. Social change and crime rate trends: a routine activity approach. Am. Sociol. Rev. 44, 588–608.

Collins, A., Cornelius, C., Sokolowski, J., 2017. Agent-based model of criminal gang formation. Proc. Agent-Dir. Simul. Symp. Artic. No 9.

Crooks, A., Castle, C., Batty, M., 2008. Key challenges in agent-based modelling for geo-spatial simulation. Comput. Environ. Urban Syst. 32, 417–430. https://doi.org/10.1016/j.compenvurbsys.2008.09.004

Elffers, H., van Baal, P., 2008. Realistic spatial backcloth is not that important in agent based simulation research: an illustration from simulating perceptual deterrence, in: Liu, L., Eck, J. (eds.), *Artificial Crime Analysis Systems: Using Computer Simulations and Geographic Information Systems*. Hershey, PA: IGI Global, pp. 19–24. https://doi.org/10.4018/978-1-59904-591-7

Farrell, G., 2015. Crime concentration theory. Crime Prev. Community Saf. 17, 233–248. https://doi.org/10.1057/cpcs.2015.17

Frank, R., Andresen, M.A., Brantingham, P.L., 2012. Criminal directionality and the structure of urban form. J. Environ. Psychol. 32, 37–42. https://doi.org/10.1016/j.jenvp.2011.09.004

Frank, R., Andresen, M.A., Cheng, C., Brantingham, P., 2011. Finding criminal attractors based on offenders' directionality of crimes, in: 2011 European Intelligence and Security Informatics Conference. Presented at the 2011 European Intelligence and Security Informatics Conference (EISIC), IEEE, Athens, Greece, pp. 86–93. https://doi.org/10.1109/EISIC.2011.34

Furr-Holden, C.D.M., Milam, A.J., Nesoff, E.D., Johnson, R.M., Fakunle, D.O., Jennings, J.M., Thorpe, R.J., 2016. Not in my back yard: a comparative analysis of crime around publicly funded drug treatment centers, liquor stores, convenience stores, and corner stores in one mid-Atlantic city. J. Stud. Alcohol Drugs 77, 17–24. https://doi.org/10.15288/jsad.2016.77.17

Griffiths, E., Tita, G., 2009. Homicide in and around public housing: is public housing a hotbed, a magnet, or a generator of violence for the surrounding community? Soc. Probl. 56, 474–493. https://doi.org/10.1525/sp.2009.56.3.474

Groff, E.R., 2007. Simulation for theory testing and experimentation: an example using routine activity theory and street robbery. J. Quant. Criminol. 23, 75–103. https://doi.org/10.1007/s10940-006-9021-z

Groff, E., 2011. Exploring "near": characterizing the spatial extent of drinking place influence on crime. Aust. N. Z. J. Criminol. 44, 156–179. https://doi.org/10.1177/0004865811405253

Groff, E.R., Lockwood, B., 2014. Criminogenic facilities and crime across street segments in Philadelphia: uncovering evidence about the spatial extent of facility influence. J. Res. Crime Delinquency 51, 277–314. https://doi.org/10.1177/0022427813512494

Groff, E., McCord, E.S., 2012. The role of neighborhood parks as crime generators. Secur. J. 25, 1–24. https://doi.org/10.1057/sj.2011.1

Herbert, D.T., Hyde, S.W., 1985. Environmental criminology: testing some area hypotheses. Trans. Inst. Br. Geogr. 10, 259. https://doi.org/10.2307/622177

Holloway, S.R., McNulty, T.L., 2003. Contingent urban geographies of violent crime: racial segregation and the impact of public housing in Atlanta. Urban Geogr. 24, 187–211. https://doi.org/10.2747/0272-3638.24.3.187

Homel, R., Clark. J. 1994. The prediction and prevention of violence in pubs and clubs, in: Clarke, R. V. (eds.), *Crime Prevention Studies*, Monsey, NY: Criminal Justice Press, Vol. 3, pp. 1–46.

Houser, K.A., McCord, E.S., Sorg, E.T., 2019. The multilevel impacts of proximate crime generators and attractors on individual-level perceptions of crime risk. Crime Delinquency 65, 1798–1822. https://doi.org/10.1177/0011128718763129

Irvin-Erickson, Y., La Vigne, N., 2015. A spatio-temporal analysis of crime at Washington, DC Metro Rail: stations' crime-generating and crime-attracting characteristics as transportation nodes and places. Crime Sci. 4:14. https://doi.org/10.1186/s40163-015-0026-5

Johnson, S.D., 2010. A brief history of the analysis of crime concentration. Eur. J. Appl. Math. 21, 349–370. https://doi.org/10.1017/s0956792510000082

Kim, Y.A., Hipp, J.R., 2018. Physical boundaries and city boundaries: consequences for crime patterns on street segments? Crime Delinquency 64, 227–254. https://doi.org/10.1177/0011128716687756

Kinney, J., Brantingham, P., Wushcke, K., Kirk, M., Brantingham, P., 2008. Crime attractors, generators and detractors: land use and urban crime opportunities. Built Environ. 34, 62–74.

Kumar, N., Waylor, C.R.M., 2003. Proximity to alcohol-serving establishments and crime probabilities in Savannah, Georgia: a statistical and GIS analysis. Southeast. Geogr. 43, 125–142. https://doi.org/10.1353/sgo.2003.0015

Kurland, J., Johnson, S.D., Tilley, N., 2014. Offenses around stadiums: a natural experiment on crime attraction and generation. J. Res. Crime Delinquency 51, 5–28. https://doi.org/10.1177/0022427812471349

Newton, A.D., Partridge, H., Gill, A., 2014. In and around: identifying predictors of theft within and near to major mass underground transit systems. Secur. J. 27, 132–146. https://doi.org/10.1057/sj.2014.2

Ratcliffe, J., 2012a. How near is near? Quantifying the spatial influence of crime attractors and generators, in: Andresen, M., Kinney, B. (eds.), *Patterns, Prevention and Geometry of Crime, Crime Science*. Abingdon, Oxon: Routledge. pp. 101–117.

Ratcliffe, J.H., 2012b. The spatial extent of criminogenic places: a changepoint regression of violence around bars. Geogr. Anal. 44, 302–320. https://doi.org/10.1111/j.1538-4632.2012.00856.x

Ratcliffe, J.H., Breen, C., 2011. Crime diffusion and displacement: measuring the side effects of police operations. Prof. Geogr. 63, 230–243. https://doi.org/10.1080/00330124.2010.547154

Rengert, G., Lockwood, B., McCord, E., 2012. The edge of the community: drug dealing in a segregated environment, in: *Patterns, Prevention and Gemoetry of Crime, Crime Science*. Abingdon, Oxon: Routledge, pp. 43–53.

Song, J., Andresen, M.A., Brantingham, P.L., Spicer, V., 2017. Crime on the edges: patterns of crime and land use change. Cartogr. Geogr. Inform. Sci. 44, 51–61.

Song, J., Spicer, V., Brantingham, P., 2013. The edge effect: exploring high crime zones near residential neighborhoods. 2013 IEEE International Conference on

Intelligence and Security Informatics, Seattle, WA, 2013, pp. 245–250, doi: 10.1109/ISI.2013.6578828.

Weisburd, D., 2015. The law of crime concentration and the criminology of place. Criminology 53, 133–157. https://doi.org/10.1111/1745-9125.12070

Weisburd, D., Braga, A.A., Groff, E.R., Wooditch, A., 2017. Can hot spots policing reduce crime in urban areas? An agent-based simulation. Criminology 55, 137–173. https://doi.org/10.1111/1745-9125.12131

Wortley, R., Mazerolle, L., 2008. Environmental criminology and crime analysis: situating the theory, analytic approach and application, in: Wortley, R. and Mazerolle, L. (eds.), *Environmental Criminology and Crime Analysis*. London: Routledge, pp. 1–19.

4 Examining guardianship against theft

Elizabeth R. Groff and Jennifer Badham

> *routine activity patterns can influence crime rates by affecting the convergence in space and time of the three minimal elements of direct-contact predatory violations: (1) motivated offenders, (2) suitable targets, and (3) the absence of capable guardians against a violation. We further argue that the lack of any one of these elements is sufficient to prevent the successful completion of a direct-contact predatory crime...*
>
> (Cohen and Felson, 1979, p. 589)

Introduction

Social scientists have long been interested in how to prevent crime from happening. As the above quote illustrates, the routine activity (RA) approach offers a clear framework for identifying and studying the elements necessary for a crime to occur. Using this framework, many studies have focused on changing the motivation of offenders; others have tried to better protect potential targets. Relatively few scholars have investigated capable guardianship. Efforts to examine guardianship have produced theoretical advancements. Two of these advancements developed new subtypes of capable guardians, handlers, and place managers. Handlers (Felson, 1986) are people who leverage their relationship with a potential offender to influence the potential offender's behavior. Place managers (Eck, 1995) are people who, through ownership or employment, control specific places. Another advancement emphasized the measurement of guardianship capability as perceived by potential offenders (Reynald, 2009, 2010, 2011a, 2011b).

Despite these theoretical and methodological developments, quantifying guardianship remains a difficult and time-consuming endeavor. As a result, most existing studies have used indirect measures such as owner-occupied housing units, persons per household, and employment outside the home to represent guardianship (Reynald, 2010). Survey data has also been used to measure frequency of occupancy (Garofalo and Clark, 1992). Neither of these approaches produces data adequate for representing micro-level levels of guardianship intensity nor capable of capturing the dynamic interaction of the three core elements of crime events: motivated offenders, suitable targets, and guardianship intensity.

To address that gap, this chapter develops and implements a theoretically based model of guardianship in a computational laboratory. The conceptual model is informed by several criminological theories important to understanding and representing crime opportunity and offender decision-making. A base model illustrates crime patterns in a virtual world where offenders do not consider the level of guardianship, which is equivalent to invisible (level 0) guardianship from guardianship in action (GIA) (Reynald, 2009). That base model is compared to three additional model scenarios that implement the available (level 1) level of guardianship intensity.

Theoretical foundations for modeling crime events

Together, RA (Cohen & Felson, 1979), crime pattern theory (CPT) (P. J. Brantingham & Brantingham, 1984; P. L. Brantingham & Brantingham, 1993b, 1995), rational choice perspective (RCP) (Clarke & Cornish, 1985), and GIA (Reynald, 2009, 2010) provide the framework for representing human activity patterns, offender decision-making, and guardianship (Figure 4.1). RA and CPT offer explanations of how transportation, land use, and facilities structure human activity to bring together offenders, opportunities, and guardians, as well as how offenders interpret those patterns. RCP explains situational decision-making. Finally, GIA provides the operationalization of guardianship intensity.

Routine activity theory

Cohen and Felson (1979) formulated the RA approach to explain macro-level crime patterns. One key contribution of their work was to emphasize

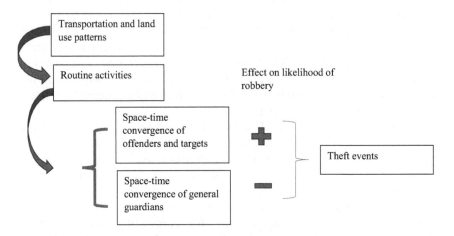

Figure 4.1 Conceptual model of convergence from criminological foundations.

how changes in the spatio-temporal patterns of human activity shaped the opportunities for crime events. Another key contribution was to identify the three essential roles people in criminal situations might play: offender, target, and guardian. In the original work, the theorists noted that crime required a likely offender, a suitable target, and the absence of capable guardianship (Figure 4.1). Crime opportunities arise from the convergences of potential offenders, targets, and guardians in space–time. The lack of any one of these elements can prevent a crime from occurring.

Since the original work there have been extensions to the concept of capable guardianship to explicitly acknowledge two important types of guardians – place managers and handlers – in addition to general guardians. Place managers are individuals who have authority over places and can regulate policies and behavior in places (Eck & Weisburd, 1995; Madensen & Eck, 2013). For example, bar owners can establish a policy that they will not serve visibly inebriated patrons. Handlers are individuals who can alter the behavior of potential offenders because of their relationship via social bonds (Felson, 1986, 1995). For example, a coach can be a handler if her presence alters planned delinquent behavior by a team member. Bystanders who are neither place managers nor handlers are part of the "general guardians" category.

Crime pattern theory

CPT covers some of the same ground as RA but expands the treatment of place and human activity. In CPT, the notion of place characteristics is encompassed in the "urban backcloth" which is defined as the social, cultural, and physical characteristics of the place (Figure 4.1). CPT addresses in more detail how the urban backcloth shapes human activity – specifically, how the transportation system and land use patterns funnel people along certain paths and to certain places. Places that are more accessible or attract many people will have more offender–target convergences and, in the absence of differential guardianship, more opportunities for a crime to occur. In this way, the urban backcloth explains much of the disparity in the number of convergences experienced by places.

The number and type of people present in a situation can largely be explained by the land use patterns, presence of certain facilities (such as schools, grocery stores, etc.), and the transportation network. Land use is important because it describes how the opportunities for work, housing, education, and recreation are arrayed across the landscape. Locations where there are housing units determine the starting point for many trips taken. Locations where there are quite a few facilities attract large numbers of users and thus are part of many people's RA spaces. Transportation networks channel human activity along certain routes. The greater the number of people who use a route, the more who are familiar with the places along that route.

Rational choice perspective

RCP offers the most complete description of criminal decision-making (Clarke & Cornish, 1985). Both RA and CPT rely on the RCP to explain offender decision-making. RCP views crimes as purposeful acts that are committed by individuals using bounded rather than perfect rationality. In other words, an individual considers the information at hand, even if incomplete, to evaluate potential risks and rewards. According to RCP, the decision to commit a crime has two stages, involvement and event. The involvement decision draws from the individual's background and life experiences as they decide whether they consider crime a viable path to meet needs or achieve goals. This decision occurs each time an individual considers how to meet needs or achieve goals with criminal activity as an option.

Once an individual has made a positive initial involvement decision, he or she begins to consider the crime potential of situations and to make event decisions. RCP assumes that offenders make the decision to commit a particular offense based on the characteristics of the specific situation using bounded rationality (i.e., imperfect knowledge). The evaluation of specific situations for their criminal opportunity is an event decision. The event decision involves temporal constraints such as whether there is enough time to commit the crime before returning to work, and external factors such as the characteristics of a situation (i.e., potential risk, potential reward, etc.). Potential offenders consider the risks in terms of the likelihood someone will challenge them and/or call the police. Characteristics of situations in which crimes are successful contribute to the offender's template and are used to evaluate future situations (P. L. Brantingham & Brantingham, 1993a; Clarke & Cornish, 1985).

Guardianship in action

Concentrating on the crime of residential burglary, Reynald (2009) proposed the GIA framework for understanding and measuring how burglars perceive the level of general guardianship present on a street. She defined four levels of resident guardianship intensity: invisible (no evidence the property is occupied); available (evidence that the property is occupied); capable (occupant looking out the window and monitoring); and intervening (direct action).[1] She hypothesized that the stronger the intensity of guardianship in situations, the less crime. She measured guardianship intensity using structured observations and surveys. Her hypothesis was supported; more guardianship intensity was associated with lower crime levels. Additionally, she found that the biggest drop in crime came between the invisible and available intensities, suggesting the importance that simply being available has on the deterrence value of guardians.

Situational aspects of the guardianship role

Situationally then, RA suggests that increasing numbers of people supplies both more targets and more potential guardians and thus could increase or decrease the opportunity for crime. At issue is whether the additional people are perceived by potential offenders as targets or capable guardians. Parsing the empirical relationship between increased numbers of people present and crime is very challenging. Direct measurement of situational dynamics including guardianship is difficult due to the lack of dynamic, micro-level data (O'Sullivan, 2004). Crime data only provides information about the result of convergences; no data exists that describes convergences that did not produce a crime. Consequently, we do not know when potential offenders and suitable targets converge, nor do we know when capable general guardians are present.

GIA introduces the notion of guardianship intensity in determining whether general guardians in situations are perceived as capable by individuals who are considering committing a crime. GIA holds that greater guardianship intensity (e.g., visibly watching from inside is more intense than simply being present but not visible) is associated with lower crime. Guardianship intensity is a measurable concept, but it is costly to collect. However, the perceptions of people who may potentially commit a crime is not measurable. Finally, almost all the existing guardianship literature infers how guardianship affects an offender's decision whether to take advantage of an existing crime opportunity from area-level residential population characteristics.

Agent-based modeling offers an alternative methodology that allows the exploration of dynamic interactions among individuals who are present in situations that result in a crime and in situations that do not. The numbers of people who are present in situations and how they are perceived can be collected and used to explore the relationship between the numbers of people, guardianship intensity, and crime events. The theoretical literature reviewed leads to a set of core assumptions that form the basis for agent behavior in the model (Table 4.1).

Guardianship in existing agent-based models of crime

Several existing agent-based models (ABMs) have explicitly included guardianship. Some represented only formal guardians such as police officers (Bosse, Elffers, & Gerritsen, 2010; Bosse, Gerritsen, & Treur, 2013; Devia & Weber, 2013; N. Wang, Liu, & Eck, 2014; X. Wang, Liu, & Eck, 2008). Others included informal guardianship such as passers-by on the street (Birks & Davies, 2017; Groff, 2007a, 2007b, 2008; Peng & Kurland, 2014).

Approaches to modeling informal guardianship have varied. In two models, the aggregate guardianship influenced the decisions of potential offenders (Groff, 2007a; Peng & Kurland, 2014). The earliest model examined street

Table 4.1 Conceptual model assumptions

Theoretical concept	Perspective
Activities and convergence	
• Theft requires space–time convergence of motivated offenders and suitable targets	RA, CPT, GIA
• Capable guardians can prevent theft when present at the space–time convergence of motivated offenders and suitable targets	RA, GIA
• Convergence frequency is shaped by routine human activity patterns	RA, CPT
• Human activity patterns are shaped by the transportation system and land use patterns	CPT
Offender decision-making	
• The decision to offend is based on bounded rationality	RCP, CPT, RA
• Individuals who have made the initial involvement evaluate crime opportunities during their routine activities	CPT, RA
• Motivated offenders evaluate theft opportunities based on perceived risks and rewards from stealing	RCP
• Event decisions to commit an offense consider: (1) target presence/perceived attractiveness; and (2) perceived level of guardianship (risk)	RA, RCP, CPT, GIA
• A motivated offender's perception of guardianship in a situation considers the presence of person(s) on the street only	RA, RCP
• A motivated offender's perception of guardianship in a situation considers both the presence of person(s) on the street and those who are available inside (displaying visible signs of occupancy)	RA, RCP, GIA

Notes: CPT, crime pattern theory; GIA, guardianship in action; RA, routine activity; RCP, rational choice perspective.

robbery and represented both formal (police) and informal guardianship (Groff, 2007a). Informal guardianship was conceptualized as the presence of additional civilian agents in a situation and operationalized by counting the number of other civilian agents present (in addition to the offender and a potential target) and then used a random number (uniform random between −2 and 2) to represent unknown components in the perception of that guardian as capable by the offender. If the guardianship value was ≥ 1, the offender was deterred. Drawbacks of this approach included: (1) potential offenders perceived all guardians as equally likely to intervene; (2) the model did not account for the effect of familiarity on the interpretation of guardian capability; and (3) potential guardians were not given agency to actively intervene. Peng and Kurland (2014) examined residential burglary patterns. They assigned formal guardians (those in their awareness space) a likelihood of intervening of 100%. Informal guardians (those not in their awareness space) had a 20% likelihood of intervening. All informal guardians were additive. For example, if there were five informal guardians present, the likelihood of intervention was 100%. The offender decided whether to proceed by comparing a randomly drawn number to the total guardianship. If a random number draw was lower than the total amount of guardianship in the situation, the potential offender did not commit the burglary. Neither of these models focused on examining the impact of guardianship on crime outcomes.

In contrast, Birks and Davies (2017) set out to explore the enclosure versus encounter debate which hinges on guardianship. The enclosure hypothesis suggests fewer people translates into fewer targets and thus less crime (Cozens & Love, 2015; Newman, 1972). More people will increase targets and thus increase crime. The encounter hypothesis is that more people equal more "eyes on the street" and thus reduce the likelihood of crime (Jacobs, 1961). In other words, more people translate into less crime. They did not attempt to quantify an aggregate amount of guardianship present in situations. Instead, they assigned each guardian a probability that they would deter the crime. Then they varied the probability by whether the agent was in their awareness space or not. For guardians who were not in their awareness space, the probability of deterring the crime was 0.20. For those who were in their awareness space, three probability values were tested, 0.20 (baseline comparison), 0.33 (empirically based), and 0.50 (stronger effect, to check sensitivity). These values translated to 1 in 5, 1 in 3, or 1 in 2 probabilities of preventing a crime respectively.

Birks and Davies' (2017) conceptualization of guardianship reduced the number of simplifications used in earlier models by incorporating the existence of a guardian's place attachment and giving guardian agents agency to intervene. They found that, as the population using high traffic streets increased, the number of guardianship events (where a guardian chose to intervene) on high-traffic streets increased but so did the number of crime events. Thus, the increases in the numbers of people meant more people acted as guardians but also that more potential offenders chose to commit a crime. In other words, the increased guardianship was not able to counteract the increased exposure to potential offenders.

Current study

This research creates a virtual world in which the behavior of inhabitants is informed by mechanisms specified in environmental criminology theories; specifically, RA, crime pattern, rational choice, and GIA. The model is populated with offenders and guardians whose behavior is identical except that potential offenders are assumed to have made the involvement decision and are actively aware of theft opportunities. Those opportunities arise from both the static environment and the presence of other people. The goal of the model is to explore how offender perceptions of different levels of guardianship intensity change the patterns of theft.

The crime of larceny-theft is modeled. By definition, larceny-theft is the "unlawful taking, carrying, leading, or riding away of property from the possession or constructive possession of another" (FBI, 2018). It is experienced by victims as missing property; a tool disappears from the front yard, a backpack is gone after the owner returns from playing Frisbee on the green, or a bicycle vanishes from the rack where the owner left it. This model focuses on thefts that occur in public or semi-public places such as purse snatching, bicycle theft, or theft from auto, but excludes pickpocketing and shoplifting because of their more specialized nature.

Two reasons guided the choice of larceny-theft for modeling here. First, many people are victims of theft each year. In 2017, the National Crime Victimization survey found that 87 out of 1000 households reported theft victimizations (Morgan & Truman, 2018). In the same year, over 3,362,107 thefts were reported to police in the USA. Given the low reporting rate for property crime, it is very likely that reported theft events represent a fraction of the thefts committed. Second, where and when larceny-theft events occur is heavily dependent on opportunity (Anderson & Kavanaugh, 2009; Lynch & Cantor, 1992). Since thefts are relatively frequent events that are primarily driven by opportunity, they are likely a good crime type for understanding how crime might be affected by relatively minor changes in guardianship.

The overall model purpose is theoretical exposition; it establishes a set of hypotheses about the theorized mechanisms related to guardianship intensity that underlie crime events (Edmonds et al., 2019). The specific goal of the model is to examine how capable guardianship might influence the number and concentration of theft events. The model accounts for the separate contributions of agents outside on the street and those who are inside but visibly present. This approach allows a more nuanced representation of an offender's perception of situational guardianship intensity.

This exposition through modeling allows us to examine the interplay of opportunity and guardianship arising from RA. Opportunities for purse snatching, theft from auto, and other larceny-thefts can only occur where there are people with purses, leaving their cars parked or otherwise providing a target for theft. In this way, land use and transportation determine baseline opportunity levels by concentrating people (and their associated property) via the uneven distribution of places where people live, work, shop, have recreation, and socialize. In addition, dynamic opportunity for theft fluctuates with the time of day and the day of the week as people move into and out of places. However, this dynamic component also contributes to guardianship. Offenders perceive other agents as both adding to theft opportunities and increasing the risk of acting on those theft opportunities. No quantitative data exists that can separate these two influences.[2]

Methodology

This research systematically examines the impact of perceived guardianship intensity on thefts via an ABM programmed in NetLogo 6.1.1 (Wilensky, 1999).[3] Broadly, simulated individuals move throughout a neighborhood in accordance with typical patterns of commuting and daily activity behavior. Those individuals are either offenders or guardians. Offenders will steal when presented with an opportunity unless they are deterred by the presence of enough guardians. Additional model detail is provided in the supplementary materials available at https://osf.io/5vhks/

Model environment and agents

Characteristics of the urban backcloth determine the distribution of opportunities for housing, recreation, shopping, and employment (CPT). The model uses a 39 × 39 grid of patches, each representing a city block. Assuming a city block length of 125–150 meters, this corresponds to about four to eight neighborhoods in the downtown core of a large city. Time is scaled so that each patch can be walked in one tick (time step) of the simulation, and the default setting of 30 ticks per modeled hour equates to a walking speed of about 4 km/h (or 2.5 mph).

Each patch has varying amounts of commercial and/or residential use. Some patches have both and represent mixed-use blocks. High- and low-density commercial or residential patches are constructed so as to be qualitatively similar to a "typical" larger city in the northeastern USA (see supplementary materials at https://osf.io/5vhks/). This area contains both high-density main axes and a small number of secondary areas of high-density commercial and/or residential areas.

All patches on the main axes are assigned as high commercial density, together with four randomly selected squares of 3 × 3 patches, to represent office buildings and shopping malls. In addition, 200 individual patches are assigned as mixed use with low-density commercial, to represent convenience stores, local professionals, and other retail or office spaces that are located within residential areas. Of the 77 main axes patches, 20 are assigned as high residential density (in addition to their high commercial density), together with 20 randomly selected squares of 2 × 2 patches. All remaining patches that are not high commercial density are assigned as low residential density (Figure 4.2).

Twelve thousand agents are created, with some number (specified by the user, set at 500 for this study) as offenders and the remainder as guardians. Home patches for each agent are randomly selected in proportion to residential density and, for the employed, work patches are assigned in proportion to commercial density. Commercial and residential density also contribute to opportunities for theft (explained in more detail below).

Agent movement patterns

Because theft opportunities arise from both static characteristics of place and dynamic ones, the daily rhythms of individual activity are represented (Birks & Davies, 2017). The model is calibrated to represent typical patterns

80 *Elizabeth R. Groff and Jennifer Badham*

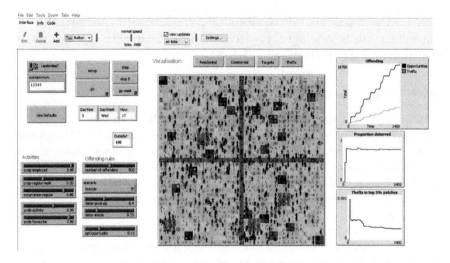

Figure 4.2 One potential distribution of residential population. Guardians (black figures) and offenders (orange circles) are moving around the environment near the beginning of a typical evening commute. Darker background patches are areas of higher commercial or residential density.

of behavior rather than the full range of behavior. These typical patterns are described by the timing, destination, and mode of transportation used. The mode of transportation also sets whether the agent is considered to be outside or inside during the activity, which is relevant to the calculation of theft opportunities and guardianship.

Theoretical specification

Human activity patterns are shaped by transportation mode/network and the land use configuration of an urban place. Consequently, individual agents have RA spaces that describe the places they travel to and through, and the routes they take. These routines have both spatial and temporal elements and have a great deal of stability over time. Weekdays are more like other weekdays and weekend days are like other weekend days, but there are significant differences between weekday and weekend activities. People who are unemployed have routines that are different from people who are employed.

Model specification

There are two broad categories of movement: commuting to and from work, and other activities. These are represented in the model in distinctly different

Table 4.2 Master schedule

Day	Triggered	Start	Agents	Activity initialized
Mon to Fri	07:00	Up to 08:30	Employed	Commute to work
Mon to Fri	12:00	Up to 13:30	Employed	Lunch
Mon to Fri	16:30	Up to 18:00	Employed	Commute to home
Mon to Fri	07:00	Up to 13:00	Unemployed	Long activity
Mon to Fri	19:00	Up to 20:00	All	Short activity
Sat to Sun	09:00	Up to 10:00	All	Short activity
Sat to Sun	13:00	Up to 17:00	All	Long activity

ways and are available at specific times of the day controlled by the master schedule (Table 4.2). The master schedule sets multiple specific periods during the week when agents may be mobile: 24 periods for employed and 14 for unemployed. To avoid model artefacts, commuting and activities both include some timing randomness. These timing variations allow interaction between agents who are on slightly different schedules. The schedule periods are of varying duration and are set to broadly reflect those reported in the 2011 American Time Use Survey (analyzed in Haberman & Ratcliffe 2015, p. 461). However, activity periods are somewhat compressed compared to real-world travel times and only the most common travel patterns are represented. This increases the level of interaction in the model as agents are moving around at similar times, which reduces the number of agents required.

At creation, each agent is assigned an employment status and, if employed, a travel mode for commuting. There are three travel modes: walk, public transport, or drive. Regular commuting patterns are implemented through a fixed delay for each agent, randomly selected up to 90 minutes. That delay is used to set the number of ticks after 07:00 that the agent leaves home each morning, and the number of ticks after 16:30 that it leaves work in the evening. Agents who walk to work move in a straight line between their home and work. Agents who are driving do not interact with other model entities while driving except as they leave their home and after they park at their destination.

Unlike the point-to-point movement for commuting, other activities involve leaving a patch (usually home) and then returning to the same patch. Activities are represented in the model with a list of key characteristics (Table 4.3): where the agent is going (destination), the average wait outside once the destination is reached (delay, for example at a bus stop), whether the agent then moves inside (inside?), and the number of ticks the agent remains at the destination (duration). The activities are archetypes rather than strict descriptions. For example, the "Home 1 hour" (Table 4.3) could be gardening or having a barbecue in the back yard or playing with children. What is important to the model is the patch where the agent is located and whether

Table 4.3 Representation of available activities

Activity	Destination	Delay	Inside?	Duration
Regular walk	Random patch distance 8–15	0	No	0
Lunch	Random patch distance 0.5–3	0	No	15–30 minutes
Favorites				
Walk 30 minutes	Random patch distance 5–10	0	No	0
Home 1 hour	Home patch	0	No	0.5–1.5 hours
Park	One of the three closest patches with a park	0	No	15–45 minutes
Shop	Random patch within distance 5 with commercial (or closest if none)	0	Yes	15–30 minutes
Other				
Walk 60 minutes	Random patch distance 10–17	0	No	0
Home 3 hours	Home patch	0	No	0.5–3.5 hours
Bus short	One of the three closest patches with a transport stop	3	Yes	1–2 hours
Bus long	One of the three closest patches with a transport stop	3	Yes	1–4 hours

the agent is inside or outside, which affects a guardian's contribution to theft opportunities and offending deterrence.

There is the opportunity for a short activity every day (evening on weekdays, morning on weekend days). Some agents are regular walkers and usually go for a 32–60-minute walk in this time. Any agents not doing a regular walk have a chance of doing a randomly selected short activity, with some activities assigned as favorites to provide a mix of consistency and variation in activities. There are five short activities available in the model, the four available as favorites plus "Bus short."

A different mix of activities are available on weekend days for the employed (afternoon) and any day for the unemployed. Each agent has a probability of doing an activity and, if successful, randomly selecting from five long activity options: park, shop, walk 60 minutes, home 3 hours, and bus long. The final activity is lunch (available only to the employed).

Offender decision-making and guardianship

There are two types of agents in the model, potential offenders and guardians. Offenders have made a positive involvement decision. Guardians do not commit theft but can be potential targets. The activities of offenders and guardians are represented in the same way (CPT and RA), with identical modeling rules and decision-making probabilities. That is, potential offenders do not make any additional trips or otherwise differ in their activities from guardians.

Theoretical specification

Offenders in the model represent people who consider theft opportunities as they go about their routine activities (CPT and RA). Consistent with RCP, the decision to offend uses "bounded rationality." In other words, offenders base their decision on their perception of potential rewards and potential risks rather than on perfect knowledge of them.

Offender agents consider the opportunity for theft in situations to obtain money or possessions. The offender considers: (1) the target opportunity (which combines availability and attractiveness of targets); and (2) the potential "general" guardianship in the situation (Figure 4.1). From GIA, scenarios represent guardianship intensity as either invisible (only outside agents count toward guardianship) or available (inside agents count either 0.1 per agent or 0.25 per agent toward guardianship in the situation). In this way the concept of guardianship intensity is included in different scenarios of the model (Table 4.4).

Model specification

Target opportunity reflects the number of potential targets at the patch, including the static contribution of the residential density and the commercial density, and the dynamic contribution of the number of other agents. At

Table 4.4 Translation of guardianship intensity

Level (L) in GIA	ABM level	Description	Operationization
None	Invisible	No visible guardian present	Offenders are not deterred; all opportunities become thefts
L0: Invisible	Outside	People who are inside are not perceived by offender	Only outside guardians on the same patch contribute to deterrence
L1: Available	Available 0.1 Available 0.25	Available to act as guardian	Both inside and outside guardians on the same patch contribute to deterrence
L2: Capable	Not modeled	Available and capable of acting as guardian	Future work: offenders to consider place awareness and/or social ties in deterrence decisions
L3: Intervening	Not modeled	Available, capable, and willing to actively intervene	Future work: guardians may intervene to actively deter thefts

Notes: ABM, agent-based modeling; GIA, guardianship in action.

every tick, any offender who is outside identifies an opportunity to steal with a probability that is a weighted sum that combines the commercial and residential density and the number of (other) people outside. The mean weighted static environment contributes approximately 0.12 to the opportunity probability. Each guardian agent who is located on the same patch and outside adds a further 0.15 to the opportunity probability.

If an opportunity is successfully identified, it is then assessed for whether a theft occurs or is deterred. Under the baseline scenario (named "invisible"), all opportunities are converted to thefts. Under other scenarios, the offender will decide whether to pursue the opportunity or be deterred by the presence of guardians. The probability of deterrence is given by:

$$p(\text{deterrence}) = 1 - (1-d)^G \quad (4.1)$$

where d is deterrence per guardian (an experimental parameter) and G is number of guardians on the same patch.

This equation represents each guardian as independently contributing to total deterrence with a fixed probability. Note that the number of guardians may be non-integer for the "available" scenario, where guardians who are inside count less than a full guardian. There is no empirical evidence related to the deterrence value per guardian, so that value is systematically varied during the experiments.

Experiments and outcome measures

Three types of outcomes were analyzed in this study. The first evaluated the model in terms of empirically based stylistic facts to ensure the real world is represented with adequate fidelity. The second evaluated theoretically based expectations related to routine activities and guardianship, to ensure relevant theories were appropriately implemented. The third explored the interaction between theories. Agents who are outside for any reason (such as walking to their destination, outside at home as their activity, or waiting at a bus stop) increase both guardianship and opportunities for theft. Simulation results allow the complex relationship between opportunity and theft to be understood in the context of represented theories about activity (RA and CPT) and deterrence (RCP and GIA).

While the questions considered by these outcome groups differ, the relevant information to respond to the questions is similar. Key measures are opportunities and thefts (and hence proportion deterred), both overall and at patch or offender level.

A set of experiments was used to systematically vary the assumptions of the model that are critical for theory: choice of guardianship intensity, level of agent activity, and the deterrence per guardian. Additional experiments held these critical parameters constant for a subset of values, but varied other settings to assess sensitivity, to ensure any observed results do not rely on other features of the model implementation.

Stylistic facts

There is strong empirical evidence supporting stylistic facts related to the concentration of crime events: (1) across space; and (2) among offenders. The observation that crime is concentrated at relatively few places has been around for hundreds of years (Guerry, 1833; Quetelet, 1842 [1969]). A recent systematic review of the literature found strong evidence for crime concentration (Lee et al., 2017). Crime concentration is typically measured using a cumulative frequency distribution or the Gini coefficient.

Specific to theft, a Canadian study found that, in 2006, 6.81% of spatial units (street segments and intersections) accounted for 50% of thefts (Table 4.3 in Andresen, Curman, & Linning, 2017). Some scholars have proposed that the finding is so consistent that it should be considered a law of crime concentration (Weisburd, 2015). Several studies of variation across street blocks/segments (both sides of a street between two intersections) have found that approximately 5% of places account for 50% of crime.

Similarly, the frequency of offending is concentrated among offenders. Empirical research suggests approximately 18% of offenders in a Philadelphia birth cohort committed about 50% of offenses (Wolfgang, Figlio, & Sellin, 1972). Another study found that roughly 6% of offenders account for 50% of offenses (Wolfgang, 1958).

Since the presence of guardians and their consequent effect on theft are situation-specific, guardianship may affect the degree of concentration of crime. To allow simulated concentration to be assessed, the model tracks thefts by individual offenders, and opportunities and thefts at individual patches. As well as total opportunities and thefts, these statistics are used to calculate several measures of theft concentration. We use as measures the Gini index (over offenders and patches) and the proportion of thefts within the highest counts (5% or 10%) of offenders or at patches. Only the 5% proportion is presented in this chapter, but additional measures are available in the supplementary materials at https://osf.io/5vhks/.

Theoretical expectations

Total opportunities and thefts, and the derived proportion deterred, cannot be assessed as there is no data about opportunities. The model is therefore not calibrated. However, the outcomes can provide evidence that the model is exhibiting the behavior expected from theory.

Related to the representation of guardianship, theory and empirical evidence suggest the model results will be the following. From RCP, the proportion deterred would be expected to increase as the deterrence per guardian increases (d in Equation 4.1), all other things being equal, since the same set of guardians would be perceived as making the situation more risky. From GIA, the proportion deterred would be expected to increase as guardian intensity increases and result in fewer completed thefts. Recall that guardianship intensity is a function of which guardians are being counted (outside only or both inside and outside) and how much deterrence each adds (0.1 or 0.25). Further, the biggest impact on reducing theft would occur between invisible guardianship and available guardianship (Reynald, 2009). Related to the routine activity levels of the agents, as the percentage of time spent away from home increases, the number of opportunities generated would increase (RA).

Experiments

As the theories of interest concern the influence of RA and guardianship, the parameters affecting activity and deterrence are varied in the experimental simulations. From the discussion of theoretical expectations, these are guardian intensity, deterrence per guardian, and activity levels.

This research implements general representations of the first two stages of the GIA model: invisible and available. The higher levels of guardianship, capable and intervention, are not implemented. There are four sets of offending rules that describe the guardianship intensity: a base condition under which guardianship is not considered at all (invisible) and three for different intensities of the available level.

Invisible:	Offenders do not consider guardianship in their calculations
Outside	Only bystanders on the street count as guardians. Potential inside guardians are all invisible (guardianship in action (GIA) level 0 (L0))
Available (0.1)	Both bystanders on the street and those inside buildings count toward guardianship in situations. All agents outside are perceived by the offender as available. Inside agents count as 0.1 (available 0.1) toward situational levels of guardianship (GIA L1)
Available (0.25)	Both bystanders on the street and those inside buildings count toward guardianship in situations. All agents outside are perceived by the offender as available. Inside agents count as 0.25 toward situational levels of guardianship (GIA L1)

In the base model, offenders do not consider guardianship levels when deciding whether to steal and thus are never deterred. This version provides a convenient baseline for examining the impact of guardianship (Birks & Davies, 2017). It is analogous to a world where all potential guardians are invisible. The remaining experimental settings implement three different versions of available guardianship intensity. One operationalizes GIA level 0 as only guardians outside are available. Guardians who are inside are invisible to potential offenders and thus do not contribute to the perceived level of guardianship in a situation. Only those agents who are visible on the street contribute to perceived guardianship and thus to the riskiness of a situation. The other operationalizes GIA level 1 as considering both outside and inside guardians as available with two different levels for guardianship contributed by inside guardians. Agents who are home are available to be guardians and they act in conjunction with agents on the street to provide guardianship against theft. Note that the outside scenario is equivalent to the available scenario with a 0 contribution from inside agents.

For activity and deterrence per guardian, parameter values are varied systematically over plausible ranges. Overall activity level has three values, one higher and the other lower than the model default. Deterrence per guardian has ten levels. This strategy allowed the investigation of their influence on the outcomes of total thefts, theft concentration across places, and theft concentration within offenders.

BehaviorSpace (Wilensky, 1999) functionality was used to run the experiments and to generate the measures calculated for each simulation. Each parameter set was simulated ten times for a period representing four weeks. Table 4.5 summarizes the simulations. Graphs are used to compare the effects of the experimental manipulations on the outcome variables.

Supplementary simulations were run to provide insight into why the observed patterns occurred. These experiments used a fixed seed for the random-number generator (set at 12345) and ran for (simulated) seven days. As for the main experiments, simulations were run with each combination of the offending rules and deterrence per guardian values. However, activity level was fixed at 0.3. As well as the overall measures reported for the full experimental set, individual patch data was exported.

Table 4.5 Experimental design

Parameter(s)	Number	Values
Offending rules	4	Scenario: invisible (1) Scenario: outside (1) Scenario: available (2): 0.1 or 0.25 contribution by inside
Deter per guardian	10	0.1 to 1 by 0.1 (for outside and available scenarios only)
Probability of activity	3	Activity level medium (default = 0.3) or low (0.15) or high (0.45)
Duration	1	28 days (20,160 ticks)
Repetitions	10	
Total simulations	930	(1 + 3 × 10) × 3 × 10

Note: number in parentheses represents the number of scenarios.

The experimental design for the sensitivity analysis follows a different structure and focuses on five variables that were not varied in the experiments but influence activity patterns. While all four offending rules were used, activity was set at 0.3 and only three values of deterrence per guardian (0.4, 0.7, and 1) were selected.

The results from the sensitivity analysis are not reported here but are available in the supplementary materials at https ://osf.io/5vhks/, together with a more detailed description of methodology. Varying these parameters did not affect the measures of interest except that total thefts and proportion deterred both increased as proportion employed and proportion walking regularly increased. These results are consistent with expectations that activity levels are associated with opportunities and no further analysis is required.

Findings

A key advantage of ABM is that the model generates behavior at the system level from the interaction of the individual decisions of the agents in the situations they encounter. Complex interactions, such as the interplay of opportunities arising from activity (RA and CPT) and offending decisions (GIA and RCP) can be simulated and measured. As these complex results are not obvious from the model inputs (or simulation would not be required), the adequacy of the model's representation must first be established from simpler results (Gilbert & Troitzsch, 1999; Groff & Birks, 2008).

The findings are discussed from two perspectives. The first assesses the model against the empirical stylistic facts and theoretical expectations. These findings demonstrate the credibility of the model as adequately representing the theories of interest. Additionally, these descriptions provide a baseline of understanding for interpreting more subtle findings that address how guardianship intensity influences model outcomes. An ABM is well suited for examining this question since the presence of guardians contributes to both the opportunity for theft and the likelihood of deterrence. Such complex relationships are impossible to adequately model statistically.

The experimental setup systematically varies input values and behavioral conditions, which leads to multiple values for each measure (such as total thefts). Model results are therefore interrogated using graphs that display the patterns of the outcome variables across combinations of input parameter values.

Each figure for investigating the main measures has three panels. The leftmost panel depicts the results under a low-activity scenario (0.15 probability of undertaking activities outside work). The center panel shows results under an assumption of medium-activity levels (0.3 probability) and the right-most panel provides high-activity level (0.45 probability) results. The x-axis of each graph in the panel reveals how systematically changing the amount of deterrence per guardians affects the results (d in Equation 4.1). Four different lines represent the four different guardianship intensity levels; essentially these represent four different behavioral realizations. The yellow line depicts the results for a scenario in which offenders do not consider guardianship when making the decision to offend. This "invisible" condition provides a baseline for comparison. The green line represents a scenario in which offenders consider "outside" guardians only. The blue and purple lines depict the results if offenders consider all "available" guardians including both on-street guardians and visible guardians, but the amount that inside guardians contribute to the total amount of guardianship is 0.1 and 0.25 respectively.

Each figure depicts a different outcome variable of interest, which is shown on the y-axis. This setup is particularly helpful for understanding the interplay of guardianship intensity, RA, and the deterrence value of each guardian and the outcomes of thefts, crime concentration across places, and crime concentration within offenders.

Stylistic facts and theoretical expectations

Looking first at the effect of increasing activity on thefts, theory predicts that as guardians/targets and offenders spend more time spent away from home the number of thefts will increase (RA). Recall that, in the model, the presence of guardian/target agents makes it more likely that offenders will recognize an opportunity to commit a theft. At the same time, each additional guardian present increases the risk perceived by an offender and makes it less likely a theft will occur, given an opportunity. Thus, the dynamic influence of guardianship means that opportunities may increase but the influence of guardian presence could keep them from becoming thefts.

The findings reflect these countervailing forces. As expected, when guardianship is not considered ("invisible" condition), the thefts increase with greater RA levels (Figure 4.3, yellow line). Note that this line also indicates opportunities since without guardianship all opportunities are converted to thefts. Also as expected, including guardians decreases the number of thefts per day as compared to no guardianship for any given activity level. Additionally, increasing the guardianship intensity decreases the number of thefts per day (RA and GIA). Finally, as the deterrence per guardian value increased, thefts decreased (RC). These relationships persisted regardless of activity level.

From Figure 4.3, thefts per day per offender increase as activity increases even for scenarios where guardians are included. That is, the increased activity of guardians deters thefts to a lesser extent than the increase in opportunities. Said another way, when the same number of guardians spend more time out and about, the effect is a net increase in theft – a finding that is consistent with Birks and Davies' (2017) model of guardianship.

Additional simulations with different numbers of agents (Figure 4.4) further illuminate this result. For a fixed activity level (0.3 in this case) and guardianship intensity, increasing the population of the simulation led to a decrease in thefts despite an increase in opportunities. This opens up the possibility

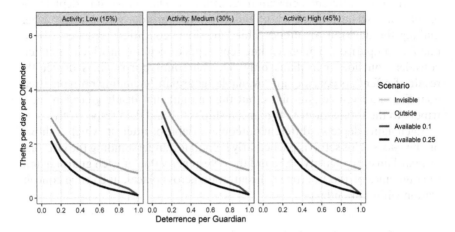

Figure 4.3 Thefts per day per offender ("invisible" scenario also shows opportunities).

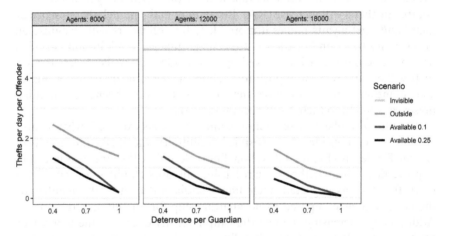

Figure 4.4 Effect of increasing numbers of agents on thefts per day per offender ("invisible" scenario depicts opportunities).

that population density is an important factor to consider when evaluating the effect of guardianship on theft.

These results also demonstrate the value of including both the inside guardians who are visible to the offender as well as the guardians outside (GIA). With high deterrence per guardian, the outcomes for the two model conditions using available guardianship converged, indicating that increasing the value of inside guardians did not reduce thefts further.

Consistent with the law of crime concentration, theft patterns were concentrated across patches, with between 17% and 45% of thefts occurring

Examining guardianship against theft 91

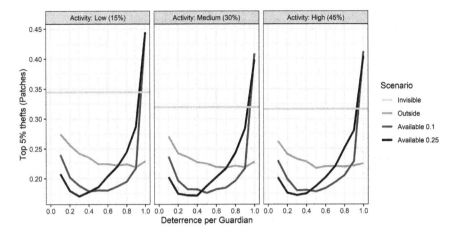

Figure 4.5 Concentration of thefts across patches ("invisible" scenario depicts opportunities).
Note: *y*-axis does not go to zero.

at the top 5% of patches (Figure 4.5). However, theft concentration across patches shows a complex relationship with guardianship intensity and deterrence per guardian. When only agents outside were considered as potential guardians, the highest level of concentration observed was 27.5% and occurred at low deterrence per guardian. When both inside and outside agents were considered as potential guardians, the highest level of concentration observed was 44% and occurred at high deterrence per guardian.

At low levels of deterrence per guardian (< 0.4), as activity increases, the concentration of theft decreases. As deterrence per guardian increases beyond 0.4, the patterns for guardianship intensity diverge. When only outside guardians are considered, the concentration across places stabilizes. When all available guardians are included, the concentration across places begins to increase. At high levels of deterrence per guardian (> 0.6 for 0.25 and > 0.8 or 0.9 for 0.1), increases in the deterrence per guardian produced steep increases in theft concentration, to much higher levels than outside guardians alone. This pattern occurred for all activity levels. Patch level data was used to explore this relationship further (reported below).

Model results showed that thefts were concentrated in a relatively small proportion of offenders (Figure 4.6). The top 5% of offenders in the model committed between 9% and 30% of all thefts. As activity level increased from low to medium, the concentration of offenses within individual offenders decreased. This was likely due to a combination of the following: lower-rate offenders encountered more opportunities in low guardianship places and offended more, which reduced the concentration among offenders overall. At the same time, higher-rate offenders encountered more theft opportunities,

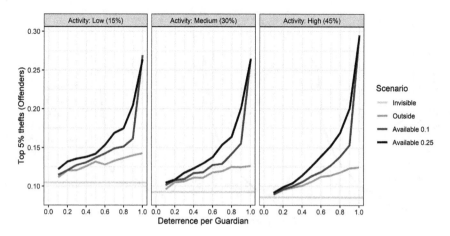

Figure 4.6 Concentration of thefts across offenders ("invisible" scenario depicts opportunities).

but their offending was tempered by increased guardianship, which also decreased concentration within offenders. This is especially noteworthy since the model did not include variation in individual offender background characteristics, motivation, or decision-making. In other words, the empirical fact was generated from environmental conditions and activity patterns alone.

Increasing guardianship intensity was associated with increased concentration of thefts within offenders as compared to the invisible guardianship condition and as compared to scenarios 3 and 4. As offenders considered opportunities they encountered, the deterrence from considering only those guardians who were outside produced a lower probability of being deterred than if the same offender in the same situation considered both outside guardians and inside guardians. The value inferred to the inside guardians was also important. At a value of 0.25 for inside guardians, the same offender was more likely to be deterred across a wider variety of places. Thus, only the smaller set of offenders whose activities occur in places with fewer guardians continued to offend and at a much higher rate than previously, which increased the concentration of offending within offenders.

Spatio-temporal patterns

Opportunistic theft has substantial spatio-temporal features because it requires the convergence of a motivated offender, target, and absence of capable guardian. In this model, convergence is operationalized as an offender occupying a patch with an opportunity. The probability of an opportunity is higher on patches with greater residential or commercial density, and with more agents present. However, the presence of more agents (as guardians)

Examining guardianship against theft 93

also increases the probability of deterrence. The complexity of convergence is already apparent from the discussion of the results related to the concentration of thefts across patches. In this section, we explore more deeply the spatio-temporal patterns that generate those concentration values.

Distribution of guardians across space and time

The space–time distribution of guardians and whether they are inside or out influences the situational probability of opportunity and deterrence. Recall the routine activity of agents (both offenders and guardians) is different based on whether it is a weekday (Monday–Friday) or a weekend (Saturday and Sunday). Figures 4.7 and 4.8 provide histograms summarizing the number of guardians per patch for both inside guardians (left panel) and outside guardians (right panel) at hourly intervals. Figure 4.7 shows a typical Monday (which represents weekday activity) and Figure 4.8 shows a typical Saturday (which represents weekend activity). On weekdays, most patches with agents have one to two guardians outside during the morning commute, lunch, evening commute, and the early evening. Some patches have many guardians present but most have none or few. In the morning and on weekends, there are many more patches with just one or two guardians outside but five to eight guardians per patch inside. There are typically many more guardians inside than outside.

Spatial relationship between opportunities and theft

To interpret the concentration of thefts over patches as deterrence per guardian changes (Figure 4.5), the model was run with the same seed and different deterrence settings. Using the same seed controls the patterns of activity so that the convergence of offenders, opportunities, and guardians is identical for each run. For the seed used, the top 5% of patches generate 32% of opportunities (at medium-activity level of 30%). Two figures display the thefts per opportunity at patch level under the "outside" scenario (Figure 4.9) and the "available" scenario (Figure 4.10). These patch maps allow exploration of the relationship between guardianship and the rate at which offenders capitalized on theft opportunities.

Recall that guardians present in a situation each contribute toward a total amount of guardianship, depending on the guardianship intensity scenario. Each outside guardian "counts" as 1 in both "outside" and "available" scenarios. Each inside guardian counts either 0.1 or 0.25 toward the total number of guardians for "available" scenarios only (Figure 4.9 only considers "outside" guardians, and Figure 4.10 counts "inside" guardians at 0.1). The deterrence per guardian is exponentiated by the number of guardian agents present (Equation 4.1). The shading of the patch indicates the conversion rate of opportunities to thefts. The scale goes from dark blue, indicating 100% of the opportunities become thefts, to yellow, indicating none of the opportunities become thefts.

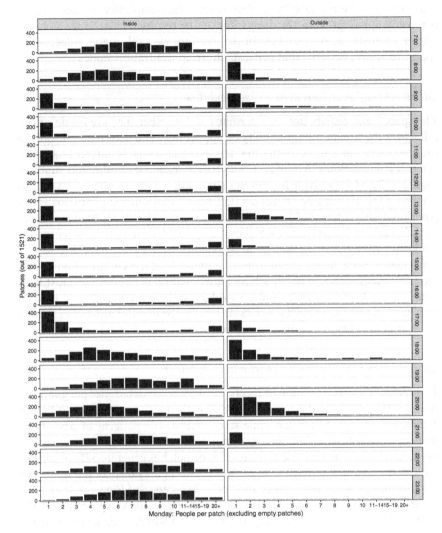

Figure 4.7 Weekday distribution of agents (Monday).

In Figure 4.5, when only outside guardians are considered, the concentration of thefts across patches decreases as deterrence per guardian increases before leveling off at about 0.5. In Figure 4.9, it is the areas with high commercial density that are lighter colored (with a lesser effect for high residential density), indicating guardians are effective at deterring crime in busy places even at very low levels of deterrence per guardian. Despite the effectiveness of guardianship, the high number of opportunities in these busy places means that these are also the locations with the greatest number of thefts for very low

Examining guardianship against theft 95

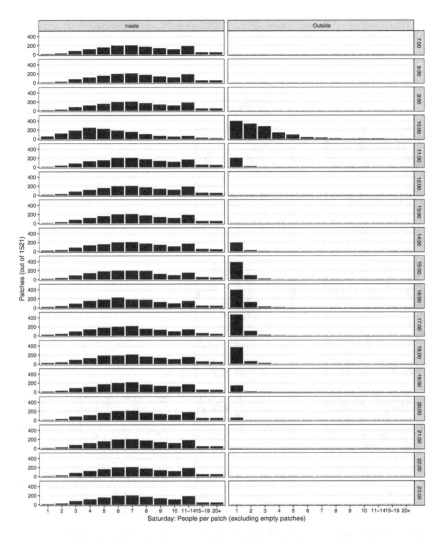

Figure 4.8 Weekend day distribution of agents (Saturday).

deterrence per guardian. As deterrence increases from 0.1 to 0.5, the number of guardians leads to decreasing rates at which opportunities are converted to thefts, these patches are less dominant in the theft results, and the overall concentration of crime decreases. Values of deterrence per guardian above 0.5 do not result in greater deterrence in busy places because opportunities are already being deterred (yellow). At all levels of deterrence per guardian, there are some dark blue patches, identifying those locations where all opportunities become thefts because there are no guardians present. At higher

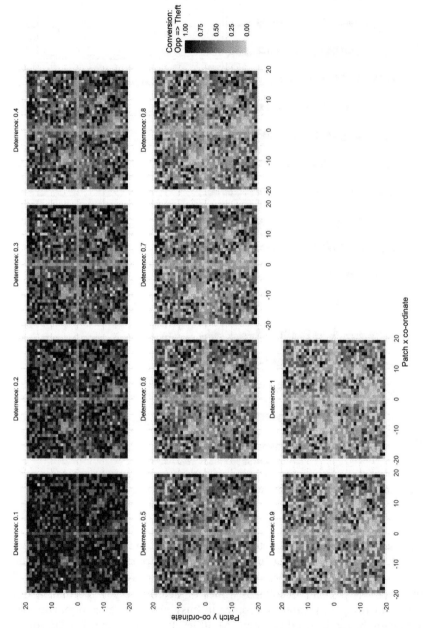

Figure 4.9 "Outside" condition (opportunities into thefts).

Examining guardianship against theft 97

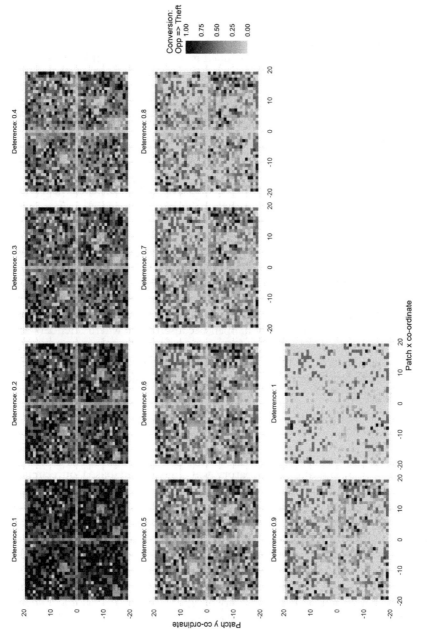

Figure 4.10 "Available" condition (each inside guardian counts 0.1).

deterrence levels, thefts occur disproportionately in these and other less busy patches, where opportunities occur without guardians to deter the offender. Such patches are distributed widely, with consequently lower concentration of thefts.

Turning now to the "available" condition of guardianship intensity, recall that in Figure 4.5 the concentration of crime across patches had a U-shape for the available conditions that included guardians inside and outside. Also recall from Figure 4.3 that, as deterrence per guardian increased, the number of thefts per day dramatically decreased. Looking at the graph for medium activity, at 0.1 through about 0.4, as deterrence per guardian increased, the concentration of thefts across patches decreased. In Figure 4.10, at low deterrence per guardian levels, busy places (such as the main roads) have a lower conversion rate because more guardians are present. This reduces the concentration level of the theft distribution. This decrease occurs more steeply than for the "Outside" scenario because busy patches are even busier if inside guardians are considered.

When the deterrence per guardian increases beyond 0.5, the concentration in theft across patches begins to increase because more thefts are deterred in the same places that a lower deterrence value per guardian failed to deter the offender. At the same time, thefts continue to occur in situations with no guardians or very few guardians, which increases the concentration at those patches. Said another way, the effect of combined guardianship (inside and outside) at higher deterrence per guardian levels is to deter crime in busy patches (where it would usually happen because that is where offenders and potential targets converge), which means they become less "hot" as compared to all other patches. By the time deterrence per guardian reaches 1.0, very few thefts are occurring in a very small number of patches with no guardian agents present.

Discussion

This study examines the role of guardianship intensity in generating theft patterns. A computational laboratory was constructed based on criminological theory and empirical evidence. The agents in the model have routine activities consisting of a commute and other activities that reflect shopping, recreation, and socializing. The agents undertake these activities in a virtual world that is stylistically consistent with the urban environment in a large city. The offenders are agents who have made the involvement decision. Offender agents use bounded rationality and consider risk and reward when making the decision to steal. Risk is operationalized as the presence of guardians and reward is represented as the availability of a potential target. Guardian agents can be targets or guardians when they converge. The results of the model provide interesting opportunities for exploring interactions between guardianship, human activity, and theft.

Using ABM allows examination of the two well-known and contradictory influences of more people on the amount of crime. More people at places increases the opportunity for crime while also increasing the number of potential guardians. These offsetting effects are clearly visible in the simulation results. More agents increase the potential for a theft to occur because they add to the number of dynamic opportunities. At the same time, guardian agents decrease the potential for a theft to occur because they increase the amount of guardianship and therefore reduce the likelihood that an offender will pursue an existing opportunity. In this study, we found that increasing guardianship intensity was associated with an increasing concentration of crime across offenders. The effect on concentration of theft across patches was U-shaped. At low levels of deterrence per guardian, increases in deterrence per guardian decreased crime concentration (up to about 0.4). At mid to high levels of deterrence per guardian (considering all available guardians), the concentration of crime increased rapidly. As guardianship intensity increased, the number of thefts per offender per day decreased. Finally, we discovered a higher deterrence in busy places even at low deterrence per guardian levels. As deterrence per guardian increased, theft opportunities were more widely deterred.

Although the model results were generally consistent with both theoretical and empirical expectations, Groff (2015) suggests the current version leaves two important components of situational guardianship unexplored. Both components are related to the routine activities of people. The first is the role provided by familiarity with place in the intensity of guardianship. As people go about their routine activities, they become familiar with and attached to places (Taylor, 1988). This place attachment contributes to how invested individuals are in places. People who are familiar with a place also understand the social norms at work, which contributes to the social legibility they perceive (Taylor, 1988, p. 180). Both the attachment and the familiarity with social norms increase the likelihood that individuals will actively surveil a place and further, that they will feel comfortable intervening when necessary.

A second theoretically relevant component of guardianship that was left unexplored is the influence of "weak social ties" (Granovetter, 1973) that originate from unplanned social interactions (i.e., passive contacts; Taylor, 1988). These passive contacts develop over repeated intersections of individuals in space–time. Noticing other place users leads to recognizing them which leads to saying "hello," which leads to short conversations. In this way, proximity and space–time convergence facilitate passive contacts and strengthen bonds through "mere exposure" (Taylor, 1988, p. 173). These social connections reinforce an individual's sense of understanding the way a place works and to a sense of belonging (recognizing and being recognized by other users). Eventually, this familiarity with both the users of the place and the norms of the place contributes to a potential guardian's likelihood of active surveillance and intervention. As Jacobs (1961) notes, individuals will intervene when they feel as if others who are present in a situation will support them. In these ways, place attachment and mere acquaintances are the foundation for the active exercise of informal social control/guardianship.

Finally, a more nuanced representation of offender decision-making could be developed. One direction for that development would be to add offender motivation. This would provide a mechanism for offenders to pause from noticing opportunities or identify an opportunity but choose not to act on it regardless of potential risk or reward because their need for cash is low (Groff, 2015).

Some weaknesses inherent in ABM should be mentioned. First, the results represent one potential mechanism. There may be others that could explain the results. Second, we compared model results with stylistic patterns in empirical crime patterns from official crime data which has known shortcomings.

This initial model of guardianship intensity examines the conflicting hypotheses generated (more people increases targets increases crime and more people increases guardianship which decreases crime) by interrogating the results from a number of different angles. Although the results cannot simply "support" or "reject" the theory, they add to our understanding of the underlying dynamics that give rise to theft patterns under different guardianship and activity regimes. Thus, the model provides a foundation on which to build more theoretically sophisticated representations of guardianship and to do so in a way that allows scholars to understand the dynamics that each new component adds. The potential for using guardianship intensity to prevent crime, even when opportunities exist, offers far greater return on investment than attempting to staff up police force size (Groff, 2015).

Acknowledgments

The authors thank Cory Haberman for his assistance with the American Time Use Survey data.

Notes

1 In later work, Reynald (2010, 2011a, 2011b) refined her stages of guardianship intensity to: (1) occupancy (presence must be detectable by potential offender); (2) monitoring (visibly monitoring street); and (3) intervention (taking direct action). Our operationalization of 'available' is analogous to 'monitoring' under the new group of stages. We use the original guardianship in action category labels and focus on how offenders perceive guardians.
2 Qualitative work is available (Wright & Decker, 1994, 1997).
3 The model will not run on version 5 of NetLogo as it uses the recently added cf extension for code clarity, and version 6.0 has a bug that affects this model.

References

Anderson, T. L., & Kavanaugh, P. R. (2009). Theft and Shoplifting. In J. M. Miller (ed.), *21st Century Criminology: A Reference Handbook* (pp. 541–548). Thousand Oaks, CA: SAGE Publications. Retrieved from http://sk.sagepub.com/reference/criminology. doi:10.4135/9781412971997

Andresen, M. A., Curman, A. S., & Linning, S. J. (2017). The trajectories of crime at places: understanding the patterns of disaggregated crime types. *Journal of Quantitative Criminology, 33*(3), 427–449.

Birks, D., & Davies, T. (2017). Street network structure and crime risk: an agent-based investigation of the encounter and enclosure hypotheses. *Criminology, 55*(4), 900–937.

Bosse, T., Elffers, H., & Gerritsen, C. (2010). Simulating the dynamical interaction of offenders, targets and guardians. Crime Patterns and Analysis 3, 51–66.

Bosse, T., Gerritsen, C., & Treur, J. (2013). Agent-based simulation of episodic criminal behaviour 1. *Multiagent and Grid Systems, 9*(4), 315–334.

Brantingham, P. J., & Brantingham, P. L. (1984). *Patterns in Crime.* New York: Macmillan.

Brantingham, P. L., & Brantingham, P. J. (1993a). Environment, routine, and situation: toward a pattern theory of crime. In R. V. Clarke & M. Felson (eds.), *Routine Activity and Rational Choice* (Vol. 5, pp. 259–294). New Brunswick, NJ: Transaction Publishers.

Brantingham, P. L., & Brantingham, P. J. (1993b). Nodes, paths and edges: considerations on the complexity of crime and the physical environment. *Journal of Environmental Psychology, 13,* 3–28.

Brantingham, P. L., & Brantingham, P. J. (1995). Criminality of place: crime generators and crime attractors. *European Journal on Criminal Policy and Research, 3*(3), 5–26.

Clarke, R. V., & Cornish, D. B. (1985). Modeling offenders' decisions: a framework for research and policy. In M. Tonry & N. Morris (eds.), *Crime and Justice: An Annual Review of Research* (Vol. 6, pp. 23–42). Chicago, IL: University of Chicago Press.

Cohen, L. E., & Felson, M. (1979). Social change and crime rate trends: a routine activity approach. *American Sociological Review, 44,* 588–608.

Cozens, P., & Love, T. (2015). A review and current status of crime prevention through environmental design (CPTED). *Journal of Planning Literature.* doi:10.1177/0885412215595440

Devia, N., & Weber, R. (2013). Generating crime data using agent-based simulation. *Computers, Environment and Urban Systems, 42,* 26–41.

Eck, J. E. (1995). A general model of the geography of illicit retail marketplaces. In J. E. Eck & D. Weisburd (eds.), *Crime and Place* (pp. 67–93). Monsey, NY: Willow Tree Press.

Eck, J. E., & Weisburd, D. (1995). Crime places in crime theory. In J. E. Eck & D. Weisburd (eds.), *Crime and Place* (pp. 1–33). Monsey, NY: Willow Tree Press.

Edmonds, B., Le Page, C., Bithell, M., Chattoe-Brown, E., Grimm, V., Meyer, R., ... Squazzoni, F. (2019). Different modelling purposes. *Journal of Artificial Societies and Social Simulation, 22*(3), 6. doi:10.18564/jasss.3993

FBI. (2018). Crime in the U.S. 2017. *Uniform Crime Report.* Retrieved from www.fbi.gov/ucr/cius2008/data/table_25.html

Felson, M. (1986). Linking criminal choices, routine activities, informal control, and criminal outcomes. In D. B. Cornish & R. V. Clarke (eds.), *The Reasoning Criminal: Rational Choice Perspectives on Offending* (pp. 119–128). New York: Springer-Verlag.

Felson, M. (1995). Those who discourage crime. In J. E. Eck & D. Weisburd (eds.), *Crime and Place* (pp. 53–66). Monsey, NY: Willow Tree Press.

Garofalo, J., & Clark, D. (1992). Guardianship and residential burglary. Justice Quarterly, 9(3), 443–463.

Gilbert, N., & Troitzsch, K. G. (1999). *Simulation for the Social Scientist*. Buckingham: Open University Press.

Granovetter, M. S. (1973). The strength of weak ties. *American Journal of Sociology*, 78(6), 1360–1380. doi:10.2307/2776392

Groff, E. R. (2007a). Simulation for theory testing and experimentation: an example using routine activity theory and street robbery. *Journal of Quantitative Criminology*, 23(2), 75–103.

Groff, E. R. (2007b). 'Situating' simulation to model human spatio-temporal interactions: an example using crime events. *Transactions in GIS*, 11(4), 507–530.

Groff, E. R. (2008). Adding the temporal and spatial aspects of routine activities: a further test of routine activity theory. *Security Journal*, 21, 95–116.

Groff, E. R. (2015). Informal social control and crime events. *Journal of Contemporary Criminal Justice*, 31(1), 90–106. doi:10.1177/1043986214552619

Groff, E. R., & Birks, D. (2008). Simulating crime prevention strategies: a look at the possibilities. *Policing: A Journal of Policy and Practice*, 2(2), 175–184.

Guerry, A.-M. (1833). *Essai sur la Statisticque morale de la France*. Paris: Crochard.

Haberman, C. P., & Ratcliffe, J. H. (2015). Testing for temporally differentiated relationships among potentially criminogenic places and census block street robbery counts. Criminology, 53(3), 457–483.

Jacobs, J. (1961). *The Death and Life of Great American Cities*. New York: Vintage Books.

Lee, Y., Eck, J. E., SooHyun, O., & Martinez, N. N. (2017). How concentrated is crime at places? A systematic review from 1970 to 2015. *Crime Science*, 6(1), 6. doi:10.1186/s40163-017-0069-x

Lynch, J. P., & Cantor, D. (1992). Ecological and behavioral influences on property victimization at home: implications for opportunity theory. *Journal of Research in Crime and Delinquency*, 29(3), 335–362.

Madensen, T. D., & Eck, J. E. (2013). Crime places and crime management. In F. T. Cullen & P. Wilcox (eds.), *The Oxford Handbook of Criminological Theory* (pp. 554–578). New York: Oxford University Press.

Morgan, R. E., & Truman, J. L. (2018). *Criminal Victimization, 2017* (NCJ 252472). Washington, DC: U.S. Department of Justice, Bureau of Criminal Statistics.

Newman, O. (1972). *Defensible Space: Crime Prevention Through Environmental Design*. New York: Macmillan.

O'Sullivan, D. (2004). Too much of the wrong kind of data: implications for the practice of micro-scale modeling. In M. F. Goodchild & D. G. Janelle (eds.), *Spatially Integrated Social Science* (pp. 95–107). New York: Oxford University Press.

Peng, C., & Kurland, J. (2014). *The agent-based spatial simulation to the burglary in Beijing*. Paper presented at the International Conference on Computational Science and its Applications.

Quetelet, A. J. (1842 [1969]). *A Treatise of Man*. Gainesville, FL: Scholar's Facsimiles and Reprints.

Reynald, D. M. (2009). Guardianship in action: developing a new tool for measurement. *Crime Prevention and Community Safety*, 11(1), 1–20. doi:http://dx.doi.org/10.1057/cpcs.2008.19

Reynald, D. M. (2010). Guardians on guardianship: factors affecting the willingness to supervise, the ability to detect potential offenders, and the willingness to intervene. *Journal of Research in Crime and Delinquency*, 47(3), 358–390. doi:10.1177/0022427810365904

Reynald, D. M. (2011a). Factors associated with the guardianship of places: assessing the relative importance of the spatio-physical and sociodemographic contexts in generating opportunities for capable guardianship. *Journal of Research in Crime and Delinquency, 48*(1), 110–142. doi:10.1177/0022427810384138

Reynald, D. M. (2011b). *Guarding Against Crime: Measuring Guardianship Within Routine Activity Theory*. Surrey: Ashgate Publishing.

Taylor, R. B. (1988). *Human Territorial Functioning: An Empirical, Evolutionary Perspective on Individual and Small Group Territorial Cognitions, Behaviors and Consequences*. Cambridge: Cambridge University Press.

Wang, N., Liu, L., & Eck, J. E. (2014). Analyzing crime displacement with a simulation approach. *Environment and Planning B: Planning and Design, 41*(2), 359–374.

Wang, X., Liu, L., & Eck, J. E. (2008). Crime simulation using GIS and artificial intelligent agents. In J. E. Eck & L. Liu (eds.), *Artificial Crime Analysis Systems: Using Computer Simulations and Geographic Information Systems* (pp. 209–224). Hershey, PA: IGI Global.

Weisburd, D. (2015). The law of crime concentration and the criminology of place. *Criminology, 53*(2), 133–157. doi:10.1111/1745-9125.12070

Wilensky, U. (1999). NetLogo (Version 6.0.4). Evanston, IL: Northwestern University. Retrieved from http://ccl.northwestern.edu/netlogo/

Wolfgang, M. E. (1958). *Patterns in Criminal Homicide*. Montclair, NJ: Patterson Smith.

Wolfgang, M. E., Figlio, R. M., & Sellin, T. (1972). *Delinquency in a Birth Cohort*. Chicago, IL: University of Chicago Press.

Wright, R. T., & Decker, S. H. (1994). *Burglars on the Job*. Boston, MA: Northeastern University Press.

Wright, R. T., & Decker, S. H. (1997). *Armed Robbers in Action: Stickups and Street Culture*. Boston, MA: Northeastern University Press.

5 A simulation study into the generation of near repeat victimizations

Wouter Steenbeek and Henk Elffers

Introduction

Repeat victimization refers to the ubiquitous empirical finding that some targets are victimized at higher rates than other targets (e.g., see Farrell and Pease 1993; Pease and others 1998). As a generalization of the concept of repeat victimization, Morgan (2001, 112) proposed the term "near repeats" for the phenomenon that often after an initial victimization a second one may occur within a short distance from the earlier one, both in time and in geographical distance. Many researchers have also demonstrated that such near repeat phenomena indeed occur, for a variety of crimes, and for various distances and time periods: these empirical studies often focus on burglary (e.g., Townsley, Homel, and Chaseling 2003; Johnson et al. 2007; Bernasco 2008; Wu et al. 2015), but also gun assault (Ratcliffe and Rengert 2008; Wells, Wu, and Ye 2012; Sturup et al. 2018), robbery and auto theft (Youstin et al. 2011; Melo, Andresen, and Matias 2018), and even maritime piracy (Marchione and Johnson 2013).

The identification of targets that are victimized repeatedly may have great practical relevance. For example, having 50% of all crime incidents occur in just 2.1% of all street segments in a city, and 25% of all crime incidents in 0.4% (Weisburd 2015, Fig. 4 on p. 144), implies that a specific focus on a small number of places may greatly impact the total number of crimes. The existence of a repeat or near repeat pattern may help to identify such street segments. The phenomenon of repeat victimization and near repeat victimization can also be used to *predict where future* crimes are likely to happen: after a first crime event, chances are a new crime will occur close by in time and space. In anticipation of this, law enforcement may patrol these areas more than others. Indeed, the processes of repeat and near repeat victimization are a key assumption of PredPol, a popular predictive policing solution, and the underlying predictive model (see Mohler et al. 2011 and www.predpol.com/technology/).

In this chapter, we are interested in *how* near repeat patterns might be generated. While there is evidence that some offenders return or go on to targets nearby in place and time, and such behavior by offenders might explain the repeat and near repeat victimization patterns, there has not been put forward a clear process theory on *how* offender decision-making will result in a choice for a target near the original location. Near repeat victimization is envisaged to be the result of consecutive decisions on target choice by serial offenders, made under the condition that targets may have different attractiveness values that are perceived by offenders, but much of the mechanism is unspecified in the prevailing verbal theories.

Given several models of offender decision-making, and a world with a number of potential offenders and a number of potential targets for a number of consecutive points in time, what do we predict to happen? Note that in the vein of testing theories by means of the empirical cycle, we have to confront predictions with actual observations (*cf.* Gerritsen & Elffers, Chapter 1, this volume). However, analytically this task seems to be too difficult. To be able to derive predictions to test against empirical data in the real world, we would first need detailed information about all offenders, not just those who were caught (e.g., number and geographic position of anchor points, velocity of changing awareness and of perception of attractiveness). In addition, we would need similarly detailed information about targets (e.g., the distribution of targets over space and the autocorrelation of their attractiveness levels). Second, we would need to work out analytically which macro phenomenon will result from the individual decision-making of a number of offenders. However, the number of parameters in such a model is large and the dynamical probabilistic consequences of different choices are too complex. An analytical solution is out of reach.

Because of the aforementioned challenges, we therefore turn to using computer *simulation* as an alternative method. An agent-based model (ABM) allows us to specify the decision-making process of individual offenders and lets these offenders interact with their environment, which results in a spatio-temporal distribution of crime events. Thus we specify the *micro*-level behavior of agents and how they affect their own environment, and the simulation produces the spatio-temporal distribution of crime events as a *macro*-outcome. In this contribution we will build a number of offender decision-making models, for which we will test whether they can or cannot produce near repeat patterns of crime. If a model cannot produce such patterns (either not at all, or when making unreasonable assumptions about offender behavior), we can reject that model as an explanation of near repeat victimization.

Near repeat victimization

Before we continue, it is important to reflect on the definition of *repeat* victimization. Above, we stated that "some targets are victimized at higher rates than other targets." This statement is not quite specific enough, because *even by chance alone* some targets are likely to be victimized at higher rates than others. If 20 crimes are distributed completely at random across ten targets, it

Table 5.1 Example of five victimization distributions, generated by a random process (20 crimes are randomly distributed across ten targets)

Ten targets

A	B	C	D	E	F	G	H	I	J
3	0	3	1	1	1	4	4	1	2
4	1	1	4	3	2	2	1	1	1
1	4	0	3	3	3	2	2	0	2
0	2	1	3	5	2	3	1	2	1
4	0	3	2	2	0	1	5	1	2

is indeed quite unlikely that all targets are victimized at the same rate, i.e., that all targets are targeted twice. While it is a possibility, a much more likely outcome is actually that some targets are victimized multiple times while others are never victimized. Table 5.1 shows five possible realizations of a *random allocation process* of 20 crimes to ten targets labeled A through J. Crime distributions such as in Table 5.1 do not necessarily indicate a process other than randomness.[1]

Given the above, we need to adjust our earlier statement to one that emphasizes how disproportionate the pattern of near repeat victimization is to our expectation. A better definition of repeat victimization is therefore that *some targets are victimized at higher rates than other targets, over and above the effect of chance*. Please note that this definition of repeat victimization *does not* include that targets are at disproportionate higher risk of victimization during a short time interval after a previous victimization: the timing of the events need not be correlated to denote a phenomenon as "repeat victimization." In addition, repeat victimization does not directly imply a *spatial* pattern of crime concentration, i.e., that targets cluster near each other. Repeat victimization only refers to the fact that crime concentrates, but not where or when.

Near repeat victimization, as Morgan (2001) introduced it, refers to a phenomenon of spatial *and* temporal interaction: targets are close by in both time and space. Note that, as per the discussion above, a random process might also lead to a near repeat pattern: even if crime incidents are randomly distributed across space and time, just by chance it is possible that some crime incidents cluster spatially and temporally. Thus, similar to above, the definition of near repeat victimization should read *an increase of risk for some limited time period in an area close by a previous victimization, over and above the effect of chance*.

How to identify near repeat victimization?

Near repeat patterns of victimization are identified using a set of crime events with three characteristics: (1) *x*-coordinate of where the event occurred;

(2) *y*-coordinate of where the event occurred; and (3) time of event. Usually these empirical data are extracted from police registration files. Notice that no information on the offender is available, as in most cases the offender is unknown. The *Knox test for space–time interaction* (Knox 1964) is widely used in criminology (and other scientific disciplines) to then identify whether the risk of victimization is disproportionate within some particular spatial and temporal distance of a previous crime event.

The Knox test considers the set of all *pairs* of crime events: for n crime events, this refers to $n(n-1)/2$ crime pairs. The Knox tests analyzes whether the temporal difference between the two events in a pair is associated with the spatial distance of those two events. Or, formulated differently, are pairs close in time also close in space? The association between temporal difference and spatial difference is analyzed by a cross-tabulation of crime pairs, categorized by a number of "difference in time" slices (the columns of the cross-table), and a number of "spatial distance" slices (the rows of the cross-table).

The substantive research question should drive the choice of spatial and temporal bandwidths, and therefore many different cross-tabulations can be found in the literature. Some researchers also include a special spatial slice for "no distance" pairs (pairs falling into that slice denote "repeat victimization," i.e., the exact same target has been targeted again). Note that in practice it is often difficult to establish the exact time that a victimization took place, e.g., in burglary cases when a home is victimized when the family is away, which may complicate near repeat analysis considerably (Peeters et al. 2013).

If we see a rather large number of pairs in the cells with small distances both in time and space, we conclude that the risk of victimization is large after a previous victimization in the recent past and nearby. Figure 5.1a shows an example cross-tabulation of spatial distances (in 100-meter increments) and temporal distances (1-day increments) of crime event pairs. However, in line with our definitions of repeat and near repeat victimization, we are not so much interested in the actual number of pairs in the cells of that cross-table, but in *how many more crime pairs are observed compared to the number of crime pairs that could be expected to occur anyway, just by chance*.

A Monte Carlo permutation procedure (originally suggested by Mantel 1967) can be used to generate, for each of the spatial and temporal windows, a distribution of the pairs of crime we expect to happen by random chance alone (as per the definitions of repeat and near repeat victimization). How many more pairs we actually observe than expected is expressed in a ratio, in this context usually called a Knox ratio. A Knox ratio of 1 means that there is no difference between observed and expected number of pairs.

Figure 5.1b shows the Knox ratios, with cells highlighted if they are at least 1.2 and significant at the $\alpha = 0.05$-level (Ratcliffe 2009). The observed number of crime event pairs in a number of cells may have seemed high (left), but the results of the significance test show that these numbers are actually not unexpected under the null hypothesis (right). We can also see where these numbers were unexpected under H_0. For example, the Knox ratio of 1.82 at

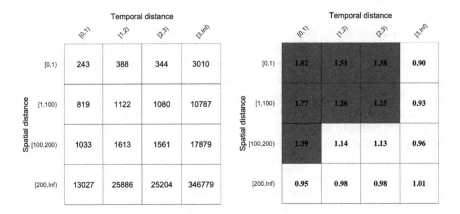

Figure 5.1 Cross-tabulation of spatial distance and temporal distance of all crime event pairs: frequencies (a) and Knox ratios, with highlighted cells at least 1.2 and significantly larger than 1 at the $\alpha = 0.05$-level (b).

the same location (defined as within 1 meter of the original location) and on the same day as the first victimization is an unexpected finding by a chance process alone, leading us to conclude that there is evidence of repeat victimization very shortly after the first event. Similarly, we conclude that the data show evidence of repeat victimization up to and including two days after the first event, and evidence of near repeat victimization up to and including two days after a first crime and within a range of 100 meters, as well as same-day revictimization up to 200 meters.

Stylized fact: the Knox Sloping-down Index (Ksi)

An ABM has a probabilistic element: repeating the simulation will generate a different macro-level outcome. Repeating a certain instance of the ABM a great number of times then gives us an estimate of the distribution of the crime pattern. The simulated (distribution of) macro-level outcome then needs to be compared to empirical crime patterns: the empirical crime patterns will fit into the simulated distribution (model corroborated!) or not (model rejected!). The snag in this argument lies in "the empirical crime pattern." Usually there is no direct correspondence between simulated and real world. The ABM is a *simplified model* of reality, and therefore it will never capture exactly the complexity of the real world.

The way to solve this issue is to investigate what *stylized facts* the study of the real world in a given area has produced. A stylized fact is one that has been observed in all (or very many) comparable studies. Let us say that all relevant studies' crime patterns show some characteristic, than we infer that it should hold in a simulated simplified world as well. The art of identifying stylized facts lies in abstracting from irrelevant differences between existing empirical studies, and concentrating on their commonality.

The stylized fact we focus on here is the existence of a near repeat pattern. However, while the color coding presentation of Knox ratios in Figure 5.1b shows where and when we observe more pairs of crimes than expected under H_0, it doesn't give us a simple overall answer to our question: does the study area exhibit evidence of repeat and near repeat victimization or not? We need a single metric characterizing a full Knox table, as an "index of near repeatedness." We can then generate a distribution of that index for many replications of agent-based simulations, to be able to conclude which models of offender decision-making can and cannot generate near repeat patterns of crime.

Previously published studies have not suggested such an overall index. Typically, when in some cells Knox ratios turn out to be statistically significant, conclusions are drawn, such as: "The analysis of all shootings across the entire city identified significant and meaningful near-repeat patterns of shootings" (Wells, Wu, and Ye 2012). Similarly, Sturup et al. (2018), upon finding a number of cells with significant Knox ratios, write: "the analyses of near-repeat patterns show significantly increased risks for a new shooting." Continuing, authors often discuss the results in detail, focusing on the cells in the Knox table where significant Knox ratios are found, e.g., "In the case of Stockholm, there were also significant near-repeat patterns between 200 and 300 m from a first incident within the first 2 weeks, and between 100 and 200 m after 3–4 weeks" (Sturup et al. 2018). As a final example, consider Youstin et al. (2011):

> The analysis for individual robbery did not show a near repeat pattern at the 14-day, 7-day, or 4-day temporal bands. The 1-day temporal band did reveal a spatiotemporal pattern indicative of spree offending, although the increased risk of offending was not directly connected to the original location (the zero- to one-block cell was not significant).

We have found three examples where authors have hinted at a clearer metric, albeit informally. Johnson et al. (2007), focusing on burglary, compare their Knox tests across ten different study areas in five different countries. Their description of findings works towards a synthesis of the overall evidence of a near repeat pattern. First, they emphasize the importance of the cell denoting the smallest spatial and temporal bandwidth:

> As a minimum, for every dataset, there was an over-representation of burglaries occurring within 100 m and two weeks of each other for every area ... the Knox ratio for this cell was consistently the largest in the contingency table for every area analyzed. This demonstrates the ubiquity of the near-repeat phenomenon at the shortest spatial and temporal bandwidths examined.

Second, they inspect the ten Knox ratios for different spatial intervals with time held constant, and for different temporal intervals with space held constant. Again emphasizing an expected downward trend, they note: "the areas with the highest Knox ratios for the first interval were not necessarily those that had the highest Knox ratios for the others" (p. 213).

Block and Fujita (2013) state:

> In only one distance gap (1201–1500 feet) did a relationship emerge at 95 per cent confidence using 14-day categories, yet this does not constitute a near repeat pattern. According to Ratcliffe (2009), a cell with a statistically significant Knox ratio should be part of the gradient-like decay pattern in order to be considered a near repeat. There should be no gap from the initiator incident in space and time.

Thus, they argue that a near repeat pattern is characterized by a gradient-like decay pattern of statistically significant Knox ratios. That is, a Knox table with several significant Knox ratios in the lower-right corner does not count as a near repeat pattern.

In Ratcliffe (2009), we could not find the exact argument for a gradient-like decay pattern as described in Block and Fujita (2013), but the importance of such a decay pattern is noted:

> It shows that once a location has been burgled, the chance of the same location being targeted again within 30 days in 311 percent (the 3.11 value) greater than if there were no discernible pattern in offender behavior. ... Importantly, there is also a near repeat pattern that exists for the first 30 days after a burglary. There is increased risk to nearby homes for up to 300 meters (about 1000 feet) – at least for the first 30 days. These values are also statistically significant and so not likely to be the result of chance. The ratio of these results decreases over space, so the risk to a house within 100 meters of the initial burgled home is 89 percent (the 1.89 value) greater than the general risk level, and the risk to a house 201 to 300 meters from the initial burgled house is about 49 percent greater.

In summary, although most scholars do not go into detail on exactly what kind of Knox table signifies a near repeat pattern, some have argued that what matters for near repeat patterns of crime is not only that there is evidence of space–time interaction, but also that this should be *most* apparent in short spatial and temporal distances from the trigger event. That is, there should be even higher than expected pairs of events within very short distances than at distances farther away (in time and space). That is, they seem to imply that one can only speak of a near repeat pattern when the Knox ratios in the contingency table have a gradient-like decay pattern both in space and time, as shown in Figure 5.2.

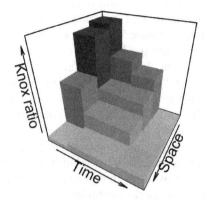

Figure 5.2 Three-dimensional representation of Knox ratios, showing gradient-like decay in space and time.

Let us be more specific on what counts as a "gradient-like decay." This is the case when

1. in each column, Knox ratios decrease over rows, and
2. for each row, Knox ratios decrease over columns.

In order to quantify the degree to which it indeed displays such a downwards slope, we define the "Knox Sloping-down Index" ξ. For the formal definition of ξ, we introduce some notation. A Knox table has r rows (bands of spatial distances), c columns (bands of temporal distances), with in each cell a Knox ratio $K_{i,j}$, with i the row index and j the column index.

1. First we count for each row i, how often Knox ratios in the cells of that row decrease over columns, that is, *how often $K_{i,j} > K_{i,j+k}$ for all $j = 1,...,c-1$ and $k = 1,...,c-j$. We then sum these values over $i = 1,..,r$.*
2. Secondly, we count for each column j, how often Knox ratios in the cells of that column decrease over rows, that is *how often $K_{i,j} > K_{i+k',j}$ for all $i = 1,...,r-1$ and $k' = 1,...,r-i$. We then sum these values over $j = 1,...,c$.*

Finally ξ is the sum of the two values as computed under (1) and (2), divided by the total number of inequalities checked, i.e., $rc(r+c-2)/2$. Thus, ξ is the fraction of times that two compared Knox ratios indeed display decay.[2] The full formula reads:

$$\xi = \frac{2\left\{\sum_{i=1}^{r}\sum_{j=1}^{c-1}\sum_{k=1}^{c-j}I(K_{i,j} > K_{i,j+k}) + \sum_{j=1}^{c}\sum_{i=1}^{r-1}\sum_{l=1}^{r-i}I(K_{i,j} > K_{i+l,j})\right\}}{rc(r+c-2)}$$

where r refers to the number of rows, c refers to the number of columns, and I is the index function on a Boolean argument, i.e., $I(\mathit{true})=1$, $I(\mathit{false})=0$.

Take for example the 4 × 4 Knox table in Figure 5.1b. For each row, there are a total of six comparisons where we expect the Knox ratios to decrease: {1,2}, {1,3}, {1,4}, {2,3}, {2,4}, and {3,4}. This leads to a total of 4*6 = 24 comparisons row-wise. Because the Knox table also has four columns, there are also 24 comparisons column-wise, for a total of 48 comparisons. By a simple but tedious count, we observe that in total 37 of the 48 comparisons show a decrease, hence the Knox Sloping-down Index $\xi = 0.75$.

We like to refine the index a bit, by recognizing statistical variance that is relevant for comparing two Knox ratios. Indeed, when computing ξ, we presently rather bluntly observe whether Knox ratios in two relevant cells are decreasing, e.g., whether $K_{i,j} > K_{i,j+k}$. However, acknowledging the statistical variability of both quantities, it may be better to first test whether indeed $K_{i,j}$ is *significantly* greater than $K_{i,j+k}$. If that is not be the case, we will not count that comparison as decreasing, even if indeed the raw values are in the right direction. We thus introduce a significance-corrected Knox Sloping-down Index, called ξ^{sc}. It holds that $\xi^{sc} \leq \xi$.

We propose to determine statistical significance as is necessary to compute ξ^{sc} by using a Monte Carlo permutation test, using the 999 permutated datasets that are the foundation of the Knox table. Specifically, we first calculate 999 Knox tables by dividing the observed frequencies table of crime pairs by the 999 frequencies table of crime pairs for each of the permutated datasets. Next, we calculate all $rc(r+c-2)/2$ inequalities as above, but on these *vectors* of Knox ratios. As a result, for each inequality check we get a vector of 999 values (true/false). If more than 95% of these are true, then we consider this particular comparison a statistically significant decrease (at the $\alpha = 0.05$-level). For Figure 5.1, using this procedure we compute $\xi^{sc} = 0.65$.

We conclude this section with several critical remarks about ξ and ξ^{sc}. First, the index measures the presence of a (statistically significant) qualitative change in Knox ratios over spatial and temporal slices, *not its magnitude*. This means the absolute size of the Knox ratios is not captured by the indices: i.e., if the magnitude in the top-left cell is much higher for one process than the other, but decreased in the same way for the remainder of the Knox table, this leads to the same value of ξ. Second, even as a summary of measure of qualitative change in Knox ratios, ξ and ξ^{sc} have an important caveat: similar to a Knox table, our indices are sensitive to the number, widths, and spacing of the various spatial and temporal slices. Therefore it is incorrect to naively compare ξ values across studies that use different spatial and temporal bandwidths.[3] This also implies that it is not possible to propose a universal threshold value for these coefficients—that can be applied across studies—above which evidence of near repeat victimization is indisputable. Investigating the implications of number, width, and spacing of the spatial and temporal bandwidths on the ξ value is outside the scope of this chapter.

Here, we can use ξ^{sc} because we only use it in *a comparative way* for the same simulated environment and the same number and spacing of spatial and temporal slices: does a given model produce a stronger near repeat pattern than another model?

Explanations of near repeat victimization

Knox ratios such as in Figure 5.1b and our proposed ξ only identify the presence of a near repeat victimization pattern in a dataset of crime incidents. They do not and cannot provide an answer as to *how* this pattern is generated. In order to come up with a more precise explanation of near repeat patterns of crime we should address the mechanism that leads offenders to choose nearby targets, which points to offender decision-making. In a spatial context, the dominant approach to offender decision-making is crime pattern theory (CPT) (Brantingham and Brantingham 1993a, 1993b), which itself pays tribute to the routine activity approach. The latter emphasizes that, for crime to occur, a motivated offender must converge with a suitable target in the absence of a capable guardian (Cohen and Felson 1979). While the origin of the routine activity approach aimed to explain macro-level changes in crime levels, the key concepts are now also applied to very micro-level situational explanations of crime occurrence.

CPT adds the explanation as to *where* these convergences occur. A key assumption is that people have a number of spatial anchor points around which their lives are centered, such as home, work, and leisure nodes. CPT further posits (inter alia) that people move along fairly predictable paths between these nodes of routine activity. The nodes and paths between them are one's awareness space, and crime can by definition only occur where an offender's awareness space overlaps with opportunities for crime. Note that some targets are likely more attractive—a combination of the potential gains, costs, and risks of victimizing them—than other targets. In practice, as we often don't know the nodes of routine activity of individual offenders, the most likely locations of crime are proxied by measuring the "environmental backcloth" of target attractiveness and additional assumptions on which environmental features are most likely to lead to a convergence of motivated offenders and suitable targets (Brantingham and Brantingham 1993a, 1993b).

According to CPT, serial offenders offend within their awareness space and by taking criminal opportunities into account. At first glance, it may seem that the target selection process is therefore not changing over time: offenders have an awareness space, and within that awareness space they see a number of more or less attractive targets. However, a time-stable awareness space is not very realistic. People tend to spend their routine activities at the same locations—otherwise they would not be routine—but people's habits can also change over time (Wortley and Townsley 2016, Chapter 5). Thus, in line with CPT, we expect people to gain knowledge of new locations and therefore new potential targets. Because one cannot be knowledgeable of all possible locations, awareness spaces also shrink, by forgetting places they used to know before.

All ABMs that will follow are therefore based on a dynamic version of CPT, which we will call *DAS*: the *Dynamic Awareness Space* model (to be specified in detail later on). The dynamics in DAS are only driven by the existing awareness space, not by where the offender has committed crime before. Specifically, we will implement a process that allows an agent's awareness space to grow (shrink), which will be more (less) likely near his current awareness space. We think it is unlikely that the mechanisms of DAS alone will generate near repeat patterns of crime, but at the very least DAS is a benchmark process against which to compare all other models. We now discuss three other offender spatial decision-making models that we hypothesize might generate near repeat patterns of victimization.

Previous crime as a cause of awareness space change

In the previous section we introduced the idea of a DAS, which was driven by the idea that people are most likely to extend their awareness with places adjacent to their existing awareness space. In this section we may continue our hypothesizing by making use of the scarce pieces of knowledge we have about unknown offenders: we know for a fact where they were at the previous time points, i.e., the targets that they victimized. We assume that being somewhere is an active mechanism in producing awareness of an area. The actual targets were already in the awareness space, otherwise they could not have been victimized, but what about places around these targets? If offenders visited a place of a target, it is likely that they will have seen at least something of the places neighboring that target. If those neighboring places had not been in their awareness space before, it is likely that they will extend their awareness space with one or more of these neighboring places.

In summary, we consider it more likely that new additions to one's awareness space will be made near previous crime locations, while forgetting places is more likely far away from recent crime locations. We will call this model *CAS*: the *Crime-affected Awareness Space* model. We think it reasonable for CAS to generate near repeat patterns, as it increases the offender's awareness close to his previous targets, and therefore enhances the likelihood of a new victimization close to previous targets.

"Flag" and "boost"

In previous research, two specific explanations have been proposed to explain *repeat* victimization, referred to as "flag" and "boost" (Pease and others 1998; Tseloni and Pease 2003; Johnson 2008). "Flagging" is simply the idea that some targets are more attractive than others. We have already introduced this concept earlier as a core component of CPT. Because offenders (presumably) are more likely to victimize attractive targets than unattractive targets, target attractiveness heterogeneity results in a disproportionate victimization rate for some targets. That is, part or all of the repeat victimization we observe over and above the effect of chance might be caused by differences in target attractiveness.

The flag account *cannot* be a sufficient explanation of *near* repeat patterns of victimization. Suppose targets differ in attractiveness. At t_0 the targets with the highest attractiveness value are most likely to be victimized; at t_1 these targets have the same attractiveness value and thus the same targets are as likely to be victimized; and so on for $t_2..t_n$. If targets with similar attractiveness values are clustered in space, we will then observe a spatial hotspot of crime that remains more or less in the same place across time. However, this pattern does *not* exhibit near repeat, i.e., an increase of risk *for some limited time period in an area close by a previous victimization*. After all, the decision-making process at each time point is independent of the decision-making process at the next time point. Thus, a victimization near a previously flagged one is just as likely to be near in time as distant in time, and this holds also if the occurrence of flags is spatially auto-correlated. For this reason we will implement two target attractiveness distributions, but this is not a separate decision-making model that we need to investigate.[4]

The second explanation of *repeat* victimization is the "boost" account, i.e., that crime exhibits event dependency. After a first crime, the risk of that particular victim is temporarily boosted for that particular offender, inviting a repeat offender to return to the same target. For example, a residential burglar might return to the same house to target replaced goods or because they now know how to access the property. Boosting seems a likely mechanism for producing near repeats if we assume that attractiveness values of targets *near* a previously victimized target are temporarily increased for that specific offender as well. Note that boosting can be seen as a temporary increase of flag values, and as such is a special case of spatio-temporal risk heterogeneity.

Authors have indeed suggested that a near repeat pattern is the result of the same offender selecting nearby targets (e.g., Bowers and Johnson 2004). Bernasco (2008) analyzed solved burglary cases for which he could identify whether the same offender had victimized various targets at various time points. He showed that near repeat pairs of solved burglaries are more often targeted by the same offender than other pairs. A number of rather small-scale interview data with convicted burglars have found some evidence of offenders looking again at previously victimized targets, but these interviews did not address near repeats (Van Burik, Van Overbeeke, and Van Soomeren 1991; Bennett 1995; Porter 1996). Optimal foraging theory argues that the offender has invested time and effort in scouting the area, making these costs for a number of targets. Targeting one of these nearby targets instead of others shortly thereafter saves him having to make those costs again, or what amounts to the same, the attractiveness value is temporarily increased (Bowers and Johnson 2004; Bernasco 2009; Johnson, Summers, and Pease 2009; Mehlbaum and van der Weele 2011; Peeters et al. 2013; Johnson 2014).

In this chapter, we will implement the "boost" explanation in the *Crime Boosts Attractiveness* model, or *CBA*. Specifically, our process increases attractiveness values of targets in the offender's awareness space close to his recent crime locations. To be clear, the grid cells near recent crime locations are only perceived to be more attractive by the offender who committed those crimes—it is *not* the case that these grid cells then become more attractive to all offenders.

Spates of crime

Quite another mechanism that has been proposed is the mechanism of "spates of crime"—also known as "crime sprees" or "runs." A spate of crimes refer to an offender who, after having victimized an initial target, immediately continues committing more crimes against a number of nearby targets. The standard example is a thief who tries to steal valuable electronics out of parked cars in a parking lot, who goes on until he has a bag full. Another example is an offender who burglarizes dwellings in a high-rise apartment building, until he has enough loot.

In the spate mechanism, the offender first makes an initial target choice, but then *does not stop* and make his next target choice on the following day (or after some other period of time). He also does not return to his home location or another location in his awareness space. Instead, he continues offending, immediately victimizing a number of new targets nearby at almost the same time as the initial offense.

Some authors have suggested that perhaps near repeat patterns are only the effect of unrecognized spates of crime, and that indeed we would not observe near repeats if we discarded spates from the crime dataset (Peeters et al. 2013). Of course, because we often cannot tie the same offender to a spate of crimes *in practice* it's often not possible to filter spates from the crime dataset. In order to investigate this suggestion we will therefore compare models with and without a spate mechanism in place.

Agent-based simulation

Near repeat victimization is envisaged to be the result of consecutive decisions on target choice by serial offenders, made under the condition that targets may have different attractiveness values that are perceived by offenders. Each of the explanations discussed above is a different mechanism exploring this main idea. As said, our underlying model across all explanations is an explicitly dynamic version of CPT, namely DAS. On top of DAS, several other explanations are investigated. First, we propose that the often posited "boost" explanation of crime, in which target attractiveness patterns for an offender change for a short time after a first victimization, may not be a necessary ingredient of near repeat patterns of crime. We argue that, because *awareness spaces* of offenders change over time, these changes in themselves might be sufficient to produce the near repeat phenomenon. This is implemented in CAS. Continuing, CBA is our model of the "boost" mechanism, while *CASBA—Crime-affected Awareness Space and Boosted Attractiveness*—is a combination of CAS and CBA. Finally, each of these models will also be used with and without a spate mechanism in place. Thus, starting from the DAS model and adding one or both of the additional mechanisms of adapting the awareness space or boosting the attractiveness values based on previous crime locations, our aim is to test whether each of these models can produce near repeats in a series of target choices, by a number of offenders.

Our simulations consist of a playing field and agents that commit crime at locations on this playing field, according to behavior rules we specify and that are different for the different models. For each of the decision-making models (for 20 offenders and 50 ticks, see below) we repeat this process 100 times because the random starting state of one particular simulation might affect results: replicating all simulations 100 times generates a distribution of potential outcomes per model. In short, each agent performs the following steps in each tick: (1) gain awareness space (i.e., "learn" new locations); (2) lose awareness space (i.e., "forget" locations); (3) commit crime at a location within his awareness space. A semi-comprehensive overview of all steps is given in pseudocode below, and each of these steps is discussed in detail for the various models in the next sections. For each of the 100 replications a dataset is created with the X and Y locations of all chosen crime locations, with the ticks of the simulation used as the *time* variable. We then calculate ξ^{sc} values for all datasets.

The agent-based simulations are programmed in R (R Core Team 2019). As we were not aware of any existing ABM packages that are easily adaptable for our purposes, code was written specifically for this paper but kept general enough so that other researchers can re-use and build upon our work. Our ABMs are built primarily using Hijmans (2019) to build the world environment, Dowle and Srinivasan (2019), Microsoft Corporation and Weston (2019), and Gaujoux (2018) to rerun many ABMs using parallel processing, and Wickham, François, et al. (2019) for data wrangling. Code from Steenbeek (2019) was adapted to perform the Knox tests, and plotting of figures and tables was facilitated by Wickham, Chang, et al. (2019), Clarke and Sherrill-Mix (2017), and Lemon et al. (2019).

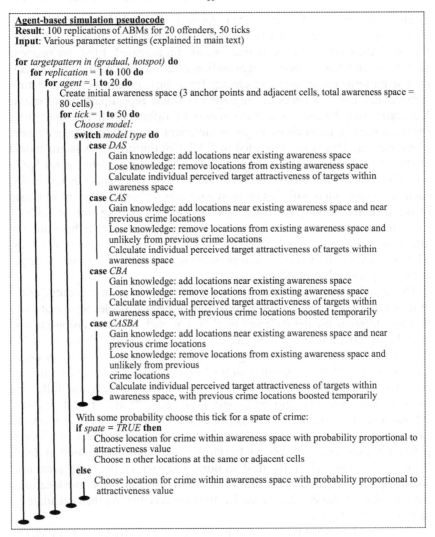

```
Agent-based simulation pseudocode
Result: 100 replications of ABMs for 20 offenders, 50 ticks
Input: Various parameter settings (explained in main text)

for targetpattern in (gradual, hotspot) do
  for replication = 1 to 100 do
    for agent = 1 to 20 do
      Create initial awareness space (3 anchor points and adjacent cells, total awareness space =
      80 cells)
      for tick = 1 to 50 do
        Choose model:
        switch model type do
          case DAS
            Gain knowledge: add locations near existing awareness space
            Lose knowledge: remove locations from existing awareness space
            Calculate individual perceived target attractiveness of targets within
            awareness space
          case CAS
            Gain knowledge: add locations near existing awareness space and near
            previous crime locations
            Lose knowledge: remove locations from existing awareness space and
            unlikely from previous crime locations
            Calculate individual perceived target attractiveness of targets within
            awareness space
          case CBA
            Gain knowledge: add locations near existing awareness space
            Lose knowledge: remove locations from existing awareness space
            Calculate individual perceived target attractiveness of targets within
            awareness space, with previous crime locations boosted temporarily
          case CASBA
            Gain knowledge: add locations near existing awareness space and near
            previous crime locations
            Lose knowledge: remove locations from existing awareness space and
            unlikely from previous
            crime locations
            Calculate individual perceived target attractiveness of targets within
            awareness space, with previous crime locations boosted temporarily
        With some probability choose this tick for a spate of crime:
        if spate = TRUE then
          Choose location for crime within awareness space with probability proportional to
          attractiveness value
          Choose n other locations at the same or adjacent cells
        else
          Choose location for crime within awareness space with probability proportional to
          attractiveness value
```

Playing field

The agents operate in an abstract gridded world of 16 × 25 (that is not a torus), i.e., 400 different locations. A real-society backcloth—i.e., a copy of a real city with houses in streets—may be interesting, but here we concentrate on the underlying mechanism without being distracted by the idiosyncratic pattern of local autocorrelation of characteristics that targets in real circumstances tend to have (Elffers and Van Baal 2008). To translate our world to a realistic setting: if we suppose that each grid cell is of size 150 × 150 meters (or a little less than 500 × 500 feet), then our world spans 3.75 km west to east and 2.4 km north to south.

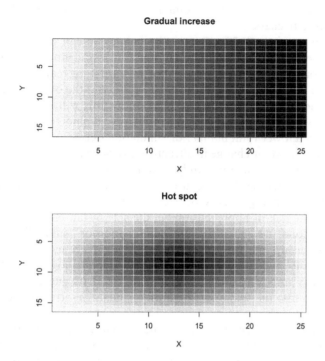

Figure 5.3 Two target distributions (a and b) (darker is more attractive).

As per the "flag" account of repeat victimization, each location has an attractiveness value—i.e., the utility a location has for a burglar—that is not constant across the playing field. In reality, whether or not a location is seen as a suitable target is a combination of the potential gains of a successful crime and the likelihood of a successful burglary. Potential gains could be modeled in terms of, for example, size of the house, or signs of wealth. Burglars also tend to look at potential risks: the difficulty they anticipate for breaking and entering, the likelihood that easy-to-transport loot will be there, levels of guardianship in the direct environment, probability of escape when being seen, and sum up this information into a likelihood of being successful (Nee and Meenaghan 2006). Here, we will simply use two different spatial distributions of target attractiveness, as depicted in Figure 5.3: (a) a gradually increasing target attractiveness from west to east; and (b) a hot spot of target attractiveness.

Agents

The agents in our model are (always) motivated offenders. These offenders each have an individual awareness space that evolves over time, and the offenders commit crime only within their own awareness space. Within their awareness space, they are more likely to commit crime in locations of higher perceived target attractiveness.

Each simulation consists of 20 agents. In principle, we can model just one offender and see if this results in the stylized facts we define a priori. However, we opt for more offenders for two reasons. First, in reality, more offenders are active in the same space at the same time, and the overall near repeat pattern is therefore "blurred" as well. Secondly, this will lead to 20 crime events in every tick, meaning that to get enough event pairs to calculate Knox ratios we need a lower total number of simulation ticks.

The targets do not move or change in attractiveness value over time—e.g., these are dwellings and the crime we study is home burglary. As such they are not agents that we need model.[5] We also do *not* model law enforcement officers as separate (or moving) agents for two reasons. First, we know from empirical data that the risk of apprehension "in the act" by law enforcement is extremely low. Second, we encompass the combination of "suitability of target" and "guardianship" (be it formal guardianship by place managers or law enforcement of informal guardianship by neighbors) in the target attractiveness value, thereby imposing a crime-dampening effect of guardianship on crime when we choose the spatial distribution of the target attractiveness values.

Finally, the agents (i.e., offenders) are assumed to *not* affect each other. That is, an agent's routine activity nodes and awareness space are generated independently of those of other agents; his awareness space changes over time, but irrespective of the awareness space or actions of other agents; and he commits crime at locations unaffected by the crimes of others. Thus the spatio-temporal pattern of offending is the sum of the actions of independently operating offenders.

Initial awareness space

An awareness space is the area (and some buffer around that area) that a person knows well, due to repeatedly spending time at nodes of routine activity (such as one's home, work, and preferred leisure activity). While the *paths* between nodes of routine activity are also considered to be part of one's awareness space, we allow the agents to have a non-contiguous activity space—i.e., pockets of knowledge. Offenders can add any new grid cell without necessarily also adding a contiguous connection to already known cells.

We do not include the paths between nodes for a number of reasons. First, time diary research shows that people spend most of their time at particular locations (especially their home) and not traveling. Second, people may take different paths depending on conditions such as time of day, traffic on the popular paths, and so on—therefore it is unclear to what extent specific paths truly become part of one's awareness space. Third, even if the above two reasons do not hold, the inclusion of paths presupposes that people spend enough time at the paths to build a mental map of attractive targets on these

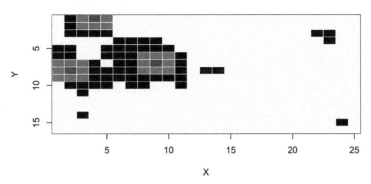

Figure 5.4 Example of initial awareness space.

routes, which we think is not a tenable assumption in many cases. Fourth, many people do not walk from one node of routine activity to another, but travel there by bike, tram, bus, subway, car, and so on. Each of these modes of transportation offers different levels of engaging with the environment along the way, but it is obvious that many modes prohibit interaction with the environment. Simply put, we are not convinced that the path between node A and node B should be part of one's criminal awareness space if one travels by train or car.

In Figure 5.4 the initial awareness space (at t_0) is depicted for one offender. The colored cells are the offender's awareness space. We set the size of the awareness space as 20% of the total number of cells: 80 cells. The offender has three fixed anchor points: key nodes of routine activities that are generated at random on the playing field and cannot be removed/forgotten from the awareness space (such as home, work, and leisure), namely at (2, 8), (4, 1), and (9, 7), shown in dark purple. The number and locations of the anchor points remain fixed over the time period of the simulations. The reason for using these key nodes is twofold. First, this is a direct implementation of the key tenet of CPT that offenders have a number of anchor points (Brantingham and Brantingham 1993a, 1993b). Second, if we were to start the simulations with a random awareness space, we expect to need a rather long "firing-up" period before offenders behave naturally.

We prohibit the offender to forget the locations directly adjacent to his key nodes (using queen contiguity), shown in light purple.[6] Because the anchor points are spaced far enough apart in this example, the light purple cells do not overlap. Note that (4, 1) is on the border of the simulation environment and therefore has five cells directly adjacent to the anchor point, for a total of 21 light-purple neighbors. (If the three key nodes were located directly next to each other, the total number of adjacent cells would be 12.)

The dark-green locations are the locations the offender also knows but are neither his key nodes of routine activity nor adjacent cells. In this case, because the awareness space is set to consist of 80 cells and 24 cells are already reserved for the anchor points and adjacent cells thereof, these are 56 cells.

This initial awareness space is built from just the three key nodes of activity and their adjacent cells using the same rules as used in the ABM ticks to "gain" and "lose" knowledge of cells, and these are explained in detail in the next sections. Note that, because the combined model CASBA consists of the combination of CAS and CBA, this model is not discussed separately in the next sections.

Gain knowledge: expansion of awareness space

In every tick, an offender can attain new knowledge of `gain_loss` new locations, specified as a proportion of the number of cells in the awareness space. Thus for a proportion of 6%, this leads to .06*80 = 5 cells (rounded). How does the offender choose which five new cells to learn? We implemented three different strategies (of which we actually use one). These are, five cells are chosen:

1. completely *at random.*
2. He is *more likely* to choose cells to gain full knowledge of *adjacent cells* already in his awareness space. This strategy in turn can be implemented in two ways:
    A. all five cells are chosen at once
    B. the five cells are chosen iteratively: first one cell is chosen; then the probabilities of choosing all unknown locations (minus the new one) are updated; the second one is chosen, and so on.

We reject the random learning of new locations (strategy #1), as this is counter the tenets of CPT. A randomly changing awareness space would be characterized by sudden (dis)appearance of pockets of knowledge all over the place. Instead, we aim to simulate an awareness space that evolves over time by gradually expanding and moving. The simplest way to implement this is to make it more likely for an offender to choose cells near the cells he already knows, as per strategy #2. Finally, we choose the iteratively changing awareness space (strategy #2B): this mimics a foraging offender whose time and effort to learn a new location are lowered after he has added an adjacent cell to his awareness space nearby.

Dynamic Awareness Space model

For every cell that is not part of one's awareness space, we calculate the number of neighbors that are in awareness space + 1 (`n_neighbors_in_awareness_space + 1`). So, if a cell is completely surrounded by one's awareness space (but itself not part of the awareness space), this leads to

Simulation of near repeat victimizations 123

8 + 1 = 9 (using queen contiguity). From all locations not yet in the awareness space, we then sample one location using unequal probabilities based on the numbers generated. For example, suppose one cell is chosen from a set of three cells called `choice_set`, and these have values of `n_neighbors_in_awareness_space + 1` as follows: $\{9,4,3\}$. These are converted into relative probabilities: $\left\{\dfrac{9}{9+4+3}, \dfrac{4}{9+4+3}, \dfrac{3}{9+4+3}\right\}$ or $\{0.5625, 0.25, 0.1875\}$ (these add to 1), and then we use `sample(choice_set, size = 1, prob = c(0.5625, 0.25, 0.1875))` to select one location using the specified probability weights.

Before we continued with the actual simulations it seemed wise to find out whether the above actually produces "realistically" evolving awareness spaces, defined as quite, but not necessarily completely, connected that do not change too quickly over time. Upon visual inspection of this stylized fact, we conclude that the initial awareness spaces still looks too haphazard spatially: the probability weights need to increase more steeply with increasing number of already known neighbors. That is, cells near existing awareness space should have an even greater increased chance of being selected to gain knowledge of. We achieved this by changing the `n_neighbors_in_awareness_space + 1` into `(n_neighbors_in_awareness_space + 1)^Multiplier`, by which we can affect this non-linear relationship using the parameter `Multiplier (M)`.

Suppose there are nine cells from which the offender might choose to gain knowledge. Each has $\{0,1,\ldots,8\}$ neighboring cells that are already present in the offender's awareness space. That is, the ninth cell is more likely to be chosen than the eighth cell, and so on. Figure 5.5 shows the probability a cell is chosen to add to the awareness space depending on the number of neighboring cells that are already part of the offender's awareness space (these can range from

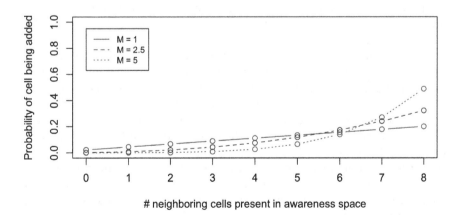

Figure 5.5 The effect of number of neighboring cells that are already present in the awareness space on the probability that a cell is added, for various values of *M*.

0 to 8, using queen contiguity), for three different values of M. In the original formulation, the relationship between the number of neighboring cells that are already in the awareness space and the probability of a cell being chosen to be added to the awareness space is linear, while for $M > 1$ this relationship is acceleratingly non-linear.

The differences in Figure 5.5 for the presented values of M may not seem like significant. It may be helpful to think about the impact of the multiplier in terms of the odds of a cell being added to the awareness space depending on the number of neighboring cells already present in one's awareness space, for various values of M. Suppose the offender can choose one of two cells to add to his awareness space. The first cell has eight neighboring cells that the offender knows already—i.e., this cell is completely surrounded by his awareness space—while the second cells has 0. For $M = 1$, the odds of choosing the former over the latter is 9 to 1. For $M = 2.5$, the odds shift to 243 to 1, while for $M = 5$, the odds are 59049 to 1. In conclusion, even these relatively low values of M will impact substantially the choice of new cells. To show this, Figure 5.6 depicts three initial awareness spaces for an offender that have the same three fixed nodes and adjacent cells, for different values of M. The awareness space was iteratively built to a total of 80 cells. Based on visual inspection of such awareness spaces, we then decided to use $M = 2.5$.

Crime-affected Awareness Space model

We introduce a new process in the CAS model. Specifically, we allow the location of the previous crime(s) to affect the processes of knowledge gain of new locations. The location of previous crime(s) affects the evolving awareness space: an offender is *more* likely to add cells to his awareness space near locations where he previously offended. To model this, we introduce the parameter `CAS_effect`. `CAS_effect` specifies the extent to which cells next to the previous crime location(s)—that are not already present in the offender's awareness space—have an elevated chance of being selected to add to the awareness space.

The value of `CAS_effect` specifies that the neighboring cells of a crime location (that are not already part of the awareness space) are treated *as if* they are surrounded by the number of locations already in the awareness space (as in the DAS model) *plus* `CAS_effect`. We investigate two values of `CAS_effect`: 8 and 20. A value of 8 refers to the maximum number of known neighbors as per the DAS model: each cell is surrounded by a maximum of eight cells. We also set `CAS_effect` to 20, meaning that the neighboring cells of a crime location are treated as if they are surrounded by an extra 20 cells on top of their actual adjacent awareness space locations, a steep boost (as compared to a cell that has 0 neighbors, as per above, this leads to an almost 2021 to 1 odds of being chosen to be added to the awareness space).

Implementing a process in which previous crime locations affect future awareness space growth raises two questions: (1) how many of the previous

Simulation of near repeat victimizations 125

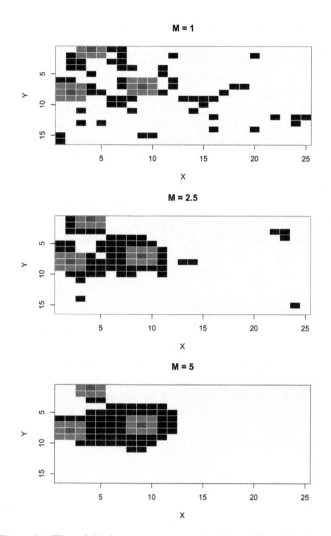

Figure 5.6 Three initial awareness spaces (a–c), as affected by the value of *M*.

crime locations affect the growth of one's awareness space? and (2) do crimes longer ago affect awareness space growth differently than recent crimes? We introduce two new parameters regarding the offender's crime history, or more specifically, how many of the previous ticks' crime locations affect the current tick, and the decay of that effect: memory and CAS_decay. Parameter memory refers to the number of previous ticks that affect the current tick. In DAS the previous crime locations had *no* effect on the current tick, or, equivalently, memory = *0*. For the simulations we set this to 2 and 4.

CAS_decay refers to a process of memory decay, in which recent crimes affect the awareness space growth more strongly (CAS_decay = true).

Specifically, for a memory of two ticks, we define the "impact" on the awareness space growth for the most recent round and the second-most recent round as 0.89 and 0.11, respectively. For a memory of four ticks, the last four rounds impact the current round with proportions 0.64, 0.27, 0.08, 0.01. This impact in turn is assigned to the neighboring cells (that are not already present in the awareness space) of the previous crime locations. For example, the most recent crime occurred at (5,2) and the crime before that at (5,15). Suppose that many of the cells adjacent to these location are already present in one's awareness space, except for (6,2) and (5,16). In this case, these cells receive impact scores 0.89 and 0.11 respectively. In the next step, the cells get a (temporarily) inflated `n_neighbors_in_awareness_space` value (see the explanation in the DAS model), namely `n_neighbors_in_awareness_space + CAS_effect * impact`. Thus, cells that are adjacent to most recent crime locations get the largest impact boost for the current tick, being treated as if it has `n_neighbors_in_awareness_space + CAS_effect *` that impact adjacent cells that are already present in one's awareness space.

Lose knowledge: reduction of awareness space

After gaining knowledge on five cells (or 6% of the total number of cells in one's awareness space), the offender also forgets five cells. That is, the offender has a limited capacity to remember all possible targets in detail and limited budget to travel around, and therefore he also has to forget some locations if he has added new ones. The number of locations to be forgotten is the same as the number of locations that are added to the awareness space, because otherwise we end up with an ever-expanding or ever-shrinking awareness space.[7] We next discuss the specifics of this process, for DAS and CAS.

Dynamic Awareness Space model

The DAS implementation is the exact inverse of the knowledge gain described earlier: the offender is less likely to forget locations that are adjacent to other cells in his awareness space. That is you are less likely to lose knowledge in an area that you know well than one in which you have isolated knowledge. The formula now reads `((8 - n_neighbors_in_awareness_space) + 1) ^ Multiplier` (using 8 because of queen contiguity).

Crime Affects Awareness Space model

In DAS, removing grid cells from the awareness space occurs based on the number of neighbors present in the awareness space, and *independently* of the previous crime locations. Instead, in CAS it is unlikely for an offender to forget his previous crime location and neighboring cells. No new parameters are needed as we also use `CAS_effect`, `memory` and `CAS_decay` to model the loss of awareness space.

The value of `memory` indicates the number of previous ticks for which the offender's crime locations (and neighboring cells thereof) affect the awareness space loss in the current tick, while `CAS_decay` specifies whether the more recent crime locations are more likely to be retained than crime locations longer ago (`true/false`). The crime location(s) and the neighboring cells of crime locations are treated *as if* they are surrounded by `CAS_effect` *plus* the true number of adjacent locations already in the awareness space.[8] As per the knowledge gain process, this is actually rather tricky to model due to the memory (decay) also modeled. Following the CAS model discussed earlier, cells that are in an offender's awareness space and adjacent to a (previous) crime location are first assigned an adjusted value `n_neighbors_in_awareness_space = n_neighbors_in_awareness_space + CAS_effect * impact`. Then, following the DAS formula in the previous section, the adjusted CAS formula reads: `((max(8, n_neighbors_in_awareness_space) - n_neighbors_in_awareness_space) + 1) ^ Multiplier`.

Committing crime

Where to commit crime within one's awareness space? One of the key propositions of CPT is that a criminal commits crime at those locations where his awareness space overlaps with attractive opportunities for crime (i.e., suitable targets). Thus, the simulation limits the criminal choice set to the awareness space's grid cells. Here we may either go for a deterministic choice model—always choose the most attractive target—or for a probabilistic model—choose a target with a chance proportional to its value. A deterministic model is not very attractive, as it would result in an absorbing state as soon as an offender gets knowledge of the most attractive target (and if the offender is prohibited to "forget" the grid cell he just offended in). We therefore implemented a probabilistic model.

Following the earlier example in Figure 5.4, and assuming a hotspot spatial distribution of targets, this means that this particular offender perceives the spatial distribution of targets (light grey = not in awareness space, hence no knowledge of target attractiveness) as in Figure 5.7. The targets just right of his right-most anchor point are most attractive, while the targets near his far left and top anchor points as well as on the outskirts of his awareness space (right) are not very attractive (though by definition still have a non-zero value). Note that this particular offender does not perceive the other very promising targets in the center of the playing field (*cf.* Figure 5.3) because he is not aware of them.

Crime is committed at every tick. The offender chooses where to attack: one cell is chosen, with cells of higher attractiveness more likely to be chosen. The logic is similar to before: an offender chooses a target within his awareness space with a probability proportional to its attractiveness value within the set of all attractiveness values of targets in his awareness space. (Targets outside the awareness space have an attractiveness value of zero for that offender.)

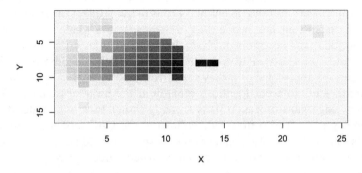

Figure 5.7 Awareness space and target perception within this space (darker is more attractive).

We also implemented a crime multiplier cM, i.e., the probability weights follow the function targets_perception ^ cM, with cM set to 3. When using no crime multiplier crimes are already more likely to be committed in the locations with the highest attractiveness values. This likelihood is further increased by setting cM to 3, as we do in all simulations.

Crime Boosts Attractiveness value model

In DAS and CAS, committing a crime has no direct effect on the perceived attractiveness of targets or their neighbors. In CBA, we start with DAS but then implement a "boost" effect: this elevates the attractiveness of previous crime locations and neighbors (temporarily, as defined by memory).[9] How does this work? As discussed in the section on playing field, above, the attractiveness of all targets is defined by $A = G * L$. For DAS and CAS, we used the same value for L for all targets. Crime locations were chosen with probability in proportion to the attractiveness value A, which was therefore equivalent to using G. In CBA, we change this set-up: for recent crime locations and neighbors, we adjust the likelihood of committing a crime at these locations (L) using parameter CBA_boost. We investigate two values: $L*5$ and $L*10$, meaning the attractiveness value of these locations increases by a factor of 5 or 10. Analogously to the implementations thus far, it seems reasonable that more recent crime locations might affect these attractiveness boosts more strongly. Parameter CBA_decay = TRUE turns on such temporal decay.

Spates of crime

The spate process can be activated "on top" of each of the models of DAS, CAS, CBA, and CASBA. With some probability spate_prob, an offender will decide to commit a spate of crimes. We investigate 0.1 and 0.25 in this chapter (although, to be honest, we think it's rather unrealistic to think that there's a 25% chance that an offender will commit multiple crimes in one go). If the spate does indeed happen, how many crimes are committed in the same tick? We have chosen four and eight crimes here (parameter spate n), but this is a first suggestion on our part and the literature discussing spates of crime is not helpful in providing estimates of how many crimes are likely to be committed in a row.

Our implementation of the spate process works as follows. An offender first chooses a crime location within his awareness space, as per our explanations earlier. After this first crime, the offender's awareness space is temporarily shrunk to that crime location and its queen neighbors, i.e., nine cells. The offender is myopic, seeing only the immediate environment near his crime. Note that the offender temporarily gains knowledge of each of these eight neighboring cells, even if they were not present in his awareness space before. Continuing with his crime spree, within this myopic environment he then chooses three (for spate n = 4) cells or seven cells (for spate n = 8) to commit crime. The choices are in proportion with the attractiveness values of the targets, i.e., he is more likely to choose the most attractive target out of these nine targets. Note that the choices are made with replacement, i.e., he could for example also choose to commit his spate of crimes at the same location. Afterwards, the offender's awareness space returns to its normal state: he still has knowledge of the original crime location (because this location was present in his awareness space), but he forgets the neighboring cells (unless, of course, the neighboring cells were already in his awareness space to begin with).

Results

The different parameter settings lead to a total of 202 models (101 per target distribution). We will present a selection of 74 of these models (37 per target distribution), that give a good overview of the total output. An overview of all combinations of parameters is given in Tables 5.2 and 5.3 in the first ten columns. In Table 5.4 we also provide an overview of the settings we *do not* vary and that are equal across all simulations.

Each simulation run with a given choice of parameter settings produces at least 600 crime events: 20 offender agents each making criminal choices for 30 ticks (i.e., consecutive point on the time axis).[10] Notice that in models in which the spate mechanism is active, we may expect more crime events, as with a certain probability more than one crime occurs at a time point. These 600+ events are categorized in a Knox table, with four time slices and four spatial distance slices (*cf.* Figure 5.1). We then compute the Knox Sloping-down Index ξ^{sc} for that Knox table. Remember, ξ^{sc} indicates the degree to which the Knox table is displaying the stylized fact of a sloping down set of Knox ratios in the Knox tables, taking significance of differences into account.

For each parameter setting, we rerun the model 100 times, thus generating a distribution of 100 ξ^{sc} values for that model and parameter setting. The

Table 5.2 Overview of fixed settings

Parameter	Description	Value
nrows	Number of rows	16
ncols	Number of columns	25
neighbors	Which cells are considered "neighbors" of a focal cell?	Queen
nrounds	Number of ticks in the simulation	50
nagents	Number of agents (offenders)	20
knowledge_prop	Proportion of total number of cells an offender has in his awareness space	.2
gain_loss	Percentage of awareness space that is learned and forgotten per tick (rounded)	6
iterative	Should knowledge gain be done in an iterative manner (or all cells added at once)?	True
multiplier	The multiplier that affects to what extent offenders are more likely to add (remove) cells that are near other cells already in their awareness space	2.5
crime_multi	The multiplier that affects to what extent offenders are more likely to choose crime locations with higher attractiveness values	3
prob_act	The probability that an offender commits crime in each tick	1

Note: gain_loss = 6 thus refers to 0.06 * 80 = 5 cells.

resulting 100 values of ξ^{sc} are depicted as a so-called *bee swarm plot*, which gives a good impression of the distribution (see, e.g., Figure 5.8). Moreover a *notched box plot* is drawn as an overlay (in red); this indicates the median and two outer hinges, which have the characteristic that when the notches of two distributions do not overlap we can reject the null hypothesis of equal medians at roughly 95% confidence (McGill, Tukey, and Larsen 1978). We display results for the two settings of the attractiveness value distribution (gradual and hotspot) above each other in one figure.

We now present several figures summarizing our results. Figure 5.8 gives a global result, while the others depict details for one or more of the models. For that reason, some model results are displayed more than once, being repeated in various figures. To start, Figure 5.8 shows the DAS outcome, and for each of the three models CAS, CBA, and CASBA we present the results for one particular parameter setting relevant for such a model. We augment this with the results of one of the DAS + spate models.

We have suggested DAS as the null model in which we do not expect near repeats, as the mechanism of DAS is not expected to produce such events. Indeed, Figure 5.8 shows us that DAS has on average very low ξ^{sc} values. We immediately get an impression on what are to be considered low ξ^{sc} values: the upper boundary of a notched box for ξ^{sc} is 0.051 (gradual case) and 0.052 (hotspot case).[11] We propose to classify a result with median $\xi^{sc} < 0.05$ as no evidence of a near repeat pattern. Notice that this threshold is critically

Table 5.3 Model specifications and agent-based model results: gradual target distribution

Targets	Model	Memory	CAS effect	CAS decay	CBA boost	CBA decay	Spate	Spate probability	Spate n	Mean	Median	sd	Low CI	Upp CI
Gradual	DAS	–	–	–	–	–	False	–	–	0.043	0.042	0.041	0.035	0.051
Gradual	DAS	–	–	–	–	–	True	0.1	4	0.327	0.312	0.052	0.317	0.337
Gradual	DAS	–	–	–	–	–	True	0.25	4	0.349	0.333	0.046	0.340	0.358
Gradual	DAS	–	–	–	–	–	True	0.1	8	0.405	0.396	0.062	0.393	0.417
Gradual	DAS	–	–	–	–	–	True	0.25	8	0.459	0.458	0.062	0.447	0.471
Gradual	CAS	2	8	True	–	–	False	–	–	0.046	0.042	0.042	0.038	0.055
Gradual	CAS	4	8	True	–	–	False	–	–	0.038	0.021	0.041	0.029	0.046
Gradual	CAS	2	20	True	–	–	False	–	–	0.045	0.042	0.037	0.038	0.052
Gradual	CAS	4	20	True	–	–	False	–	–	0.038	0.021	0.038	0.030	0.045
Gradual	CAS	2	8	False	–	–	False	–	–	0.045	0.042	0.045	0.036	0.054
Gradual	CAS	4	8	False	–	–	False	–	–	0.039	0.021	0.047	0.030	0.048
Gradual	CAS	2	20	False	–	–	False	–	–	0.046	0.021	0.047	0.037	0.055
Gradual	CAS	4	20	False	–	–	False	–	–	0.042	0.031	0.043	0.033	0.051
Gradual	CBA	2	–	–	5	True	False	–	–	0.322	0.312	0.038	0.314	0.329
Gradual	CBA	4	–	–	5	True	False	–	–	0.313	0.312	0.034	0.306	0.320
Gradual	CBA	2	–	–	10	True	False	–	–	0.326	0.333	0.040	0.318	0.334
Gradual	CBA	4	–	–	10	True	False	–	–	0.324	0.333	0.035	0.317	0.331
Gradual	CBA	2	–	–	5	False	False	–	–	0.223	0.229	0.048	0.213	0.232
Gradual	CBA	4	–	–	5	False	False	–	–	0.115	0.125	0.054	0.104	0.126
Gradual	CBA	2	–	–	10	False	False	–	–	0.227	0.229	0.048	0.218	0.237
Gradual	CBA	4	–	–	10	False	False	–	–	0.106	0.104	0.055	0.095	0.117
Gradual	CBA	2	–	–	5	True	True	0.1	4	0.404	0.417	0.060	0.392	0.416
Gradual	CBA	4	–	–	5	True	True	0.1	4	0.373	0.375	0.064	0.360	0.386
Gradual	CBA	2	–	–	10	True	True	0.1	4	0.389	0.396	0.055	0.378	0.399
Gradual	CBA	4	–	–	10	True	True	0.1	4	0.359	0.354	0.051	0.349	0.370
Gradual	CASBA	2	8	True	5	True	False	–	–	0.300	0.312	0.044	0.292	0.309

(continued)

Table 5.3 (Cont.)

Targets	Model	Memory	CAS effect	CAS decay	CBA boost	CBA decay	Spate	Spate probability	Spate n	Mean	Median	sd	Low CI	Upp CI
Gradual	CASBA	4	8	True	5	True	False	–	–	0.296	0.292	0.045	0.287	0.305
Gradual	CASBA	2	8	True	10	True	False	–	–	0.310	0.312	0.043	0.301	0.319
Gradual	CASBA	4	8	True	10	True	False	–	–	0.310	0.312	0.036	0.302	0.317
Gradual	CASBA	2	8	True	5	False	False	–	–	0.208	0.208	0.049	0.198	0.217
Gradual	CASBA	4	8	True	5	False	False	–	–	0.098	0.083	0.057	0.087	0.110
Gradual	CASBA	2	8	True	10	False	False	–	–	0.209	0.208	0.047	0.199	0.218
Gradual	CASBA	4	8	True	10	False	False	–	–	0.096	0.083	0.052	0.086	0.106
Gradual	CASBA	2	8	True	5	True	True	0.1	4	0.383	0.375	0.063	0.370	0.395
Gradual	CASBA	4	8	True	5	True	True	0.1	4	0.362	0.365	0.057	0.351	0.373
Gradual	CASBA	2	8	True	10	True	True	0.1	4	0.388	0.396	0.051	0.378	0.398
Gradual	CASBA	4	8	True	10	True	True	0.1	4	0.372	0.375	0.052	0.362	0.383

CAS, Crime-affected Awareness Space; CASBA, Crime-affected Awareness Space and Boosted Attractiveness; CBA, Crime Boosts Attractiveness; DAS, Dynamic Awareness Space.

Table 5.4 Model specifications and agent-based model results: hotspot target distribution

Targets	Model	Memory	CAS effect	CAS decay	CBA boost	CBA decay	Spate	Spate probability	Spate n	Mean	Median	sd	Low CI	Upp CI
Hotspot	DAS	–	–	–	–	–	False	–	–	0.044	0.042	0.040	0.036	0.052
Hotspot	DAS	–	–	–	–	–	True	0.1	4	0.292	0.292	0.052	0.281	0.302
Hotspot	DAS	–	–	–	–	–	True	0.25	4	0.345	0.333	0.047	0.335	0.354
Hotspot	DAS	–	–	–	–	–	True	0.1	8	0.391	0.375	0.066	0.378	0.404
Hotspot	DAS	–	–	–	–	–	True	0.25	8	0.422	0.417	0.059	0.410	0.434
Hotspot	CAS	2	8	True	–	–	False	–	–	0.050	0.042	0.043	0.041	0.058
Hotspot	CAS	4	8	True	–	–	False	–	–	0.042	0.021	0.045	0.033	0.051
Hotspot	CAS	2	20	True	–	–	False	–	–	0.042	0.021	0.043	0.034	0.051
Hotspot	CAS	4	20	True	–	–	False	–	–	0.047	0.042	0.043	0.039	0.056
Hotspot	CAS	2	8	False	–	–	False	–	–	0.047	0.042	0.045	0.038	0.056
Hotspot	CAS	4	8	False	–	–	False	–	–	0.043	0.042	0.039	0.036	0.051
Hotspot	CAS	2	20	False	–	–	False	–	–	0.055	0.042	0.047	0.045	0.064
Hotspot	CAS	4	20	False	–	–	False	–	–	0.054	0.042	0.047	0.044	0.063
Hotspot	CBA	2	–	–	5	True	False	–	–	0.282	0.271	0.050	0.272	0.292
Hotspot	CBA	4	–	–	5	True	False	–	–	0.279	0.292	0.057	0.267	0.290
Hotspot	CBA	2	–	–	10	True	False	–	–	0.291	0.292	0.043	0.282	0.299
Hotspot	CBA	4	–	–	10	True	False	–	–	0.282	0.292	0.050	0.272	0.292
Hotspot	CBA	2	–	–	5	False	False	–	–	0.185	0.188	0.063	0.172	0.197
Hotspot	CBA	4	–	–	5	False	False	–	–	0.102	0.094	0.063	0.089	0.114
Hotspot	CBA	2	–	–	10	False	False	–	–	0.191	0.188	0.059	0.179	0.203
Hotspot	CBA	4	–	–	10	False	False	–	–	0.105	0.104	0.058	0.094	0.117
Hotspot	CBA	2	–	–	5	True	True	0.1	4	0.330	0.333	0.085	0.313	0.346
Hotspot	CBA	4	–	–	5	True	True	0.1	4	0.301	0.312	0.079	0.285	0.317
Hotspot	CBA	2	–	–	10	True	True	0.1	4	0.332	0.333	0.066	0.318	0.345
Hotspot	CBA	4	–	–	10	True	True	0.1	4	0.310	0.312	0.067	0.296	0.323
Hotspot	CASBA	2	8	True	5	True	False	–	–	0.199	0.208	0.070	0.185	0.213

(continued)

Table 5.4 (Cont.)

Targets	Model	Memory	CAS effect	CAS decay	CBA boost	CBA decay	Spate	Spate probability	Spate n	Mean	Median	sd	Low CI	Upp CI
Hotspot	CASBA	4	8	True	5	True	False	–	–	0.197	0.208	0.085	0.180	0.214
Hotspot	CASBA	2	8	True	10	True	False	–	–	0.206	0.208	0.069	0.192	0.219
Hotspot	CASBA	4	8	True	10	True	False	–	–	0.214	0.229	0.069	0.200	0.228
Hotspot	CASBA	2	8	True	5	False	False	–	–	0.119	0.125	0.064	0.106	0.132
Hotspot	CASBA	4	8	True	5	False	False	–	–	0.056	0.042	0.052	0.046	0.066
Hotspot	CASBA	2	8	True	10	False	False	–	–	0.115	0.104	0.063	0.102	0.128
Hotspot	CASBA	4	8	True	10	False	False	–	–	0.054	0.042	0.045	0.045	0.063
Hotspot	CASBA	2	8	True	5	True	True	0.1	4	0.245	0.250	0.088	0.228	0.262
Hotspot	CASBA	4	8	True	5	True	True	0.1	4	0.217	0.219	0.090	0.199	0.235
Hotspot	CASBA	2	8	True	10	True	True	0.1	4	0.253	0.250	0.092	0.235	0.271
Hotspot	CASBA	4	8	True	10	True	True	0.1	4	0.242	0.240	0.092	0.224	0.260

CAS, Crime-affected Awareness Space; CASBA, Crime-affected Awareness Space and Boosted Attractiveness; CBA, Crime Boosts Attractiveness; DAS, Dynamic Awareness Space.

Simulation of near repeat victimizations 135

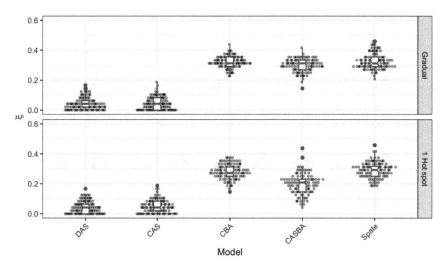

Figure 5.8 Summary of results, presenting one specific model (DAS, CAS, CBA, CASBA, DAS + spate) among the many models investigated. CAS, Crime-affected Awareness Space; CASBA, Crime-affected Awareness Space and Boosted Attractiveness; CBA, Crime Boosts Attractiveness; DAS, Dynamic Awareness Space.

dependent on number and width of time and distance slices in a Knox table, and therefore can only be used as a near repeat threshold index when comparing Knox tables of the same composition, which is what we do here.

The first substantive result is that CAS (with parameters as in line 6 of Tables 5.3 and 5.4) is not doing better than DAS (by "better" we mean producing a higher median ξ^{sc} value). In fact, the distribution of ξ^{sc} values for CAS is almost indistinguishable from that for DAS. Figure 5.9 expands on the CAS results: it depicts CAS models with different parameters for memory, effect, and memory decay. A summary of Figure 5.9 is that CAS generates near repeats for *none* of the parameter combinations (median ξ^{sc} values are at most 0.042). Perhaps CAS could generate a near repeat pattern if offenders have very small awareness spaces and these are almost exclusively determined by previous crime locations—but such parameter settings seem unrealistic.

CBA (with parameters from line 14 in Tables 5.3 and 5.4) generates much higher ξ^{sc} values. In fact, in Figure 5.8 the distribution of ξ^{sc} is almost non-overlapping for CBA and DAS/CAS, and median ξ^{sc} is 0.271 (hotspot case) and 0.312 (gradual case): the boosting mechanism seems to produce a near repeat pattern. Figure 5.10 gives a closer look into which parameter settings within the CBA model produce stronger or weaker near repeats. It seems particularly important to have the decay parameter set to `true`, which means that the influence of the location of victimized targets longer ago gradually fades away. Indeed, when agents in the CBA simulation have both a high

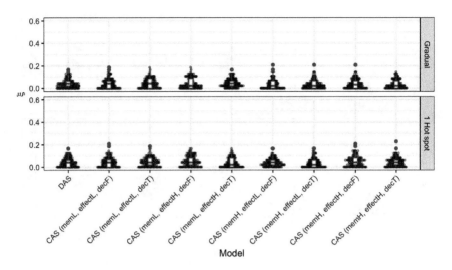

Figure 5.9 Dynamic Awareness Space (DAS) vs. Crime-affected Awareness Space (CAS).

memory parameter (which lets the offender be affected by four instead of two previous crimes when considering a new crime location) and *no* memory decay, CBA starts to lose its power to generate near repeats: in those cases median ξ^{sc} barely passes the 0.1 mark. We interpret this as that an offender has so many targets boosted, that we lose the focus around the most recent crime locations.[12] Having seen this, in the remainder of this chapter we present only models in which the decay parameter is set to true.[13]

Referring back to Figure 5.8, we now turn to CASBA. Having seen that CAS produces very low ξ^{sc} values, it does not come as a surprise that CASBA does not do much better than CBA alone, while—presumably due to its CBA component—it produces higher ξ^{sc} values than CAS. We have no explanation for the finding that CASBA is doing worse than CBA in the case of a hotspot distribution of attractiveness values. Figure 5.11 shows that this effect is roughly equal for different parameter settings (see also all outcomes for CASBA from line 26 in Tables 5.3 and 5.4).

Now, let us look at the results when we introduce spates into the models. Notice that we add a spate mechanism to the existing models, so we have DAS + spate, CAS + spate, CBA + spate, CASBA + spate. As we have already seen that CAS and DAS produce roughly similar (low) ξ^{sc} values, we save the reader from having to digest CAS + spate models here. Spate is also available in various versions (as a function of its parameters), that introduce a lower or higher intensity of the spate process. Figure 5.8 (far right) shows DAS including a low-intensity spate model (parameters from line 2 in Tables 5.3 and 5.4). We see that even this low-intensity spate process produces

Simulation of near repeat victimizations 137

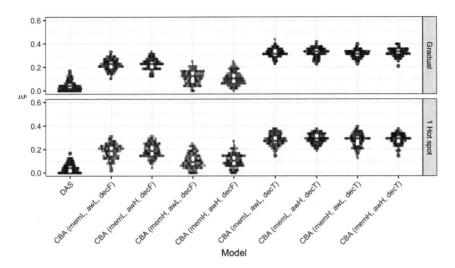

Figure 5.10 Dynamic Awareness Space (DAS) vs. Crime Boosts Attractiveness (CBA).

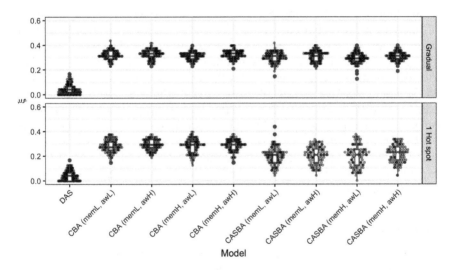

Figure 5.11 Dynamic Awareness Space (DAS) vs. Crime Boosts Attractiveness (CBA) vs. Crime-affected Awareness Space and Boosted Attractiveness (CASBA).

high ξ^{sc} values, quite comparable with the distribution of CBA. This leads to two conclusions. First, a spate model can produce near repeats without any boosting. Second, a spate model is not *necessary* to produce near repeat patterns, as we have seen that CBA produces high ξ^{sc} values as well. Notice

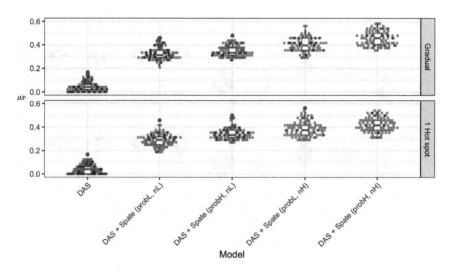

Figure 5.12 Dynamic Awareness Space (DAS) + spate.

from Figure 5.12, which shows all DAS + spate models increasing intensity of the spate process, that indeed more intense spates produce on average even higher ξ^{sc} values, with the median sometimes even larger than 0.4.

Tables 5.3 and 5.4 also present the results for CBA and CASBA models that include a spate process, which we shortly discuss here (lines 22–25 and lines 34–37, not depicted in figures). We observe that adding a spate component to CBA or CASBA seems to strengthen the near repeat patterns slightly: when offenders take notice of only a few (i.e., 2) previous targets, the median ξ^{sc} is 0.1 higher in the gradual case. This effect vanishes for cases where offenders take four previous targets into consideration, which seems to have the same explanation as given before (an "overboosting" of too large a part of the awareness space).

Conclusion

Our results show that two models of offender decision-making on target choice are compatible with stylized facts from the near repeat realm. That is a helpful result for the theory of near repeats, as for the first time we have shown that some ideas about underlying offender behavior have been corroborated, while other ideas can be disqualified. Specifically, our simulations have shown that:

- DAS *does not* produce near repeats.
- CAS *does not* produce near repeats.
- CBA *produces* near repeats, and this holds for almost all (but not all) parameter choices that govern the boosting process.

- CASBA *produces* near repeats, more than CAS, but not more than CBA.
- Spate *produces* near repeats (as an extension of DAS), and strengthens near repeats when combined with CBA or CASBA (but only when offenders don't take too many previous targets into consideration and for a gradual target distribution).

The stylized fact of a sloping-down Knox ratio in two dimensions is reproduced—to some degree—by both CBA (boosting) as well as by introducing a spate process, or by combining them. The dynamics of a changing awareness space alone, even if it is related to where crimes have been executed (CAS) is not enough to generate near repeats. In this way we have demonstrated that two possible underlying offender decision-making models are sufficient to produce near repeats. We corroborate the suggestions that the same offender returning or continuing is responsible for near repeats. However, the suggestion of Peeters et al. (2013) that without a spate process no near repeats can be found is rejected.

Finally, note that the overall patterns of all models are similar for both target distribution patterns, but generally ξ^{sc} values are slightly lower (not always significantly so) for the hotspot than for the corresponding gradually changing attractiveness values. We have no explanation for this finding.

Discussion

We hope to have contributed to our understanding of the mechanisms that lead to near repeat crime patterns. On the one hand we are confident that a process of dynamically changing awareness spaces (that may or may not be affected by previous crime locations) *cannot* produce near repeat crime patterns. On the other hand, that some of our other models (CBA and spate) are compatible with stylized facts by no means excludes that other models can be proposed that may also be able to generate stylized facts. Nevertheless, we like to point out that no other fully[14] specified models of individual decision-making of target choice have been proposed by scholars thus far. We invite the criminological community to propose other or better rival models and test them.

Modesty is also called for as all agent-based simulation research, regardless of its detail, of course focuses on some directions and a number of possible mechanisms. We discuss three ways in which further research can extend and improve upon the research discussed in this chapter. Firstly, we may speculate whether other than the currently investigated boosting mechanism would generate different results. Our results show that the number of previous target locations that are taken into consideration by offenders has quite an impact on ξ^{sc} values. In addition, memory decay (i.e., whether and how strongly crimes in the recent past have more influence than those longer ago) seems an important parameter. We think that further research diving into the boosting mechanism can be fruitful. Secondly, our spate mechanism is also just one of many possible ways to model the idea that one offender (sometimes) commits a spate or spree or crimes. Do different implementations of a spate process perhaps lead to fewer or no near repeat crime patterns? We would be surprised, but are open to different proposals for the spate mechanism. Thirdly, we propose that it would also be fruitful to further investigate the influence of the attractiveness value distribution of targets. Our research was limited to two distributions—a gradual increase of attractiveness values from west to east, and a case with one hotspot of attractiveness values—and we do not yet quite understand why the hotspot distribution on average seems to have weaker near repeat patterns of crime. We suggest that it may be worthwhile investigating systematically how the spatial distribution of attractiveness values (e.g., a random or almost random distribution, or a case with multiple hotspots) affects outcomes.

We have made several overall decisions or set fixed parameters that other researchers may criticize. In our set-up we have given all offenders exactly three fixed anchor points. Another possibility would be to take a different number of fixed anchor points; assigning different offenders a different number of anchor points; drawing the number of anchor points from a distribution; and finally, allowing for change in the anchor point locations (such as when an offender moves house). Other examples of overall decisions is that we have 20 offenders who commit crime at every tick,[15] the simulation runs for 50 ticks of which we analyze the final 30, and that the playing field consists of 16 × 25 cells. Finally, each model currently consists of just one type of offender: i.e., in a CBA model, the 20 offenders in a simulation all behave according to that same CBA specification. Alternatively, we could populate the simulation with (different distributions of) offenders with different decision-making models.

Taking a step further back from our abstract environment, at least two other critiques are possible. First, we use an abstract playing field. Instead, simulations could be done using a real-life background, such as targets that are houses in a neighborhood or city, with attractiveness values taken from the real-estate administration and/or other sources regarding value and risk. Because this is a first step towards criminal decision-making models that are specified enough to use in agent-based simulation research, we have focused on such an abstract environment. In this regard, also see Elffers and Van Baal's (2008) argument in favor of an abstract spatial backcloth. Second, our offenders do not "travel" between locations in their awareness space, meaning that there is no cost (or time) associated with committing crime far away from one's anchor points, nor are locations in one's awareness space necessarily connected by travel paths.[16] Alternatively, we could introduce travel time to targets from anchor points, introducing distance decay (in our models, this would mean that targets far away from anchor points have lower attractiveness values for that offender). As a variation on that theme, we might also introduce varying durations that offenders are present at anchor points: in our models that would mean that some locations have lower attractiveness values depending on how long the offender spends time at each of his anchor points. These alternative implementations will certainly generate different distributions of ξ^{sc} values, but would it also disturb the generation of stylized facts? It is clear that many extensions and alterations of our models may or should require further research.

We have proposed a *Knox Sloping-down Index* ξ^{sc} to measure to what degree a Knox table displays a near repeat pattern. We hope that using ξ or ξ^{sc} is an improvement over the rather impressionistic way that Knox tables have been summarized in previously published research. However, comments and criticism on the definition and use of ξ^{sc} are welcome. We are aware of the fact that more investigation in the sensitivity of ξ to the number, spacing, and width of columns and rows in Knox tables is sorely needed, so that a well-argued threshold value may be established. We might then consider a standardization of ξ depending on the size of the Knox table. Ultimately, this could lead to ξ being used to summarize previously published Knox tables.

To conclude, we are aware that many a loose end may be identified in our simulation models, and other researchers can take issue with choices we have made. We like to point out that our simulation code (in R) is publicly available for those who feel that such further research is necessary and to their liking. Nevertheless, we do claim that our effort has shown that agent-based simulation is a fruitful approach to test criminological theories.

Notes

1. Another example is a situation with fewer crimes than targets (Bernasco and Steenbeek 2017). Suppose five crimes are distributed completely at random across ten targets. Because the number of crimes is smaller than the number of targets, some targets will experience zero crimes, and thus *by necessity* some targets will be victimized more than other targets.
2. In each row we compare $(c-1)+(c-2)+...+1=c(c-1)/2$, so in total $rc(c-1)/2$ comparisons. Likewise column-wise there are $cr(r-1)/2$ comparisons, for a total of $rc(r+c-2)/2$ comparisons.
3. In addition, as ξ is a ratio of the number of (significantly) decreasing Knox ratios (numerator) to the total number of comparisons (denominator), the ratio can be lowered artificially by creating numerous spatial and temporal slices, thereby inceasing the denominator *ad infinitum*.
4. The flag explanation can only produce near repeat patterns if we change the definition of a "flag" into *spatio-temporal* attractiveness heterogeneity, that is, when the attractiveness values of different places within a study area change differently over time for all offenders. This process is outside the scope of this paper.
5. It is well known that the Knox test cannot distinguish between clustering caused by contagion and that caused by changing attractiveness of targets over time (Mantel 1967 ; Kulldorff and Hjalmars 1999). To focus on the contagion process only, we therefore keep the target attractiveness' distribution constant over time in this ABM, except when they are temporarily boosted—as in the CBA model—for *one particular offender only*.
6. Although it is outside the scope of this paper, the neighbor setting can be adjusted to "rook" or the user can input a neighbor matrix manually (Cliff and Ord 1981).

7 An alternative way is to set the # cells to be added or removed to come from the same distribution—e.g., a distribution with mean 3 and SD of 1. In that case sometimes an offender's awareness space expands slightly more than it shrinks, while at other times it shrinks slightly more than it expands. However, this is outside the scope of the present chapter.
8 Of course these locations are only treated this way if they are still present in the offender's awareness space. They could have been forgottten already one or more ticks ago.
9 Locations are only boosted when they are present in one's awareness space in the current tick, in which the decision of where to commit crime is taken. Note that when **memory** increases, chances are that some previous crime locations may no longer be present in the current awareness space.
10 In fact, we had the simulation run for 50 ticks, but the first 20 ticks are used to provide the offenders with a criminal history, which is necessary for various models. For analysis, however, only the last 30 ticks are used.
11 These values can approximately be read from Figure 5.8, but more precise values are given in Tables 5.3 and 5.4.
12 If an offender remembers four previous targets, all of them boosting eight targets around them, almost half of the awareness space (of 80 targets) becomes boosted.
13 This is one of the reasons why we do not present results of all simulations.
14 By "fully" we mean an individual decision-making model detailed enough to program an agent's behavior.
15 Another implementation would be to let agents commit crime with some probability. And yet another way is to implement a time-dependent likelihood of committing crime.
16 See also our arguments in the section on initial awareness space.

References

Bennett, Trevor. 1995. "Identifying, Explaining, and Targeting Burglary 'Hot Spots'." *European Journal on Criminal Policy and Research* 3 (3): 113–23.

Bernasco, Wim. 2008. "Them Again? Same-Offender Involvement in Repeat and Near Repeat Burglaries." *European Journal of Criminology* 5 (4): 411–31.

———. 2009. "Foraging Strategies of *Homo criminalis*: Lessons from Behavioral Ecology." *Crime Patterns and Analysis* 2 (1): 5–16.

Bernasco, Wim, and Wouter Steenbeek. 2017. "More Places Than Crimes: Implications for Evaluating the Law of Crime Concentration at Place." *Journal of Quantitative Criminology* 33 (3): 451–67.

Block, Steven, and Shuryo Fujita. 2013. "Patterns of Near Repeat Temporary and Permanent Motor Vehicle Thefts." *Crime Prevention and Community Safety* 15 (2): 151–67.

Bowers, Kate J, and Shane D Johnson. 2004. "Who Commits Near Repeats? A Test of the Boost Explanation." *Western Criminology Review* 5 (3), 12–24.

Brantingham, Patricia L, and Paul J Brantingham. 1993a. "Environment, Routine and Situation: Toward a Pattern Theory of Crime." *Advances in Criminological Theory* 5 (2): 259–94.

———. 1993b. "Nodes, Paths and Edges: Considerations on the Complexity of Crime and the Physical Environment." *Journal of Environmental Psychology* 13 (1): 3–28.

Clarke, Erik, and Scott Sherrill-Mix. 2017. *Ggbeeswarm: Categorical Scatter (Violin Point) Plots*. https://CRAN.R-project.org/package=ggbeeswarm.

Cliff, Andrew David, and J Keith Ord. 1981. *Spatial Processes: Models & Applications*. London: Taylor & Francis.

Cohen, Lawrence E, and Marcus Felson. 1979. "Social Change and Crime Rate Trends: A Routine Activity Approach." *American Sociological Review* 44 (4): 588–608.

Dowle, Matt, and Arun Srinivasan. 2019. *Data.table: Extension of 'Data.frame'*. https://CRAN.R-project.org/package=data.table.

Elffers, Henk, and Pieter Van Baal. 2008. "Realistic Spatial Backcloth is Not That Important in Agent Based Simulation Research: An Illustration from Simulating Perceptual Deterrence." In L. Liu and J. Eck (eds.) *Artificial Crime Analysis Systems: Using Computer Simulations and Geographic Information Systems*, 19–34. Hershey, PA: IGI Global.

Farrell, Graham, and Ken Pease. 1993. *Once Bitten, Twice Bitten: Repeat Victimisation and Its Implications for Crime Prevention*. London: Home Office Police Department.

Gaujoux, Renaud. 2018. *DoRNG: Generic Reproducible Parallel Backend for 'Foreach' Loops*. https://CRAN.R-project.org/package=doRNG.

Hijmans, Robert J. 2019. *Raster: Geographic Data Analysis and Modeling*. https://CRAN.R-project.org/package=raster.

Johnson, Shane D. 2008. "Repeat Burglary Victimisation: A Tale of Two Theories." *Journal of Experimental Criminology* 4 (3): 215–40.

———. 2014. "How Do Offenders Choose Where to Offend? Perspectives from Animal Foraging." *Legal and Criminological Psychology* 19 (2): 193–210.

Johnson, Shane D, Wim Bernasco, Kate J Bowers, Henk Elffers, Jerry Ratcliffe, George Rengert, and Michael Townsley. 2007. "Space–Time Patterns of Risk: A Cross National Assessment of Residential Burglary Victimization." *Journal of Quantitative Criminology* 23 (3): 201–19.

Johnson, Shane D, Lucia Summers, and Ken Pease. 2009. "Offender as Forager? A Direct Test of the Boost Account of Victimization." *Journal of Quantitative Criminology* 25 (2): 181–200.

Knox, EG. 1964. "The Detection of Space–Time Interactions." *Journal of the Royal Statistical Society.* Series C (Applied Statistics) 13 (1): 25–29.

Kulldorff, Martin, and Ulf Hjalmars. 1999. "The Knox Method and Other Tests for Space–Time Interaction." *Biometrics* 55 (2): 544–52.

Lemon, Jim, Ben Bolker, Sander Oom, Eduardo Klein, Barry Rowlingson, Hadley Wickham, Anupam Tyagi, et al. 2019. *Plotrix: Various Plotting Functions*. https://CRAN.R-project.org/package=plotrix.

Mantel, Nathan. 1967. "The Detection of Disease Clustering and a Generalized Regression Approach." *Cancer Research* 27 (2 Part 1): 209–20.

Marchione, Elio, and Shane D Johnson. 2013. "Spatial, Temporal and Spatio-Temporal Patterns of Maritime Piracy." *Journal of Research in Crime and Delinquency* 50 (4): 504–24.

McGill, Robert, John W Tukey, and Wayne A Larsen. 1978. "Variations of Box Plots." *The American Statistician* 32 (1): 12–16.

Mehlbaum, S, and W van der Weele. 2011. "Gepakt En Gestraft? Een Onderzoek Naar de Kenmerken En Afhandeling van Woninginbraakverdachten." Technical report, Regiopolitie Amsterdam-Amstelland, Dienst Regionale Informatie.

Melo, Silas Nogueira de, Martin A Andresen, and Lindon Fonseca Matias. 2018. "Repeat and Near-Repeat Victimization in Campinas, Brazil: New Explanations from the Global South." *Security Journal* 31 (1): 364–80.

Microsoft Corporation, and Steve Weston. 2019. *DoParallel: Foreach Parallel Adaptor for the 'Parallel' Package.* https://CRAN.R-project.org/package=doParallel.

Mohler, George O, Martin B Short, P Jeffrey Brantingham, Frederic Paik Schoenberg, and George E Tita. 2011. "Self-Exciting Point Process Modeling of Crime." *Journal of the American Statistical Association* 106 (493): 100–108.

Morgan, Frank. 2001. "Repeat Burglary in a Perth Suburb: Indicator of Short-Term or Long-Term Risk?" Crime Prevention Studies 12: 83–118.

Nee, Claire, and Amy Meenaghan. 2006. "Expert Decision Making in Burglars." *British Journal of Criminology* 46 (5): 935–49.

Pease, Kenneth, and others. 1998. *Repeat Victimisation: Taking Stock.* Vol. 90. London: Home Office Police Research Group.

Peeters, MP, WMEH Beijers, JJ van der Kemp, and others. 2013. "Waarom Is Besmettelijkheid Geen Besmettelijkheid?" Nederlands Studiecentrum Criminaliteit en Rechtshandhaving (NSCR) & Afdeling.

Porter, Mike. 1996. *Tackling Cross Border Crime. Crime Detection and Prevention Series,* 79. London: Home Office Police Research Group.

Ratcliffe, Jerry H. 2009. Near Repeat Calculator (Version 1.3).Philadelphia, PA: Temple University and Washington, DC: National Institute of Justice.

Ratcliffe, Jerry H, and George F Rengert. 2008. "Near-Repeat Patterns in Philadelphia Shootings." *Security Journal* 21 (1–2): 58–76.

R Core Team. 2019. *R: A Language and Environment for Statistical Computing.* Vienna, Austria: R Foundation for Statistical Computing. www.R-project.org/.

Steenbeek, Wouter. 2019. *NearRepeat: Near Repeat Calculation Using the Knox Test (Monte Carlo Permutation).* https://github.com/wsteenbeek/NearRepeat.

Sturup, Joakim, Amir Rostami, Manne Gerell, and Anders Sandholm. 2018. "Near-Repeat Shootings in Contemporary Sweden 2011 to 2015." *Security Journal* 31 (1): 73–92.

Townsley, Michael, Ross Homel, and Janet Chaseling. 2003. "Infectious Burglaries. A Test of the Near Repeat Hypothesis." *British Journal of Criminology* 43 (3): 615–33.

Tseloni, Andromachi, and Ken Pease. 2003. "Repeat Personal Victimization. 'Boosts' or 'Flags'?" *British Journal of Criminology* 43 (1): 196–212.

Van Burik, A, R Van Overbeeke, and P Van Soomeren. 1991. "*Modus Operandi Woninginbraak [Modus Operandi Residential Burglary].*" Amsterdam: Bureau Van Dijk, Van Soomeren en Partners.

Weisburd, David. 2015. "The Law of Crime Concentration and the Criminology of Place." *Criminology* 53 (2): 133–57.

Wells, William, Ling Wu, and Xinyue Ye. 2012. "Patterns of Near-Repeat Gun Assaults in Houston." *Journal of Research in Crime and Delinquency* 49 (2): 186–212.

Wickham, Hadley, Romain François, Lionel Henry, and Kirill Müller. 2019. *Dplyr: A Grammar of Data Manipulation.* https://CRAN.R-project.org/package=dplyr.

Wickham, Hadley, Winston Chang, Lionel Henry, Thomas Lin Pedersen, Kohske Takahashi, Claus Wilke, Kara Woo, and Hiroaki Yutani. 2019. *Ggplot2: Create Elegant Data Visualisations Using the Grammar of Graphics.* https://CRAN.R-project.org/package=ggplot2.

Wortley, Richard, and Michael Townsley. 2016. *Environmental Criminology and Crime Analysis*. Abingdon, Oxon: Taylor & Francis.

Wu, Ling, Xiao Xu, Xinyue Ye, and Xinyan Zhu. 2015. "Repeat and Near-Repeat Burglaries and Offender Involvement in a Large Chinese City." *Cartography and Geographic Information Science* 42 (2): 178–89.

Youstin, Tasha J, Matt R Nobles, Jeffrey T Ward, and Carrie L Cook. 2011. "Assessing the Generalizability of the Near Repeat Phenomenon." *Criminal Justice and Behavior* 38 (10): 1042–63.

6 Creating a temporal pattern for street robberies using ABM and data from a small city in South East Brazil

Eric Araújo and Charlotte Gerritsen

Introduction

High crime rates in Brazil are a consistent problem that affects the entire population both directly and indirectly. The rates of homicides and armed violence are 30 times higher than the average rates in Europe, for instance, according to the Violence Map of Brazil (Cerqueira et al. 2018). The problem of crime in Brazil is complex, and many discussions have been held in past years trying to propose solutions to increase the population's safety. Finding a consensus on the best solution is as hard and complex as the problem itself. Besides the large economic inequality, and the socially vulnerable environments where a significant percentage of young people are raised (e.g. favelas) (Sachsida et al. 2010), the efforts proposed in recent years have received a lot of criticism from many members of society, including the inhabitants of the most dangerous areas. There is a predominant set of actions that try to fight against drug trafficking, for instance, but little work on the prevention and analysis of the causes of the problems.

With much complexity and multiple factors influencing the dynamics of crime in Brazil, it is a challenge to address the question of how to define the urban space and reduce opportunity for offenders. That is, how is it possible to increase safety feelings within the Brazilian context, considering the specific history of crime within a city and the understanding of its patterns? We will take the city of Lavras as a case study. Lavras is a city with a population of 100,000 inhabitants, in the state of Minas Gerais, in South East Brazil. We present data on crime types and locations and try to define a model that can explain the temporal aspects of crime. An agent-based model (ABM) has proven to be a powerful instrument to study complex criminology phenomena in an automated manner and a very promising choice, as will be shown throughout this chapter.

We want to answer the following questions:

1. Is it possible to build an ABM that can derive temporal patterns of street robberies from stylized facts presented in real data?
2. How to use parameter tuning in order to fit a model for street robbery into a data set for a small city in Brazil?

Street robbery

Street robbery is one of the most common crimes in Brazil, and also a side effect of drug addiction and unemployment among socially and economically vulnerable citizens (Sachsida et al. 2010). Currently around 12 million people are unemployed, and drugs are a constant and permanent problem that is hard to ignore in Brazilian cities. Street robberies usually involve the use of some coercive means (e.g. guns, knives) in order to extract money or goods from a vulnerable victim. The motivated offender generally seeks a place where his action can be executed with minimal risk of getting caught.

Within this chapter two theories form the basis of our model, namely routine activity theory (Cohen and Felson 1979), and crime pattern theory (CPT) (Brantingham and Brantingham 2013). Routine activity theory distinguishes three factors that influence the probability that a crime will be successful – a motivated offender, an attractive target, and the absence of a capable guardian – that come together in time and space. Within CPT the main assumption is that crime is a complex phenomenon but it is possible to find patterns on different levels. Some locations are more prone to certain types of crime, some crimes typically occur at certain times of the day. In this chapter we propose an ABM that incorporates both theories. The ABM presented is based on a small Brazilian city centre. We make use of actual crime data, in contrast to other chapters that focus on stylized facts derived from theories. Since we use real crime data the facts are not stylized any more but were determined by reality. We adapt a data-driven approach instead of a knowledge-driven approach for our simulation, which is very much in line with developments in artificial intelligence, in which scholars increasingly make use of data-driven methods (Dubois, Hájek, and Prade 2000).

This chapter shows that our model reflects the tendency of crimes to happen at certain times of the day. The work is an initial effort to generate and validate a model useful for preventing crimes and guiding governmental decisions regarding public safety.

Related work

In this section we make a distinction between two types of related work. First, we will discuss related work that might be considered to form the foundation of our model. We based our decisions on the outcomes of these references. The second part of the related work section consists of literature that has some similarities to the work we do but addresses a different point of view and, although very relevant, has not been part of our framework.

Background of our model

The starting point of our research lies in the work by Bosse and Gerritsen (2010) in which a generic ABM to test routine activity theory was presented.

The framework they present is based on the theory and general assumptions but has not been validated based on real data. In Gerritsen (2015) an overview of the modelling and simulation process is presented that can be used for agent-based research in the domain of criminology. This cycle shows four phases, among which the final phase of the model should be compared to real-world situations to validate the model. This has been discussed by Troitzsch (2017) as well, while mainly focusing on the usefulness of ABM to replicate organized crime scenarios.

Our model is comprised of various components that form research interests of dedicated scholars. Groff, Johnson, and Thornton (2019) present an overview of ABM and urban crime research. Holston and Caldeira (1999) present some interesting analyses of the dynamics of violence in Brazil. The temporal patterns of street robbery form are discussed by Tompson and Bowers (2013) and their work supports us in our decisions in the study of street robbery in Lavras. These three publications form the basis for our geographical decisions.

We built our model in NetLogo. The decision to use NetLogo as our research tool was based on the outcomes of the work by Crooks and Castle (2012). They present a guideline for integrating GIS and ABM for simulations. They discuss a set of tools that can be used in this kind of exploration.

The definitions of the agents in a street robbery scenario, as well as a deep discussion on how to study this phenomenon, were provided by Monk, Heinonen, and Eck (2010). The most interesting actor in our simulations is the offender. Our input for this actor has been mainly based on work by Bernasco, Block, and Ruiter (2013) and Bernasco, Ruiter, and Block (2017). This helped us to decide about the radius of action of offenders. Further in their work they explored if location choices for offenders change over time of the day and day of the week by using a data set from Chicago. The authors investigated whether street robbers' crime location preferences varied across four time blocks: morning, afternoon, evening, and late night. Even though street robberies vary over the blocks of time, the findings showed that the location preferences are stable over the time scale, confirming that street robbers would rather act near cash-intensive business and other places with higher benefits and lower risks. Their outcomes helped us to discard the hypothesis that the location is affected by time in these sorts of crimes.

Other ABMs for crime approaches

Pint, Crooks, and Geller (2010) made a more generic model considering societal aspects of life in order to derive the macro changes in two neighbourhoods in Rio de Janeiro and Alkimim, Clarke, and Oliveira (2013) present a more statistical analysis of a Brazilian city with similar characteristics to Lavras.

With respect to criminological research burglary has been of interest to criminologists. Malleson et al. (2012) present a model for offender behaviour in a model of burglary and Birks and Davies (2017) presented and validated an ABM for residential burglary while using street networks and empirical data. Robbery has been the focus of Groff (2007). In her research she tried to use an ABM of the routine activity theory to describe and test street robbery. The hypothesis tested in this work was that, as time spent away from home increases, crime will increase. The framework presented is claimed to be strong enough for further explorations in a similar context.

In addition, an interesting category of ABMs makes use of spatio-temporal data on human mobility. Already in 1982, Brantingham and Brantingham exploited information on commercial burglaries known to the police in order to study crime patterns in a small town in British Columbia (Brantingham and Brantingham 1982). More recently, in the work of Brüngger, Kadar, and Pletikosa (2016) and Rosés et al. (2018), offender mobility has been simulated based on activity nodes from location-based social networks – a very interesting approach that might be incorporated into our research later.

Furthermore, some recent studies make use of data on mobility of citizens. For example, Malleson and Andresen use social media data to determine where to study spatio-temporal crime patterns in the city of Leeds, UK (Malleson and Andresen 2015). Similarly, Caminha et al. exploit a combination of geo-referenced data sets to study crime patterns in the city of Fortaleza, Brazil (Caminha et al. 2017).

In this chapter we address the main research questions and discuss what the outcomes mean for routine activity theory (Cohen and Felson 1979). We also present related work that contributed to the study of street robbery and the potential analysis performed to reduce the offenders' opportunities. The next section introduces the data set and the characteristics of the location used in the study. This is followed by the ABM based on routine activity theory and its parameters, then the next section exposes the results obtained through simulation. The discussion of the outcomes follows and, lastly, potential improvements to the model in future work are explained.

Crime in Lavras

Lavras is a Brazilian municipality in the southern part of the state of Minas Gerais, founded in 1729. It is also one of the safest cities in Brazil, being in the top ten cities with the lowest violence rates in the country (Cerqueira et al. 2018). With around 100,000 inhabitants, its economy is mostly based on agriculture and animal products. Lavras is also known for having one of the biggest universities in the country, with around 9,000 students and more than 1,000 professors and staff. For this study we are focusing on street robberies which occurred in the city of Lavras between 2014 and 2018. This is a very common crime that significantly affects the feeling of safety for citizens. Street robberies, or muggings, generally take place on streets, and in shops or houses. This section will explain the patterns of time of day when the crimes took place, as well as the characteristics of the victims and offenders. We selected the crime of mugging intending to reduce the complexity of our study, and

Table 6.1 Main robbery locations in Lavras (2014–2018)

Public street	429	49.88%
Gas station	118	13.72%
Bar/restaurant/similar	68	7.91%
Other – commerce shop / services	34	3.95%
House	33	3.84%
Supermarket/grocerys shop	28	3.26%
Bakery	26	3.02%
Diverse shops	17	1.98%
Farm	15	1.74%
Nightclub/similar	11	1.28%

also because these crimes are the majority of cases within our data set. Other types of crime can be added in the future for further exploration. The model presented in the section on modelling street robberies, below will use the information for the purpose of validation. This data was provided by Polícia Militar de Minas Gerais (Minas Gerais State Military Police), and contains the data collected by police officers using an accurate system through the use of smartphones and GPS location to register the events.

There were 862 registered cases in Lavras between 1 January 2014 and 31 December 2018. Most of the crimes of mugging happened on the streets, as shown in Table 6.1. Gas stations and bars are also common targets of offenders.

Most of the offenders used a shotgun as the coercion crime tool. This is relevant, as the number of illegal guns in Brazilian society is abnormal, being held by gangs and sold on the black market to anyone who intends to use them (Zaluar 2007). Two cases of offenders setting traps for victims, known as 'saidinha de banco' (leaving the bank), were also registered. These are situations where the victim is approached by the offender after leaving an ATM with withdrawn money. This sort of crime tends to happen on payday, the day when people receive their monthly salary. The motivated offender waits and observes an ATM in order to detect when someone has money, and then decides to commit the mugging. Table 6.2 shows the main means of coercion used by the offenders in our data set. For our model, the means of coercion were ignored as this is not part of the routine activity theory. Even though we don't take the means of coercion into account for the model, it is good to notice the prevalent use of firearms (handguns mostly) in almost half of the registered cases.

The yearly registered cases of muggings in the whole city of Lavras from 2014 until 2018 are shown in Figure 6.1. The number of robberies has been decreasing over the last two years, an inverted tendency observed from 2014 until 2016.

The time of day when the crimes occurred is what our model tries to predict. The data set shows that most of the crimes occurred after 18h00 and

Table 6.2 Means used to commit robbery in Lavras (2014–2018)

Guns	376	44.08%
Weapon (knife, sharp instrument)	184	21.57%
Physical aggression without instruments	94	11.02%
Threat	87	10.20%
Others	83	9.73%
Fake shotgun	27	3.17%
Trap (saidinha de banco)	2	0.23%

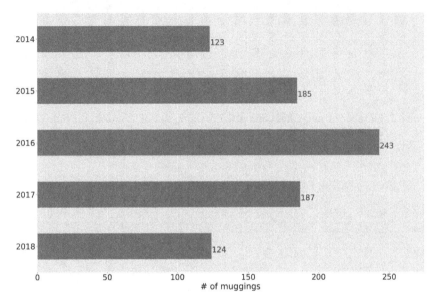

Figure 6.1 Robberies per year in Lavras (2014–2018).

before 03h00, as shown in Figure 6.2. Checking the amount of crimes on a 6-hour window basis, it is possible to observe that between 22h00 and 03h00 the cumulative sum is higher than 40% of the total crimes in the data set (Figure 6.3). The data provided by the police was used to validate the model. It shows that the time of the day is relevant to whether the offender commits a crime or not. This factor is included in the model, as shown in the section on modelling street robberies, below.

Offenders and victims: describing the characteristics of the people involved in a mugging

The data set contains the profiles of 399 offenders and suspects. As the data set is anonymized it is not possible to have a better idea of the number of

152 *Eric Araújo and Charlotte Gerritsen*

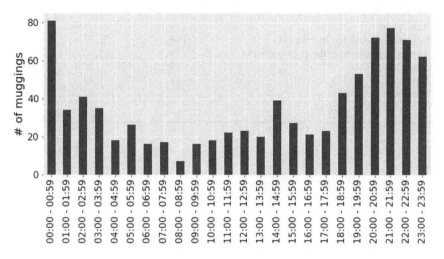

Figure 6.2 Number of muggings committed per time slot of 1 hour in the time range 2014–2018 in Lavras.

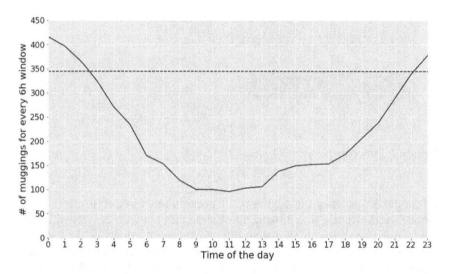

Figure 6.3 Six-hour window average of muggings in Lavras.

crimes committed by each offender, or the number of unique offenders in the data set. It also contains the profiles of 1,196 victims of mugging. Most of the victims are between 18 and 30 years old, students and male. Most of the offenders are unemployed, male and with a low educational level (incomplete secondary school). That is, there is a clear pattern for targeting victims by criminals, as well as a clear pattern for offenders.

Most muggings have only one offender involved, with a mean of 1.49 offenders per crime, and a standard deviation of 0.77. In total, 90.42% of offenders were single, acknowledging the fact that not having a family or being part of a fractured family might be relevant factors in a person turning to criminal activities. The most frequently targeted victims are students, gas station workers and shop workers, in that specific order.

Data cleaning and selection

The data analysis shown above is relevant to understanding the patterns of mugging crimes in Lavras in the time range from 2014 until 2018. Now we turn to the task of data cleaning and selection, aiming to provide more specific information to validate our model.

As we are interested in muggings that occurred on the streets, we want to know what the characteristics of the victims are who were approached in public spaces. For that, we removed registrations with missing latitude and longitude coordinates. There were 59 registrations without a geolocation of the crime, or 0.07% of the total.

After removing missing latitude and longitude coordinates, we turned to the selection of the muggings which occurred on the streets. Out of the 803 remaining registrations, 407 (50.68% of the total) occurred on the streets.

We also selected the more central area of the city of Lavras to run our simulations. The city centre is the area where more people are concentrated and where shops run their businesses. For this, we exported the GIS data provided by OpenStreetMaps (OpenStreetMap contributors, 2017) as latitude $\in [-21.2479824, -21.2360275]$ and longitude $\in [-45.0059971, -44.9870231]$. We then selected the street muggings within these spatial limits.

To support our limit selection, we compare the number of crimes in each of the three subsets: (1) the total number of robberies for the whole city; (2) the total number of robberies happening on the streets; and (3) the number of street robberies within the limits of the city centre. Figure 6.4 shows the number of events for each subset per year.

As is shown in Table 6.3, there is a correlation between the data subsets generated from the original data set regarding the time patterns. Figure 6.5 shows that a second-degree regression over the three subsets (full data set, robberies on the streets, and robberies on the streets within geographic limits) will deliver a good fit for the data. All the regressions presented a $R^2 > 0.63$ and $p < 0.01$ for the model. That means that quantitatively the three subsets present the same tendency and reducing our analysis to the subset of the street robberies within our latitude and longitude boundaries will keep a good representation of the crimes for the whole city.

The data analysis presented in this section is useful to generate the model with more realistic properties. We describe some of the crime patterns in Lavras from 2014 to 2018. The number of crimes per year and per time of day are crucial for our work as we intend to generate a model that returns a similar temporal pattern as observed in our empirical data set.

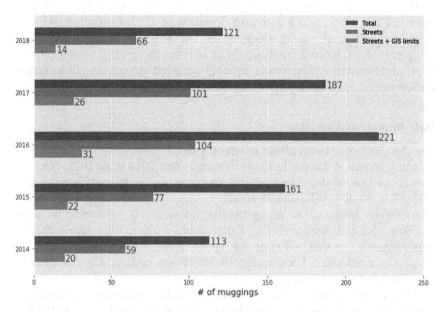

Figure 6.4 Total muggings and street muggings after cleaning and selecting data for street crimes within geographical coordinate limits.

Table 6.3 Pearson correlation and significance for the three sets of data selection on the number of crimes per hour

	Total	*Streets*	*Streets + GIS*
Total	1.000	0.961*	0.817*
Streets		1.000	0.856*
Streets + GIS			1.000

*$p<0.01$.

Modelling street robberies

Pratt (2015) presents a very relevant point when discussing how criminological theories are being created at a faster pace than the efforts to validate them. In his own words,

> To be sure, it appears that we have as many varieties of explanations as to why people break the law as ways that Wile E. Coyote has used to try to snuff out the Roadrunner.

Empirical tests of the main propositions of theories are relevant to verify which theories are better, and also for further use of the knowledge obtained

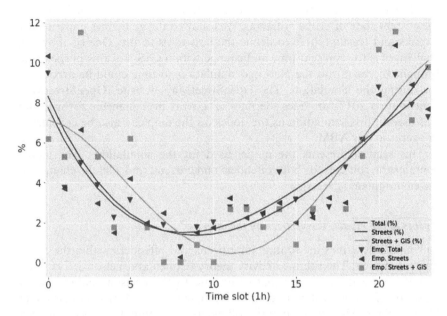

Figure 6.5 Polynomial regression over the three different data selection sets.

from the theory framework. This section is dedicated to presenting an adaptation of the routine activity theory for street robbery activities. We aim to provide a computational model and a data-based approach to validate our model.

The complexity of phenomena that involve human behaviour, environmental influences and social influences is a helpful way of being represented by ABMs. The ABM relies on a temporal scale to simulate real-life scenarios by giving autonomy to the entities called agents to make decisions based on information observed in their direct environment (Gerritsen 2015). By using ABMs, we can describe the dynamics of crime using mathematical formulae to define the decision-making system of the agents in a temporal-causal approach (usually differential equations).

The process of creating an ABM starts with a conceptual model stating what the basic questions or goals are and what the elements of the system are. The outcome measures are also identified in order to validate or define if the model is functioning according to what is expected. The definition of the model encompasses defining the types of agents, their attributes, the rules for interaction, the behaviour of the agents and the environment where the agents are going to act (Brown 2006). In this work, we model two types of agents with different routines on a map. The use of geolocation in this study requires the use of geospatial simulation combined with the ABM.

We used a data set of all the crimes of mugging in a small Brazilian city called Lavras in the period from 2014 until 2018. The data is used as a benchmark to evaluate the accuracy of our model. The ABM is tuned to match the current state of crime in Lavras. We followed the guidelines presented by Crooks and Castle (2012) to define the best tools to use. One of the main challenges is to represent time and change within GIS. For this purpose, we brought the map into the NetLogo simulation so time could be accounted for during the simulation. The OpenStreetMap website (OpenStreetMap contributors 2017) provides the map of Lavras in a shapefile format, and was used in this simulation as the nodes on the map can also be considered as agents in our ABM.

This section presents the model used for the simulations. The model contains the routines for both offenders and citizens, and also the changes in the environment (streets).

Agents in the model: the vertices on the map

Our model describes the routine for citizens and offenders within the environment chosen. The routine activity theory (Cohen and Felson 1979) states that there are three factors that contribute to the decision-making mechanism of offenders willing to commit a crime: (1) offenders; (2) targets; and (3) guardians. Therefore, potential offenders will commit a robbery if they find a suitable target in the absent of capable guardians. In this part of the chapter we will explain the agents that are part of our simulations, as well as describe their routines. Our model is adapted from the previous model presented by Bosse and Gerritsen (2010).

First, we will explain why guardians are not included in this model. The data provided by the police does not include the guardianship routines. It is also known that the crimes that happened were a result of the lack of police presence, or they wouldn't happen. So, the data set provides a good measurement of the crimes that were successful, and as the aim of this work is to define the distribution of these crimes in a spatial dimension, we considered that the distribution of the guardians was irrelevant. This is in line with several other ABM studies, which also base their model on crime data without taking guardian data into consideration (Malleson and Andresen 2015; Caminha et al. 2017). Nevertheless, some aspects of guardianship were kept in the model, as we understand that police enforcement and presence are not the only ways to construct a safe environment. That leads us to the first agents in our model: the places on the streets.

The map of the city was imported into NetLogo using the gis extension, after being pre-processed and transformed into shapefiles. This map, after being imported, is turned into a graph, where the vertices are the corners (or points of street changes), while the edges become the paths from one node to another. Figure 6.6 shows the map of the city centre of Lavras as used in the simulations. The green and red symbols represent the people on the streets. The red-coloured agents are the offenders.

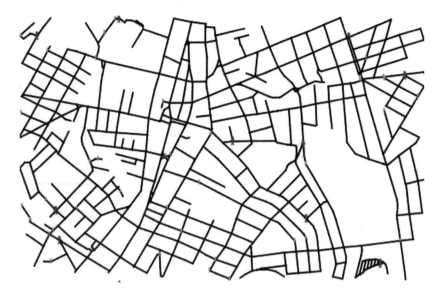

Figure 6.6 Map of Lavras city centre.

The guardianship in our model is related to the density of the places. That means that, as more people are gathered in a specific spot on the map, the less the chances of an offender to successfully commit a crime. Thus, our model is similar to a one-tailed distribution where, the higher the density, the less the probability of a street robbery. The street robberies we consider in this model are generally crimes that require action and are easily noticed by other citizens if spotted. Therefore, we believe that offenders will consider that more people significantly increase the risks, reducing their intent.

Our model also includes lighting as a factor for increasing risks of mugging. That is, daylight is a natural inhibitor for offenders. This statement is also confirmed by the data set, as explained previously, where most crimes occur at night time.

Every vertex on the map will have two attributes, called attractiveness and density. Density is calculated as:

$$density(v) = \begin{cases} 0, & \text{if } num\_people(v) = 0 \\ \dfrac{1}{num\_people(v)^2}, & \text{otherwise} \end{cases}$$

where v is the vertex. The idea to define guardianship as a measure of situational density is a common approach in computational criminology (see, e.g., Groff 2007).

158   Eric Araújo and Charlotte Gerritsen

The attractiveness ($\alpha(v,t)$) of the place v at time t is, then, given by the density of the place, and also for the light levels of the time of the day, given by the equations below.

$$lighting(v,t) = \begin{cases} 0.4, & \text{if } current\_hour > 18 \text{ or } current\_hour < 7 \\ 0.9, & \text{otherwise} \end{cases}$$

$$\alpha(v,t) = (1 - lighting) \times density$$

The lighting patterns were kept the same throughout the whole year due to the small variation in daylight duration in the regions studied. It would certainly be different for places that are not close to the equator line. The attractiveness is related to the offender's decision mechanism. The higher the value of α, the more attractive is the vertex for the criminals.

Agents in the model: the people

All agents receive a random location at the beginning of the simulation. Two sorts of agents are then generated: offenders and citizens. The routine of the agents is defined by their role.

For both types of agents, a distribution of people on the map is generated over time. The aim is to get more people on the streets at business times and during the day, and reduce the number of citizens on the streets when it gets dark. This is done by a sinusoidal function given by the equation below (*people_on_the_streets*). The function is calculated in relation to *ticks*, which is the basic step given during the simulation. Every *tick* represents 10 minutes in real life.

$$people\_on\_the\_streets(tick) = 0.51 + 0.5 \times \sin\left(\frac{5}{2} \times (ticks - 54)\right)$$

As it is expected that offenders are more frequently walking on the streets when it is more attractive to them, they have their own function that will return the percentage of offenders active at each time, as shown in the following equation (*offenders_on_the_streets*).

$$offenders\_on\_the\_streets(tick) = 0.5 - 0.5 \times \sin\left(\frac{5}{2} \times (ticks - 24)\right)$$

So each agent (citizen or offender) will be active or not based on the outcome of the equations *people_on_the_streets* and *offenders_on_the_streets*, respectively. Both citizens and offenders follow a random walk algorithm every 10 minutes (or one tick). That means that the agents move on the map by selecting a random vertex and moving to it in the next time step. The density of the map, then, is based on the amount of people distributed on the map randomly. When an agent is inactive, they don't move from their original vertex.

Many policing guides approach the importance of citizens being aware of their surroundings as a way of reducing the risks of getting robbed.[1] As Barker et al. (1993) state,

> Given that most people are attacked within a short distance of their homes, alertness and awareness on journeys home could he promoted, so that people do not fall into the trap of believing that because the area is familiar that they are necessarily safe.

Thus, in our model each citizen will have an awareness attribute. This awareness is related to their own perception of the environment where they are at a given moment. People who are more aware of the threats while on the streets tend to present a lower chance of getting robbed. The awareness of the agents is updated according to the changes in the environment, and presents a smoother pattern. The equation below shows how it is calculated:

$$awareness(c,v,t) = awareness(c,v,t-1) + awareness_{sf} \times (\alpha(v,t) - awareness(c,v,t-1))\Delta t$$

where *awareness_sf* is the speed factor that defines how fast the awareness of the agents changes, $\alpha(v,t)$ is the attractiveness of the vertex v where the agent is located in a given time t, c is the citizen agent, and Δt equals 1 for the purpose of this work.

The decision mechanism of offenders has been studied by many researchers. Bernasco, Ruiter, and Block (2017) examined the (rejected) hypothesis that the location chosen for a street robbery is dependent on the time of day and on the day of the week. Tompson and Bowers (2013) studied the influence of darkness together with temperature in street robberies. Darkness was discovered to be an important driving factor in seasonal variation of the phenomenon in a data set from London and Glasgow.

Along with environmental factors, offenders also need some level of motivation to move into committing a crime. We assume that the offender will have a much lower motivation right after succeeding in mugging a citizen, and after some time the motivation is going to return to a level that requires more action. For this situation, we define the initial motivation level of each offender as a random float number between 0 and 1, and if it reaches a threshold, there is an attempt to commit a crime. After a robbery has been successful, the level of motivation is decreased to a random value between 0 and 0.25. The motivation is readjusted and incremented by a motivation factor every time there is a step (or tick), as shown in the algorithm below.

Algorithm 1 **Motivation mechanism for offenders**

```
1:   procedure Commit_Crime
2:      if motivation > motivation_threshold then
3:      if density > 0 then
4:      if crime_succeeded then
5:      motivation ← random(0; 0.25)
6:      motivation ← motivation + 0.05 x (random(0; motivation_sf))
7:      if motivation > 1 then
8:      motivation = 1
```

The offender takes a final chance of committing the crime based on the awareness of the victim chosen (previous equation for *awareness*) and their own motivation. The risk of committing the crime is given by the equation below, where c is the citizen chosen as a target, v is the vertex where both offender and citizen are located and t stands for the time of the action.

$$\phi(c,v,t) = \frac{(1 - awareness(c,v,t)) + motivation}{2}$$

Based on the value of $\phi(c,v,t)$, the offender will commit a successful robbery or adjust their motivation until the next opportunity if the attempt fails.

Parameter tuning and validation methods

Figure 6.1 showed the total number of street robberies between 2014 and 2018 in our data set. Now we take the average number of robberies per time slot per year in order to find the best parameters that will provide a similar pattern through the model presented.

The model has many parameters that will define the pace at which events will happen. The three main parameters in the model are:

1. motivation_threshold
2. $awareness_{sf}$
3. $motivation_{sf}$

These variables and weights created are used to ensure that the model is realistic. The data provided by the police is the benchmark to assure the patterns emerging from the simulation are similar to the ones empirically collected. More specifically, the distribution of the street robberies over time is the pattern we aim to replicate in our model.

The section on crime in Lavras, above, explained how the data was selected and cleaned to be used for validation purposes. The street robberies within the geographic limits alone are used for this study. The area selected includes the city centre and some adjacent neighbourhoods. To measure the accuracy, the number of crimes during one year of simulation will be considered.

The parameters are adjusted by parameter sweeping. That is, the values for the parameters were adjusted from 0 to 1 in steps of 0.1 for *awareness*$_{sf}$ and *motivation_threshold*. The value for *motivation*$_{sf}$ was adjusted from 0 to 0.1 in steps of 0.01. Values above 0.1 for this parameter lead the simulations to drastic oscillations and unrealistic results. We used the BehaviorSpace tool in NetLogo to generate the simulations with different combinations of parameters. More than 400 scenarios were tested in order to find the best fit to the empirical data.

The spatial analysis of the crimes was ignored in this work as we selected a very specific area of the city, ignoring the other neighbourhoods. In future works we intend to explore the spatial characteristics of the crimes.

Results

This section presents the results obtained while using the model to find similar patterns of street robberies over time. We first show the parameters found to fit the data set provided by the local police. Then we provide the outcomes from this first analysis.

The parameter-tuning process was done using a parameter-sweeping approach. Four phases were done to narrow down to the parameters that fit the model the best. BehaviorSpace tool was used to sweep through the potential values for the three parameters used: (1) *motivation_threshold*, (2) *awareness*$_{sf}$ and (3) *motivation*$_{sf}$. Simulations were run from 100 days up to 365 days (1 year) in order to verify the effect of time on the results. In the end, we ran the same simulation 50 times for one year.

The goal is to fine-tune the model so the temporal crime distribution found is correlated to what is observed in the data set. Table 6.4 show the best parameters found after the four phases of parameter testing.

The graphic in Figure 6.7 shows the empirical distribution of the crimes in comparison to the average of 100 simulations using the model presented in this chapter. The correlation between the two sets of data is $0.67 (p < 0.001)$. That is, our model generates crimes in a stochastic approach that correlates with the empirical data provided by the police.

Table 6.4 Parameters adjusted according to the empirical data

Parameters	Value
awareness$_{sf}$	0.80
motivation$_{sf}$	0.01
motivation_threshold	0.90
Number of offenders	10
Number of people (maximum)	10,000

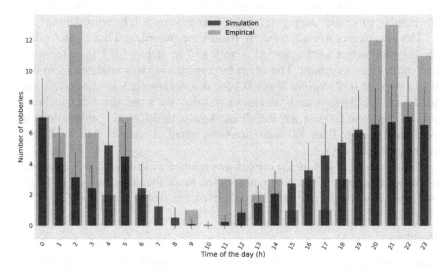

Figure 6.7 Results of the simulation of the model for 100 times compared to the empirical data.

Figure 6.7 shows that our ABM does produce a distribution over time of day that is satisfactory, similar to the actual distribution observed in police data. We may refresh the memory of the reader here that, in contrast to the other chapters in this book, we do not compare generated data with stylized facts, but with facts as observed in reality.

Discussion

This chapter presented a model using the routine activity theory to define the characteristics of the street robberies in the city of Lavras, Brazil. Besides introducing our model and the characteristics of the simulation, we have shown that we can use it to derive the time pattern of crimes throughout the day in Lavras.

Our findings showed that using real data to fine-tune the routine activity theory can improve the model for cases of street robbery. Therefore, the routine activity theory converges with real data and is corroborated by our findings.

The use of ABMs for the simulation combined with real data has been proven as a promising approach for testing a criminological theory and for the validation of models that explain the many elements of the street robbery phenomenon. More specifically, in this model the amount of muggings committed was correlated with the data obtained by the police. We also used the real map to run the simulation.

Bernasco, Block, and Ruiter (2013) examined the street robbers' location choices in the city of Chicago. They concluded that:

> The theory asserted that street robbers decide on where to attack by optimizing a combination of the perceived rewards, efforts and risks attached to potential robbery locations. Empirically, it was demonstrated that street robbers living in Chicago are most likely to attack on easily accessible blocks, where legal and illegal cash economies are present. It was also shown that the *robbery attracting effects of cash economies and accessibility spill over to adjacent blocks, but not beyond* (italics added for emphasis).

The location used for the simulation contains the city centre, where most of the shops, restaurants, banks and other cash economies are present (Figure 6.8). It is also the region where the flow of people is greater, and therefore is a constant focus of robberies.

Using data to confirm that the model is accurate brings new discussions to the crime theory test field of studies. The possibility of verifying the accuracy of the models fulfils one of the main problems presented in the introduction of this chapter, regarding the large number of theories without as many works

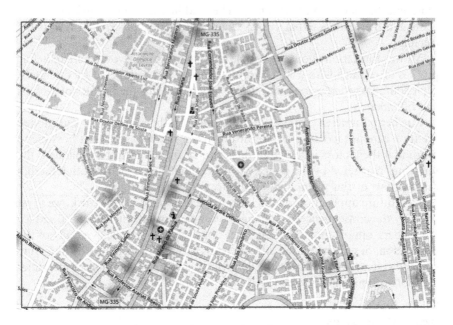

Figure 6.8 Map of the city centre of Lavras. The red square represents the cut used for the simulations. The street robberies' locations in 2018 are shown as blue marks on the map.

intending to verify if the outcomes of the models are observable in real life. As this is a new field being explored, it is natural that difficulties arise in the first efforts to provide a good explanation for the events observed in a data set of crimes. On the other hand, as we improve the methods in this direction, potential interventions and predictions would be a great contribution to the state of the art as never observed before.

Finally, the work presented in this chapter raises the question of which method is better for testing theories. The stylized facts are useful knowledge that helps in simulations for criminology's studies, but providing real observations and deriving the model from there can be a more trustworthy way of generating new scenarios for prediction of future crimes. In our case, we used data from the police to provide temporal patterns to our street robbery model based on the routine activity theory. We believe that, as more reliable and precise data is generated in the real world, the more researchers on simulations will improve their results and their models.

Potential improvements based on the results obtained

The model presented can be extended in many ways. Geographic position analysis is required to understand the spatial dimension of the crimes. In this sense, the model can acquire more details of the vertices of the graph that represent the places on the real map. These additions would consider the hot spots and the tendency that crimes usually happen in places that favour the offender.

More information about the people in our simulations would help to define profiles of citizens with a higher probability of being targeted by offenders. That could be tested using our data set which contains the profiles of victims and offenders.

Further parameter tuning could also enhance the accuracy of our model. We took care not to cause an overfitting in our model, as it is not possible to claim that the factors included in this chapter are sufficient to explain all the muggings registered by the police. We expect that, as we include other factors that are part of this phenomenon, the accuracy will be higher.

As a future application of the knowledge generated in this work, we want to study the consequences of changes on the environment, aiming to reduce the robbers' opportunity. That might be done by changing the dynamics of the population, or enhancing the attractiveness of vulnerable places by including security systems or increasing the density in those places at times when crimes are more promising for offenders.

Acknowledgements

We are very pleased with the data provided by the PMMG (Military Police in Minas Gerais). The partnership between science and the police corporation has proven to be very rich and fruitful. We look forward to the next developments from this initial work. We also appreciate the effort and help coding in NetLogo by Álvaro Martins Espíndola.

Note

1 Street Robbery. Guide No. 59 (2010) https://popcenter.asu.edu/content/street-robbery-0, accessed 20 April 2020; Metropolitan Police (UK). How to protect yourself from street robbery. www.met.police.uk/cp/crime-prevention/personal-robbery/street-robbery/, accessed 20 April 2020.

References

Alkimim, A., Clarke, K.C., and Oliveira, F.S. (2013). Fear, Crime, and Space: The Case of Viçosa, Brazil. *Applied Geography* 42: 124–32.

Barker, M., Geraghty, J., Webb, B., and Key, T. (1993). The Prevention of Street Robbery. London: Home Office Police Research Group.

Bernasco, W., Block, R., and Ruiter, S. (2013). Go Where the Money Is: Modelling Street Robbers' Location Choices. *Journal of Economic Geography* 13 (1): 119–43.

Bernasco, W., Ruiter, S., and Block, R. (2017). Do Street Robbery Location Choices Vary over Time of Day or Day of Week? A Test in Chicago. *Journal of Research in Crime and Delinquency* 54 (2): 244–75.

Birks, D., and Davies, T. (2017). Street Network Structure and Crime Risk: An Agent-Based Investigation of the Encounter and Enclosure Hypotheses. *Criminology* 55 (4): 900–37.

Bosse, T., and Gerritsen, C. (2010). Social Simulation and Analysis of the Dynamics of Criminal Hot Spots. *Journal of Artificial Societies and Social Simulation* 13(2).

Brantingham, P.L., and Brantingham, P.J. (1982). Mobility, Notoriety and Crime: A Study of Crime Patterns in Urban Nodal Points. *Journal of Environmental Systems* 11 (1): 89–99.

Brantingham, P., and Brantingham P. (2013). Crime Pattern Theory. In R. Wortley & L. Mazerole (eds.), *Environmental Criminology and Crime Analysis*. Cullompton: Willan Publishing, pp. 78–94.

Brown, D.G. (2006). *Agent-Based Models. The Earth's Changing Land*. Westport, CT: Greenwood Publishing.

Brüngger, R.R., Kadar, C., and Pletikosa, I. (2016). Design of an Agent-Based Model to Predict Crime (Wip). In Proceedings of the Summer Computer Simulation Conference, 55. Red Hook, NY: Society for Computer Simulation International.

Caminha, C., Furtado, V., Pequeno, T.H.C, Ponte, C., Melo, H.P.M., Oliveira, E.A., and Andrade Jr. J.S. (2017). Human Mobility in Large Cities as a Proxy for Crime. *PloS One* 12 (2): 1–13.

Cerqueira, D., Lima, R.S. de, Bueno, S., Neme, C., Ferreira, H., Coelho, D., and Palmieri Alves, P. (2018). Atlas Da Violência 2018. Rio de Janeiro: IPEA.

Cohen, L.E., and Felson, M. (1979). Social Change and Crime Rate Trends: A Routine Activity Approach. *American Sociological Review* 44 (4) 588–608.

Crooks, A.T., and Castle, C.J.E. (2012). The Integration of Agent-Based Modelling and Geographical Information for Geospatial Simulation. In A. Heppenstall, A. Crooks, L. See, & M. Batty (eds.), *Agent-Based Models of Geographical Systems*. Heidelberg: Springer, pp. 219–251.

Dubois, D., Hájek, P., and Prade, H. (2000). Knowledge-Driven Versus Data-Driven Logics. *Journal of Logic, Language and Information* 9 (1): 65–89.

Gerritsen, C. (2015). Agent-Based Modelling as a Research Tool for Criminological Research. *Crime Science* 4 (1): 2.

Groff, E.R. (2007). Simulation for Theory Testing and Experimentation: An Example Using Routine Activity Theory and Street Robbery. *Journal of Quantitative Criminology* 23 (2): 75–103.

Groff, E.R., Johnson, S.D., and Thornton, A. (2019). State of the Art in Agent-Based Modeling of Urban Crime: An Overview. *Journal of Quantitative Criminology* 35 (1): 155–93.

Holston, J., and Caldeira, T.P.R. (1999). *Democracy and Violence in Brazil.* 4. Vol. 41. www.cambridge.org/core.

Malleson, N., and Andresen, M.A. (2015). Spatio-Temporal Crime Hotspots and the Ambient Population. *Crime Science* 4 (1): 10.

Malleson, N., See, L., Evans, A., and Heppenstall, A. (2012). Implementing Comprehensive Offender Behaviour in a Realistic Agent-Based Model of Burglary. *Simulation* 88 (1): 50–71.

Monk, K.M, Heinonen, J.A., and Eck, J.E. (2010). *Problem-Oriented Guides for Police Problem-Specific Guides* Series No. 59. Washington, DC: Center for Problem-Oriented Policing.

OpenStreetMap contributors. 2017. Planet Dump. Retrieved from https://planet.osm.org. www.openstreetmap.org.

Pint, B., Crooks, A., and Geller, A. (2010). Exploring the Emergence of Organized Crime in Rio de Janeiro: An Agent-Based Modeling Approach. In 2010 *Second Brazilian Workshop on Social Simulation*, 7–14. Los Alamitos, CA: IEEE.

Pratt, T.C. (2015). Theory Testing in Criminology. *The Handbook of Criminological Theory* 4: 37.

Rosés, R., Kadar, C., Gerritsen, C., and Rouly, C. (2018). Agent-Based Simulation of Offender Mobility: Integrating Activity Nodes from Location-Based Social Networks. In *Proceedings of the 17th International Conference on Autonomous Agents and Multiagent Systems*. International Foundation for Autonomous Agents and Multiagent Systems, Richland, SC, 804–12.

Sachsida, A., Cardoso de Mendonça, M.J., Loureiro, P.R.A., and Sarmiento Gutierrez, M.B. (2010). Inequality and Criminality Revisited: Further Evidence from Brazil. *Empirical Economics* 39 (1): 93–109.

Tompson, L., and Bowers. K. (2013). A Stab in the Dark? A Research Note on Temporal Patterns of Street Robbery. *Journal of Research in Crime and Delinquency* 50 (4): 616–31.

Troitzsch, K.G. (2017). Can Agent-Based Simulation Models Replicate Organised Crime? *Trends in Organized Crime* 20 (1–2): 100–19.

Zaluar, A. (2007). *Crimes and Violence Trends in Rio de Janeiro, Brazil.* Case Study Prepared for Enhancing Urban Safety and Security: Global Report on Human Settlements.

7 Corruption and the shadow of the future

A generalization of an ABM with repeated interactions

Nick van Doormaal, Stijn Ruiter, and Andrew M. Lemieux

Introduction

Corruption is a widespread, complex phenomenon with detrimental impacts on social and economic development around the world (Banuri & Eckel, 2012; Transparency International, 2019; Warf, 2016). High levels of corruption lead to unfair distributions of resources and income, while undermining democracy and the rule of law. Corruption manifests itself in a variety of ways, including individual acts such as accepting bribes, and grand larceny on an organized, institutional scale (Transparency International, 2019; Warf, 2016). Ultimately, a better understanding of the effects and causes of corruption has the potential to inform corruption control and anti-corruption campaigns. Policies that seek to deter corruption can be directed at influencing individual behaviour and perception through penalties, public relations campaigns or organisational structures and procedures. Such policies have the potential to increase the perceived costs for engaging in corrupt activities and deter potential offenders.

Deterrence of corrupt behaviour

Early modern deterrence theorists argued that people weigh costs and benefits in their decision-making process (Becker, 1968). Assuming rational decision-making, individuals can be deterred from crime if the costs outweigh the benefits. This model of deterrence is known as the "economic model of rational deterrence" (Becker, 1968). The theory does not differentiate between criminals and non-criminals, and states that every individual has their own cost–benefit assessment for committing crimes (Paternoster, 2010).

Deterrence theory divides the costs of committing a crime into three components related to punishment: severity, certainty and celerity (Nagin, 2013). The severity of punishment needs to be strong enough to sufficiently reduce the benefits of a particular crime. Certainty applies to the likelihood of receiving punishment, whereas celerity applies to the timing of imposing punishment. Empirical studies on the deterrence of crime show mixed results regarding the severity and celerity of punishment. The certainty of punishment, however, is often found to play an important role in crime deterrence (Nagin, 2013).

Deterrence is general or specific. We refer to specific deterrence when an individual is deterred from committing future crimes through the experience of punishment. General deterrence refers to the idea that individuals respond to the threat of punishment; the punishment of those who commit crimes will also serve as an example to potential offenders among the general population.

Most forms of corruption are interactions between at least two individuals or groups. Choosing to behave corruptly will yield the highest rewards that the individual otherwise would not be able to get. Although the rewards of corruption are generally higher than for following the rules, the rewards could be counterbalanced by high costs. According to deterrence theory, the costs of corruption could be increased by increasing the perceived severity, certainty or celerity of punishment. Empirical studies commonly find the costs of crime can be increased by increasing the likelihood of punishment (Nagin, 2013).

Modelling corruption and deterrence

The level of corruption in a society is the aggregate-level outcome of all individual decisions. The associated costs of corruption are perceived differently among individuals and it is the perception of the severity, certainty and celerity of punishment that matters (Paternoster, 2010). The conditions to deter someone from corruption can vary depending on the individual's perception of punishment. The reciprocal relationships among these three components and its effect on deterrence complicate our understanding of what leads to higher or lower levels of corruption. To tackle the complexity of corruption and deterrence, agent-based models can be used to assess these conditions.

Agent-based modelling is a simulation technique in which the behaviour and decision-making of autonomous individuals are modelled to identify relevant factors for the entire system (Epstein and Axtell, 1996). It allows researchers to study complex systems and problems in an abstract environment, without them being influenced by specific characteristics of certain locations, and without the need for direct observations in the real world. Corruption is a widespread, complex phenomenon and difficult to observe directly in the real world. Therefore, agent-based modelling can be used to study the dynamics of corruption and its deterrence in an abstract environment. For further explanation of agent-based models and their application in criminological research we refer to the introductory chapter of this book.

Studies on corruption have used agent-based models or similar bottom-up approaches to explore the mechanisms, drivers (Farjam et al., 2015; Ye et al.,

2011; Zausinová et al., 2019) and emergence of corruption (Kim et al., 2013; Situngkir & Khanafiah, 2006; Voinea, 2013). Hammond (2000) modelled corruption as a game-theoretic interaction between two agent populations and showed the effects of general deterrence on corruption levels in an artificial society. His model showed that the effect of general deterrence or "fear of enforcement" can spread rapidly throughout society and can lead to a transition from a high corrupt society to a low corrupt one. The simulation results showed that the transition from a corrupt society to an honest one can happen endogenously. Hammond's (2000) findings contradict existing political economy and economics literature, which assumes these transitions are the result of an exogenous force like a new election, government policy or economic shock (Di Vita, 2007; Goel & Nelson, 2005).

Improving corruption research

Hammond's model offered an alternative explanation for how general deterrence can cause transitions in a corrupt society. However, his model was based on a specific instance of corruption. The interactions between agents were modelled as one-shot, random encounters. Certain scenarios can indeed be regarded as a one-time random interaction, for example citizens declaring taxes or applying for a driver's licence. However, not all interactions involving corruption can be represented with one-shot interactions. Some types of interaction involving corruption are improperly captured with one-shot interactions or even a disconnected series of one-time interactions among individuals. For example, a supplier and a purchasing agent often interact with each other multiple times and over an extended time, as do corrupt police officers who facilitate the work of local criminal groups. To better understand those forms of corruption, assuming repeated interactions between the same individuals would better reflect reality than one-shot interactions.

A key element that is omitted in one-shot interactions is some form of reciprocity (Dal Bo & Frechette, 2011; Gossner & Tomala, 2009). Corrupt individuals working together operate in a risky environment. Interaction is based on the expectation that cooperation will be beneficial to both sides (Dal Bo & Frechette, 2011; Gossner & Tomala, 2009). If one individual does not hold up his or her end of the bargain, then it is likely that the other side will not cooperate in the future. Repeated interaction favours a solid base for mutual trust, and this will also have an impact on the certainty of apprehension. An individual's cooperation in social situations depends strongly on the degree to which others cooperate, which is why offenders are more likely to co-offend with family, long-time friends and other confidants (Kleemans & de Poot, 2008). In terms of deterrence theory, repeated interactions and mutual trust can reduce the certainty of punishment as long as both parties hold up their end of the bargain. Previous studies of human decision-making in exchange relationships have noted that the possibility of there being future interactions can hold important consequences for understanding cooperation (Axelrod, 1984; Balliet et al., 2011).

Objective

In this chapter we focus on the theory of general deterrence and the certainty of punishment. The work of Hammond (2000) showed the effect of general deterrence on the spread of corruption in an artificial society, but was based on a specific instance of corruption with one-shot interactions. Repeated interactions, on the other hand, likely reduce the certainty of punishment and hence should lead to higher levels of corruption. Our stylized fact is therefore that certainty of punishment is a necessary component for the general deterrence of crime. We extend the original model by Hammond (2000) to examine if and how repeated interactions change the ability of high corrupt societies to transition into low corrupt societies. We explore several scenarios in which we systematically vary the likelihood of punishment to better understand the conditions that lead to higher or lower levels of corruption.

The following sections provide an overview of the modelling framework, and describe how we generalized Hammond's model to include repeated interactions between agents.

Model framework

Payoff structures

We first explain the model from a purely game-theoretic perspective. Every player can choose one of two strategies: "corrupt" or "honest". Their decision is based on the expected payoff of that strategy (Table 7.1). We assume that the corrupt action yields the highest payoff (x), but only if both players choose "corrupt". A game-theoretic analysis shows that choosing "corrupt" results in a strict Nash equilibrium because no one has an incentive to change their decision; the outcome with both players choosing "corrupt" is better than all other outcomes. If one or both players choose "honest", then they both receive the lowest payoff (y). Choosing "honest" leads to a weak Nash equilibrium. Neither player can do better by choosing "corrupt" if the other player chooses "honest" because both options yield the low payoff y.

Table 7.1 The 2 × 2 corruption game payoff structure: x and y are the payoffs for choosing that particular strategy

		Player 2 Corrupt	Honest
Player 1	**Corrupt**	x, x	y, y
	Honest	y, y	y, y
$x > y$			

Agent-based modelling approach

Although the decisions in the game are straightforward, it is still an over-simplification of decision-making. No two persons in reality are the same, and each individual has a unique set of values that affects their perception. Furthermore, people's decisions are not only influenced by their own set of values, but also by the behaviour of others, especially friends and family. Therefore, individuals will perceive the payoffs for engaging in corruption differently and make different decisions. The game can be played by a heterogeneous population to better reflect reality, but would also be difficult to solve under the traditional game-theoretic framework. The behaviour of heterogeneous players in a dynamic environment is difficult to predict with game theory alone, but can be captured and quantified with agent-based models. Agent-based modelling allows for heterogeneous and autonomous agents capable of exhibiting human-like behaviours, for example, corrupt behaviours.

Agent characteristics and behaviour

Morality and perceived payoff

Based on the offender motivation literature, we assume that agents possess some intrinsic core values on how to behave (McMurran & Ward, 2004; Ryan & Deci, 2000). We refer to this as an agent's "morality" (Hammond (2000) labelled it as "Honesty".) It influences how the agent perceives the payoffs for choosing "corrupt". An agent that scores high on morality gains little from a corrupt interaction, while only an agent with the lowest morality score gains the full benefits. Increasing levels of morality thus decrease the perceived payoff of corruption. Morality takes a random value between 0 and 1 and is assigned to every agent before a simulation run starts. The assigned morality value is fixed throughout the simulation run. The perceived payoff for acting corrupt (x_i) is calculated as:

$$x_i = (1 - morality) x$$

Networks

Every agent has its own network of other agents (Hammond (2000) referred to the agents within a network as "friends".) The size of an agent's network is fixed and set by the modeller at the start of the simulation. Every agent creates an undirected link with a number of other random agents until it reaches the specified network size. Agents can be part of multiple networks but will never exceed the specified network size. The size of the network is fixed and set by the modeller at the start of the simulation. We are uncertain if our network setup is the same as the one described by Hammond because little information was provided. Hammond (2000) described it as follows: "These networks are of fixed (standard) size, but the specific contents of each agent's network is randomly assigned during initialization".

The agent has access to certain information of other agents within its network. The agent can observe the most recent actions of the members within its network ("honest" or "corrupt"), and observe which members are suspended.

Agent decision-making

Each agent first calculates the perceived payoffs for acting corrupt (x_i). Next, every agent estimates the probability of encountering a corrupt agent as follows.

The agent keeps track of the actions chosen by the agents it interacted with in previous rounds and will remember those actions for a certain period of time. This is referred to as the agent's "memory". The size of memory (i.e. the number of past interactions the agent can remember) is set by the modeller at the start of the simulation and is fixed throughout the simulation run. The agent examines its memory to count the number of corrupt partners it has encountered in previous interactions. The agent calculates the probability of encountering a corrupt agent as: $A = \dfrac{n}{N}$, in which n is the number of corrupt partners encountered in N previous interactions.

Every agent also estimates the probability of apprehension for acting corrupt in this round. The agent does this by examining the behaviour and status of other agents in its social network. Every agent can only observe the most recent action chosen by all network members, and observe which network members are suspended. The probability of apprehension is calculated based on the number of suspended network members and the number of corrupt network members in the last round. The probability of apprehension for a corrupt action in a round is calculated as: $B = \dfrac{m}{M}$, in which m is the number of suspended network members and M the number of corrupt network members in the previous round.

Finally, agents know the length of suspension k. Suspended agents are removed from play for the duration of k. The decision rule for each agent to act corrupt is then:

$$(1-B)\big[Ax_i + (1-A)y\big] + B\big[y - ky\big] > y$$

The cost of being suspended is ky. The partner of the suspended agent will randomly choose another agent as its new partner. Suspended agents and agents that already have a partner cannot be chosen. It is possible that no agents will be available, because some are suspended and others already have a partner. If so, then the agent without a partner will not interact and wait until agents become available again.

Compare actions with partner

Every agent randomly chooses a partner to interact with. Only agents who are not suspended and do not have a partner at that moment can be selected. If no other agent is available as a partner, then the agent will remain without a partner until other agents become available. Depending on the model settings, the interaction between the agent and its partner may only last one round (one-shot interaction) or multiple interactions over a longer period of time (repeated interactions). Each agent decides between the two actions ("corrupt" and "honest") immediately before each interaction by using the decision rule outlined before.

Next, the agents compare their actions, which leads to one of three possible outcomes (Figure 7.1):

1. Honest interaction: both agents act honest and will receive the lowest payoff.
2. Mismatch: a corrupt agent meets an honest agent. Both agents will receive the lowest payoff and the honest agent will "report" the corrupt agent. If the number of reports reaches a certain threshold, then the corrupt agent will be temporarily suspended.
3. Collusive corruption: both agents act corrupt and will receive the highest payoff.

Enforcement

Just as in Hammond's model, a punishment component will be triggered if a corrupt agent meets an honest agent. The model keeps track of how many reports every agent has received for acting corrupt throughout the simulation run. If an agent has been reported a certain number of times, then the reported agent will be suspended temporarily. Suspended agents cannot interact with other players and therefore cannot gain payoffs. The agent is allowed to interact with other agents again and able to gain payoffs after

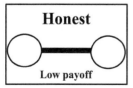  

Figure 7.1 Diagram visualizing the three potential outcomes of two agents interacting.

serving the suspension time. An agent's decision-making is unaltered after being suspended.

The agents in the model are aware that it is possible to be suspended for acting corrupt and do know the length of the suspension term. The length of suspension is set during the model initialization and can be specified by the user. Agents take the length of suspension k into account when deciding between acting corrupt or honest. However, the agents themselves do not know how many reports they have received or how many reports are required to get suspended. The next section will describe the decision-making process of the agents in the model.

A model round can be summarized as follows:

1. *Select agent*: every round, an agent will be randomly paired with another agent.
2. *Select strategy*: each agent decides simultaneously to act corruptly or honestly. The decision rule is based on the agent's bounded rationality.
3. *Receive payoff*: acting corrupt yields the highest payoff (x), but only if the other agent also chooses the corrupt strategy. If both agents choose to act honest, they both receive the lowest payoff (y). If only one of two agents acts corrupt, the honest agent reports the corrupt agent and both receive the lowest payoff (y).
4. *Suspend agents*: if an agent is reported a predefined number of times, the agent will be suspended for a period of time. A suspended agent cannot interact with other agents or gain payoffs.
5. *Release agents*: after serving the suspension time, agents are allowed to interact with other agents again.

From random one-shot to repeated interactions

In Hammond's original model, an agent was randomly paired with another available agent. Hammond did not explore if the transition from a high to low corrupt state can be reached when the same pair of agents interact for consecutive rounds. Our model extension is aimed at changing the current one-shot interaction to repeated interactions between the same agents. The decision-making of agents and model processes described earlier still works in the same way. The only difference is that agents will interact with the same agent over multiple rounds. The number of interactions can be specified by the user and applies to all agents. The number of repeated interactions will never be longer than specified, but can end earlier if one of the agents is suspended.

Agent interactions and memory weights

We expect that the length of memory will play an important role in scenarios with repeated interactions. The agent's memory in the original model reflects the different choices by the other players. The agent uses its memory to assess the likelihood of encountering a corrupt agent in the next round. However, when pairs of agents interact with each other over multiple consecutive rounds, their memory will mostly consist of interactions with that particular agent. The agent's challenge is then to assess the likelihood that its current partner will choose the corrupt action in the next round, rather than assessing the likelihood of encountering a corrupt agent in the entire population. We incorporate this by assigning a weight to the most recent interaction of the agent's memory. The higher the weight, the larger the influence of the most recent interaction on the agent's estimation of encountering a corrupt agent. When the weight is 100%, the agent will only include the most recent interaction in the decision-making for estimating the likelihood of encountering a corrupt agent and disregard all other, older memories. Our extension is built in such a way that when no additional weight is assigned to the most recent interaction, the model reflects the original model by Hammond.

Scenario simulations

Scenarios with repeated interactions were compared with scenarios with Hammond's original one-shot model settings. We run scenarios with agents repeatedly interacting with each other for two to eight consecutive rounds. We run these scenarios in combination with situations in which no addition weight, 50% and 100% weight were assigned to the most recent interaction of the agent's memory (Table 7.2). All other parameters in the model were kept constant throughout all simulation runs (Table 7.3). Each simulation run lasts no longer than 2.000 time units (called ticks in the model). The model keeps track of the number of honest and corrupt agents throughout the simulation run. The outcome variable was the number of corrupt agents at the end of each simulation run. We also recorded when a transition from high corruption to low corruption took place. This was recorded as the moment when the number of honest agents exceeded the number of corrupt agents. Each combination of settings was run 150 times.

Table 7.2 Overview of the parameters introduced to the original model and the values in the simulation runs

Parameter introduced to the original model	Description	Values
Interactions	The number of times an agent consecutively interacts with the same agent before being matched with a different agent	1–8
Weight	Percentage of weight assigned to the most recent interaction in the agent's memory. The higher the weight, the larger its influence on the agent's estimation of encountering a corrupt agent	50, 100

Table 7.3 Overview of the corruption model's defaults setting, based on Hammond (2000)

Parameter	Description	Default value
Morality	Agent variable to reflect an inherent propensity for "doing good". Increasing levels of morality decrease the perceived payoff of corruption	Randomly distributed [0,1]
Corruption payoff	Benefit an agent receives for a successful collusive corrupt action. Corruption payoff is always the highest payoff	20
Honest payoff	Benefit that an agent receives for choosing honest actions. Both players receive the honest payoff in a mismatch	1
Reports	Number of reports required to get suspended	2 reports
Suspension term	Number of rounds an agent will be suspended from interaction with other players	4 rounds
Memory	Every agent remembers a certain number of actions chosen by the other players it interacted with in previous rounds	5 rounds
Network	Represents the number of "friends" that every agent has. Agents are randomly assigned to a network	10 agents
Population	Total number of agents in every simulation round	300 agents

We used the software NetLogo version 6.1.0 (Wilensky, 1999), building upon an earlier implementation of Hammond's original model (Lonsdale, 2017). Our model and code are published online at: http://modelingcommons.org/browse/one_model/6210.

The Shapiro–Wilk test was used to test for normality. Further analyses were performed with the Kruskal–Wallis test. A post-hoc comparison using Dunn's test with the Bonferroni adjustment was performed if the Kruskal–Wallis showed statistical differences between the groups. These conservative non-parametric methods were applied to reduce the possibility of a type I error.

Results

One-shot vs. repeated interactions

The effect of repeated interactions was compared with the one-shot interactions based on the original model. All other model parameters were kept constant throughout the simulation runs (Table 7.3). The number of corrupt agents at the end of a simulation was statistically significantly different between the different number of repeated interactions (Kruskal–Wallis test; $H = 550.96$; d.f. = 7; $p < 0.001$). The number of corrupt agents was the lowest for one-shot interactions, and the two and three repeated interactions (Figure 7.2). The scenario with three repeated interactions

Corruption and the shadow of the future 177

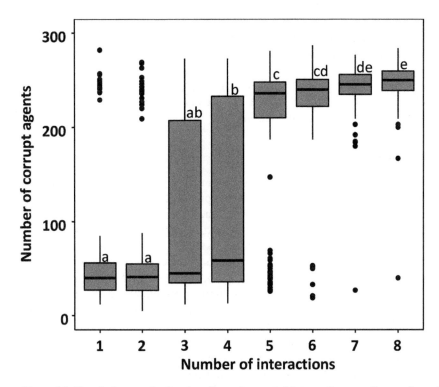

Figure 7.2 Simulation results for the effect of repeated interactions on the number of corrupt agents at the end of each simulation run. No weights to the agent's memory were assigned. For statistical comparisons, a Kruskal–Wallis test was conducted followed by a Dunn's post-hoc test. The plots bearing the same letters are not statistically significantly different at the 5% level.

showed more variation in the number of corrupt agents but it was not statistically significantly different from single- and double-shot interactions. The outliers in the one-shot and two-shot repeated interactions showed that the transition from high to low levels of corruption does not always happen; 11% ($n = 16$) of the simulation runs with one-shot interactions and 13% ($n = 20$) of the simulations with two repeated interactions did not result in a transition to low levels of corruption.

The scenarios with three and four repeated interactions showed more variation in the number of corrupt agents than the other scenarios (Figure 7.2). The majority of these runs still resulted in a transition from high to low levels of corruption, as indicated by the low median of corrupt agents (45 and 58 corrupt agents for the three repeated and four repeated scenarios respectively). For the simulation runs with three repeated interactions, 26% ($n = 39$) did not result in a transition to low levels of corruption. For four repeated interaction runs, this was 47% ($n = 71$).

The number of corrupt agents at the end of every simulation run was higher when agents repeatedly interacted for five rounds or more compared to the other scenarios (Figure 7.2). In 78% ($n = 117$) of the runs with five repeated interactions, the levels of corruption remained high and did not show a transition to low levels. Simulation runs with seven and eight repeated interactions showed the highest level of corrupt agents. A transition to low levels of corruption was observed on one occasion only for scenarios with seven and eight repeated interactions.

Weight to memory

Weights were assigned to the agents' most recent interaction to explore their effect on the transition from a high corrupt society to a low one. The higher the weight, the larger the influence of the most recent interaction on the agent's estimation of encountering a corrupt agent. The results for adding weights to the agent's memory resulted in statistically significant, but small, differences in the number of corrupt agents at the end of each simulation run (Kruskal–Wallis test; $H = 1088.5$; d.f. $= 15$; $p < 0.001$). When the weight parameter was set to 50, the results were similar to scenarios with zero weight; the number of corrupt agents was the lowest for the one-shot interactions (Figure 7.3). The three repeated interactions scenario showed more variation in the number of corrupt agents as well. The majority of those runs (55%, $n = 83$) showed a transition from high to low levels of corruption. The number of corrupt agents at the end of the simulation runs was highest for scenarios with five or more repeated interactions. Only one transition from a high level of corruption to a low level was observed for the six repeated interactions scenario, while no transition was observed for seven or eight repeated interaction scenarios.

When the weight was set to 100%, the agent will only include its most recent interaction in the decision-making for estimating the likelihood of encountering a corrupt agent and disregard all other, older memories. For these scenarios, the results look similar to the scenarios with no addition weights and 50% weights; the number of corrupt agents at the end of the simulation runs was highest for scenarios with six or more repeated interactions (Figure 7.3). Scenarios with the weight value set to 100% showed a high variability in the number of corrupt agents for the two repeated interactions. Just over half of all the simulation runs resulted in a transition from high to low corruption levels (53%, $n = 79$). Three times a transition from high levels of corruption to low levels occurred for the six repeated interactions scenario. No transition was observed for the seven or eight repeated interaction scenarios.

Time until transition

We also explored the time until transition for the different number of repeated interactions. When no weight was assigned to the agent's memory, transitions

Corruption and the shadow of the future 179

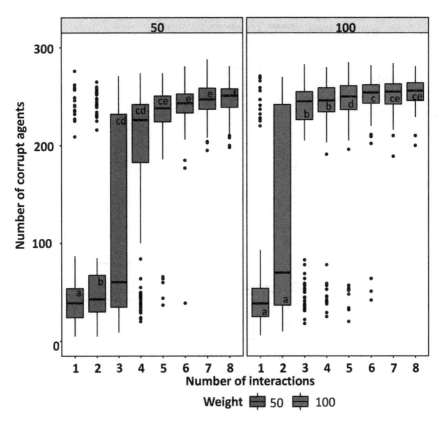

Figure 7.3 Simulation results for the effect of repeated interactions together with assigning weights to agent's memory on the number of corrupt agents at the end of each simulation run. For statistical comparisons, a Kruskal–Wallis test was conducted, followed by a Dunn's post-hoc test. The plots bearing the same letters are not statistically different at the 5% level.

from high to low levels of corruption tend to happen earlier for scenarios with one-shot interactions, followed by scenarios with two, three and four repeated interactions (Figure 7.4). The median "survival" time for a high corrupt state was 32 ticks for scenarios with one-shot interactions. For the repeated interactions, this was 71 ticks, 457 ticks and 1459 ticks for the two, three and four repeated interactions respectively (Table 7.4). For the scenarios with five or more repeated interactions not enough transitions from high to low corruption were observed to estimate a median survival time.

In scenarios with weights assigned to the agent's memory, the scenarios with two and three repeated interactions were affected most (Figure 7.5A). The median "survival" time for a high corrupt state in the two repeated interaction scenarios and a weight of 50% was 120 ticks. When the weight parameter was

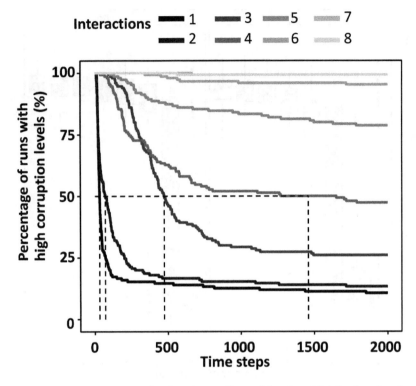

Figure 7.4 Survival curves for duration until transition from high levels to low levels of corruption for simulation runs with one and multiple repeated interactions. Each coloured line represents a different number of interactions. No weights were assigned to agent's memory. The dashed lines show the median survival time for that scenario.

Table 7.4 Summary of the median time until transition for the different scenarios.

Number of interactions	Median survival time (ticks)		
	No weight	*50 weight*	*100 weight*
1	32	33	22
2	71	120	762
3	457	1100	–
4	1459	–	–
5–8	–	–	–

Corruption and the shadow of the future 181

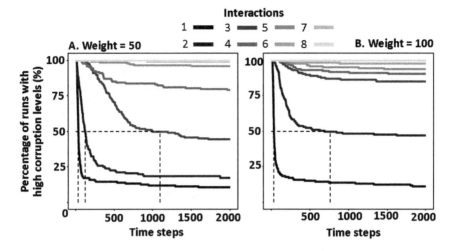

Figure 7.5 Survival curves for duration until transition from high levels to low levels of corruption for simulation runs with one and multiple repeated interactions. Each coloured line represents a different number of interactions. The left graph (A) shows scenarios with the weight parameter set to 50%; the right graph (B) has weight set to 100%. The dashed lines show the median survival time for that scenario.

set to 100%, the number of ticks increased to 762 (Table 7.4). For the three repeated interactions scenario, this was 1100 ticks for the 50% weights. When the weight parameter was set to 100%, not enough transitions occurred to estimate the median "survival" time (Figure 7.5B). The two weight values did not influence the one-shot interactions because both median survival times (respectively 33 and 22 ticks) were similar to one without the weight parameter (32 ticks).

Model sensitivity to parameter settings

To get a better understanding of how our model behaves under different parameter settings, we ran scenarios with varying parameters for corrupt payoff, honest payoff, suspension term and memory size. These results are summarized in Table 7.5. Our results for the corruption and honest payoffs and suspension terms in the one-shot scenarios were in line with the findings from Hammond (2000).

Discussion

This chapter introduces an extension of an agent-based model for corruption originally developed by Hammond (2000). The original model represents a

Table 7.5 Summary of the scenario runs with varying values of corruption payoff, honest payoff and suspension term

Parameter	One-shot interaction	Repeated interactions
Corruption payoff	Transition to low corruption less likely with increasing payoffs, but still occurs regularly. The transitions that do happen take longer	Higher corruption payoffs decrease the likelihood of a transition to low corruption even further. From six or more repeated interactions, also low payoffs do not show a transition most of the time
Honest payoff	Increased payoffs for honest behaviour always resulted in a transition to low corruption and transitions happen almost immediately	Increased payoffs for honest behaviour always resulted in a transition to low corruption, but transitions do take longer to occur with increasing numbers of repeated interactions
Suspension term	For suspension term = 3, a transition rarely occurred. When this parameter was set to 4 and 5, a transition occurred in most runs	For suspension term = 3, a transition never occurred. When set to 4, transitions only occurred in scenarios with four or fewer repeated interactions. Transitions often occurred when suspension term was set to 5 in all repeated interactions
Memory	Transition to low corruption was observed for the majority of runs for both small and large sizes of memory	Dynamics for both small and large sizes of memory start to shift from around 3–4 repeated interactions. From 5 repeated interactions onwards, a transition to low levels of corruption was not observed for the majority of runs of both small and large sizes of memory

specific instance of corruption, that of one-shot interactions. By also studying repeated interactions between agents, we could evaluate our stylized fact. Our stylized fact was based on the empirical regularity that certainty is an important component for the general deterrence of crime. Our expanded model shows that high levels of corruption were more likely to persist in scenarios with repeated interactions compared to one-shot scenarios. Transitions from high to low levels of corruption rarely occurred in scenarios with increasing number of repeated interactions. The time it took for a transition to occur also increased with increasing number of repeated interactions. We were able to reproduce our stylized fact only for the one-shot interactions and therefore found support that certainty is indeed an important component of general deterrence.

While we were able to reproduce our stylized fact, we were not able to exactly replicate Hammond's original findings. According to Hammond, all agents would eventually decide to behave honestly, until all agents within the population are honest. Our results from the one-shot interactions are similar to those described by Hammond (2000), but none of our simulation runs eventually led to a population with only honest agents. We found that some corrupt agents persisted even while the society was in a low corrupt state. Furthermore, 11% of the simulation runs did not result in a transition. It is unclear what caused these differences in results, because the original code of Hammond's model was unfortunately not published or made available elsewhere. His model was described in great detail, but still information on certain elements were missing from his description. We took NetLogo implementations of Hammond's model published by others as our starting point and were forced to make our own assumptions, for example on the exact network configuration and reporting system.

Deterrence and repeated interactions

In our model, the number of corrupt agents remained high with repeated interactions and often a transition to low levels of corruption did not happen. We interpret this result as the certainty of punishment diminishing with increasing numbers of repeated interactions. When an agent has "learned" that its partner is willing to act corruptly, the optimal decision is to act corruptly as well. Learning that your partner is corrupt removed the certainty of punishment. From that moment onwards, agents have no incentive to report their partner and no one will get suspended. The results of this are then signalled throughout society via the social networks of the agents. Agents use their own network to get a subjective estimate of how likely it is to be caught for a corrupt act in the future. If no one inside the network is suspended, then a corrupt agent has no incentive to change its strategy. The agent feels certain of encountering another corrupt agent, and believes he will not get caught for acting corruptly. Similarly, honest agents are tempted to choose the "corrupt" strategy because none of the corrupt agents inside the network are receiving punishment. Hence, repeated interactions reduce the certainty of punishment and with it the effect of general deterrence dissolves.

This chapter focused on the theory of general deterrence. The theory states that the interplay of severity, certainty and celerity of punishment can deter crime. In our model, we only varied the certainty of punishment, while the severity and celerity were held constant. Deterrence theorists argue that at least certainty of punishment is important for the deterrence of crime (Nagin, 2013; Paternoster, 2010). Empirical studies show that the effects of severity and celerity on crime are still not well understood (Nagin, 2013; Paternoster, 2010; Friesen, 2012). Therefore, we did not fully explore the interactive effects between severity and certainty. Our simulation runs do suggest that some level of severity may be required for certainty of punishment to be effective. A similar suggestion has been proposed by other researchers (Engel & Nagin, 2015; Stafford et al., 1986). The results in this chapter suggest that at least certainty plays an important role in the deterrence of corruption. Our model can be used to explore these components further to detect if a particular severity threshold is indeed needed to effectively deter corruption.

One-shots to increase certainty

Our results are in line with the current literature on behaviour in repeated interactions; cooperation becomes more likely if there is "a shadow of the future" (Axelrod, 1984; Sabater & Sierra, 2005). Cooperation, in our model, refers to two agents successfully colluding in a corrupt act. In the example of corrupt officers working together with local criminal groups, the officers routinely work together with offenders for longer periods of time. By working together, they can get a higher payoff and reduce the certainty of getting caught. To increase the perceptions of certainty of punishment, one should aim to create a setting that mimics a one-shot scenario or fewer repeated interactions. These scenarios should represent situations in which individuals do not learn about the behaviour of their partner. An example to approach this is through the introduction of rotation schemes. Abbink (2004) showed that the number of bribery attempts and their volume are cut by approximately half when an agent is paired with another random agent in every round. Staff rotation schemes have the potential to reduce levels of collusive corruption in organizational or institutional settings.

Model assumptions and improvements

The general approach in extending the model leads to two important assumptions related to the enforcement and reporting system. The strength of this general model is that these scenarios can be easily incorporated in the current model.

In our model, the model has perfect information on all agents. Although the individual agents do not keep track of the number of reports they received, the model will automatically remove a corrupt agent from the game when that agent received a certain number of reports. This assumption is related to the certainty of apprehension in deterrence theory. Our results show that, even when one has perfect information, high levels of corruption can still persist if agents repeatedly interact with one another. Only through mismatches in which an honest agent reports a corrupt agent will the system know who is corrupt. Our model can be extended further to compare with different enforcement systems – for example, a new enforcement system in which agents are randomly inspected for corrupt behaviour or by focusing only on agents who were apprehended in the past.

For simplicity, we assumed that an honest agent will always report a corrupt agent. An agent may decide not to report a corrupt agent under certain circumstances. For example, an honest agent might not blow the whistle if the reporting agent was involved in corrupt practices in the past. A possible extension would be to relate the likelihood of reporting a corrupt agent to an agent's morality, or to the number of corrupt acts in the past. These potential model extensions can provide more insights into how whistleblowing could affect levels of corruption over time.

Conclusion

This chapter improved upon the work of Hammond (2000) to test the theory of general deterrence and the role of certainty of punishment on controlling corruption in an artificial environment. Our stylized fact, that certainty of punishment is a necessary component for the general deterrence of crime, was only replicated for one-shot interactions. Repeat interactions between agents reduce the certainty of punishment and corruption is therefore more likely to persist inside the artificial society. This led us to suggest that the certainty of punishment is indeed an important component of general deterrence theory. The general framework of the model can be easily expanded to explore different elements and conditions for deterring corruption. The model presented here should be regarded as a theoretical exploration to better understand the complexity of corruption and deterrence.

References

Abbink, K. (2004). Staff rotation as an anti-corruption policy: an experimental study. *European Journal of Political Economy, 20*(4), 887–906. doi:10.1016/j.ejpoleco.2003.10.008

Axelrod, R. (1984). On the evolution of cooperation. New York: Basic Books.

Balliet, D., Mulder, L. B., & Van Lange, P. A. (2011). Reward, punishment, and cooperation: a meta-analysis. *Psychological Bulletin, 137*(4), 594. doi:10.1037/a0023489.

Banuri, S., & Eckel, C. (2012). Experiments in culture and corruption: a review. In D. Serra & L. Wantchekon (eds.), New advances in experimental research on corruption (Vol. 15, pp. 51–76). Bingley: Emerald.

Becker, G. S. (1968). Crime and punishment: an economic approach. Journal of Political Economy, *76*, 169–217.

Dal Bo, P., & Frechette, G. R. (2011). The evolution of cooperation in infinitely repeated games: experimental evidence. *American Economic Review, 101*(1), 411–429. doi:10.1257/aer.101.1.411

Di Vita, G. (2007). A note on exogenous changes in incentives for and deterrence of corruption. *European Journal of Law and Economics, 24*(1), 15–27.

Engel, C., & Nagin, D. (2015). Who is afraid of the stick? Experimentally testing the deterrent effect of sanction certainty. *Review of Behavioral Economics, 2*(4), 405–434. doi:10.1561/105.00000037

Epstein, J., & Axtell, R. (1996). Growing artificial societies: social science from the bottom up. Cambridge: Brookings Institution Press & MIT Press.

Farjam, M., Faillo, M., Sprinkhuizen-Kuyper, I., & Haselager, P. (2015). Punishment mechanisms and their effect on cooperation: a simulation study. *Journal of Artificial Societies and Social Simulation, 18*(1). doi:10.18564/jasss.2647

Friesen, L. (2012). Certainty of punishment versus severity of punishment: an experimental investigation. *Southern Economic Journal, 79*(2), 399–421. doi:10.4284/0038-4038-2011.152

Goel, R. K., & Nelson, M. A. (2005). Economic freedom versus political freedom: cross-country influences on corruption. *Australian Economic Papers, 44*(2), 121–133.

Gossner, O., & Tomala, T. (2009). Repeated games with complete information. In R. Meyers (eds.),*Encyclopedia of complexity and systems science*, pp. 7616–7630. Berlin: Springer.

Hammond, R. (2000). Endogenous transition dynamics in corruption: an agent-based computer model. Washington, DC: Center on Social and Economic Dynamics.

Kim, Y., Zhong, W., & Chun, Y. (2013). Modeling sanction choices on fraudulent benefit exchanges in public service delivery. *Journal of Artificial Societies and Social Simulation, 16*(2), doi:10.18564/jasss.2175

Kleemans, E. R., & de Poot, C. J. (2008). Criminal careers in organized crime and social opportunity structure. *European Journal of Criminology, 5*(1), 69–98. doi:10.1177/1477370807084225

Lonsdale, C. (2017). *Creating an agent-based model of Hammond's model of social inequality using netlogo.* http://charleslonsdale.co.uk/portfolio/advanced-2.php. Accessed 9 January 2019.

McMurran, M., & Ward, T. (2004). Motivating offenders to change in therapy: an organizing framework. *Legal and Criminological Psychology, 9*, 295–311. doi:10.1348/1355325041719365

Nagin, D. S. (2013). Deterrence in the twenty-first century. *Crime and Justice in America, 1975-2025, 42*, 199–263. doi:10.1086/670398

Paternoster, R. (2010). How much do we really know about criminal deterrence? *Journal of Criminal Law & Criminology, 100*(3), 765–823.

Ryan, R. M., & Deci, E. L. (2000). Self-determination theory and the facilitation of intrinsic motivation, social development, and well-being. *American Psychologist, 55*(1), 68–78. doi:10.1037//0003-066x.55.1.68

Sabater, J., & Sierra, C. (2005). Review on computational trust and reputation models. *Artificial Intelligence Review, 24*, 33–60. doi:0.1007/s10462-004-0041-5

Situngkir, H., & Khanafiah, D. (2006). Theorizing corruption through agent-based modeling. Paper presented at the 9th Joint International Conference on Information Sciences (JCIS-06).

Stafford, M. C., Gray, L. N., Menke, B. A., & Ward, D. A. (1986). Modeling the deterrent effects of punishment. *Social Psychology Quarterly, 49*(4), 338–347. doi:10.2307/2786773

Transparency International. (2019). *Corruption perception index 2018.* www.transparency.org/cpi2018. Accessed 30 January 2019.

Voinea, C. (2013). Bribery-scape: an artificial society-based simulation model of corruption's emergence and growth. *European Quarterly of Political Attitudes and Mentalities-EQPAM, 2*(1), 27–54.

Warf, B. (2016). Global geographies of corruption. *Geojournal, 81*(5), 657–669. doi:10.1007/s10708-015-9656-0

Wilensky, U. (1999). Netlogo. Evanston, IL: Center for Connected Learning and Computer-Based Modeling, Northwestern University. Retrieved from http://ccl.northwestern.edu/netlogo/

Ye, H., Tan, F., Ding, M., Jia, Y., & Chen, Y. (2011). Sympathy and punishment: evolution of cooperation in public goods game. *Journal of Artificial Societies and Social Simulation, 14*(4). Article no. 20. doi:10.18564/jasss.1805

Zausinová, J., Zoričak, M., Vološin, M., & Gazda, V. (2019). Aspects of complexity in citizen–bureaucrat corruption: an agent-based simulation model. *Journal of Economic Interaction and Coordination, 15*, 527–552. doi:10.1007/s11403-019-00240-x

8 Agent-based modeling for testing and developing theories
What did we learn?

Henk Elffers, Charlotte Gerritsen, and Daniel Birks

Our enterprise for this book: let several experienced agent-based model (ABM)-minded criminologists engage in a simulation study with the explicit goal of applying ABM to formalize, test and, where necessary, refine some component(s) of criminological theory. Doing so, we sought to better understand how the development of computational models could be used to help evaluate theoretical models commonly discussed by criminologists. In the previous six chapters, six studies with this goal have been presented. In that way, several models have been developed and several criminological theories have been put to the test, which is of course interesting in itself, but here, in this final chapter, our concern is not so much on the support or otherwise of the theories as such. Here we concentrate on the meta-question: is the methodology successful, is it a fruitful approach, what challenges does it present, how might they be met, and where is further methodological development required? Otherwise formulated: has ABM been a success as a methodology for testing and developing criminological theory?

In our introductory Chapter 1, we proposed that an ABM exercise can contribute to theory testing and development, if it conforms to the following *"ABMforCTT criteria"*, where CTT is criminological theory testing:

1. Clear criminological theory is specified.
2. A clear ABM mechanism is constructed, and it is shown which components of the theory are reflected in which rules or initial conditions.
3. A clear set of stylized facts is specified, and it is argued that they find ample support in the relevant community of criminologists.
4. In order to derive expectations from the theory through the ABM, a clear plan is specified on under what parameter settings the ABM should run and produce results. Then these results are produced, and an adequate descriptive presentation of them is given.
5. A clear statement is formulated whether or not stylized facts are reproduced by the simulated theoretical expectation.
6. The procedure of turning on and off various rules is executed in order to get insight into which components of the theory are necessary or superfluous.

Notice that step 5 of this approach is congruent but nevertheless different from the one proposed over a quarter-century ago by Axtell and Epstein (1994). They present a four-step scheme for judging whether an ABM reproduces reality on a macro-level. Their *Level 0* is that the model produces a sketch (*caricature* is their term) of *macro-level empirical findings;* level 1 represents a *qualitative agreement with empirical macro-structures*; *level 2* represents a *quantitative agreement with empirical macro-structures*; and finally *level 3* is when we get *quantitative agreement with empirical microstructures* within the agent population. Axtell and Epstein address the comparison of ABM outcomes with what can be empirically observed in real-life macro-structures. Our goal is different from theirs: it is about matching theoretical expectations, expressed as stylized facts, with the outcomes of ABMs. Nevertheless, we feel inspired by their four-step quality categorization of congruence, also for comparing ABM outcomes with theoretical expectations.

It seems fair to say that this six-step scheme of ABMforCTT criteria turned out to be rather demanding for all contributors. It may be a nice abstraction of what we hope to encounter when doing ABM research for theory testing, but reality, as we might have guessed, is more complex.

Prior to discussing these six specific criteria and our reflections regarding each of them, it would be instructive to provide a brief reiteration of the topics researched throughout this volume. In the preceding chapters quite a variety of types of crime and theories explaining their occurrence have been put to the test (Table 8.1), from burglary and theft, interpersonal violence, robbery and corruption, to all localized crime in general. Five of the six chapters investigate crimes in a spatial context, and therefore consider theories such as crime pattern theory, and use stylized facts such as crime concentration in various forms. Chapter 7, by Van Doormaal and colleagues, does not look into spatial issues, instead investigating corruption in an interpersonal context, and putting deterrence theory to the test using a stylized fact on certainty of punishment. As such, the variety of topics and therefore of ABMs is promising; indeed, it is clear our team of researchers sees lots of opportunities for applying the ABM approach to theory testing.

Specification

The first of our ABMforCTT criteria concerns the specification of theory. This initial requirement is key to our approach – it is necessary because grand criminological theories tend to be rather all-encompassing, and ABMs tend to specialize in rather concrete instantiations of the theory. So, in any given case we must derive a particular sub-theory as a special case consequence of the larger abstract, high-level theory. Moreover, as can be seen in previous chapters, not all criminological theories can boast of being sufficiently specific. For example, many chapters explore spatial and temporal crime patterns, and do so through *crime pattern theory* (CPT) (see, e.g., Andresen,

Table 8.1 Overview of research in Chapters 2–7

Chapter	Crime	Theory	Stylized fact(s)
2 Davies and Birks	Interpersonal violence	Crime generator theory (within crime pattern theory)	Crime concentration around crime generators
3 Tether et al.	All localized crime	Crime generator and attractor theory (within crime pattern theory)	Crime concentration around edges created by generators and by attractors
4 Groff and Badham	Theft	Guardianship in action	Crime concentration in places and in offenders
5 Steenbeek and Elffers	Burglary	Near repeat theory (awareness space, flag mechanism)	Occurrence of near repeat patterns
6 Araújo and Gerritsen	Robbery	Routine activity theory	Time of the day when robberies take place*
7 Van Doormaal et al.	Corruption	General deterrence theory, applied to serial two-party corruption	No deterrence without certainty of punishment

* Not a stylized fact, but an actually observed pattern within registered crime data.

2019). While this theory is decades old, no two formalizations of this theory in our volume concur completely. Even within each chapter, authors demonstrate the need to specify the rather abstractly formulated theory to make it applicable in a concrete simulation, often feeling somewhat lost when working on this task, without sufficient guidance in the literature in specifying their model. Such a critique is not unique to one particular theory. Indeed, the written and spoken models which typically define a given social science theory are, by their very nature, substantially more expressive, and thus less specific than is typically required to construct their computational equivalent. In fact, this point was further demonstrated by Van Doormaal et al. (Chapter 7), examining general deterrence theory, who struggled to reconstruct what was to be expected from the theory under the concrete case of reiterated two-party corruption. Consequently, the challenge of aligning traditional written theory with ABM was expressed as a point of concern in our workshops, and indeed reviewers reiterated this point again, when commenting on initial concepts of chapters.

Specification may have several varieties. One of them is not so problematic, the case of just selecting a subset of possible applications of a theory for investigation. So, for example, while CPT in its full generality claims to be applicable to all spatially located crime, in a given study we may just only look at interpersonal violence, or the impact of crime generators, or the presence of edge effects, and so on. That such a form of specification is necessary is not a problem for research within the empirical cycle approach. It just limits the study to subsets of all claims of CPT, and if the study corroborates this specific application of CPT, further steps will become possible, e.g., expanding the model to study property crime, or public disorder, and so on. Indeed, all chapters have – and could not have done other than that – limited their study to a specified subset of the theory under scrutiny, and applied it to a certain selection of all situations and circumstances where the theory in question would be applicable.

The second form of specification is when we need to be clearer than the available theory is on concrete behavioral aspects. CPT has put forward the relevance of crime generators. Both Davies and Birks (Chapter 2) and Tether et al. (Chapter 3) felt it necessary to be more specific on what the broad concept of a crime generator may or should contain, before it can be modeled. Both groups of authors set out to be more specific on how a crime generator works or may work. In fact, they came up with rather different specifications of different aspects of the concept. This is not necessarily a problem, as long as different specifications are at least compatible. However, it seems that the degrees of freedom authors have in specifying a broadly formulated theory are almost unlimited, which makes the accumulation of knowledge a problem. If, after reading this book, we conclude that several possible but unrelated specifications of CPT have such and such credentials, where do we find scientific progress? Notice that this is not a criticism of the individual ABM studies presented in this volume; it is a criticism of the rather unsatisfactory state of available criminological theories: too vague, too abstract, leaving room for too many unrelated specifications.

Now, lack of specificity of theories is of course not only a problem for criminologists using simulation methods, it is a point of concern for criminology as a discipline: does criminology after all have theories that deserve that name? If not, and we tend to believe that that is the case, our field is in a rather desolate state. While many theoreticians have complained that there are too many theories around and criminology needs integration of theories (e.g., Bernard & Snipes, 1996; Bruinsma, 2016; Opp, 2020), the point made here is different: what is around qua theories is not good enough to deserve the name of a theory (cf. Braithwaite, 1989). At least theories in the realm of environmental criminology are not precise enough and need first and foremost clarification. Our book has only shed light on environmental criminology theories and deterrence theory, but we venture the suggestion that vagueness of theories is a recurring problem in criminology at large. Of course, any attempt to integrate theories needs clear specification of what is supposed to be integrated.

While our efforts in this volume were directed at applying ABMs for theory testing, at the end of this book we tend to believe that this volume's first contribution to criminology is a strong exhortation to all criminologists: *stop being satisfied with vaguely formulated abstract theoretical perspectives; work towards fully specified theories.*

The second ABMforCTT criterion: constructing an ABM

All our chapters have constructed and presented a fully specified ABM of some aspect of involvement in criminal enterprises. The complete computer code, in R or in NetLogo, is made public. It is exactly when constructing an ABM that authors feel the necessity for full specification, as we have discussed in the previous section. To put it mildly, quite often theory was not exactly dictating what should be the mechanism of the behavioral decisions of individual agents, as a function of agent characteristics, previous decisions, previous experiences, and environmental influences. It is at this point that authors have come up with creative solutions to the lack of specificity of the available theory. Of course, the choices made may, nay, ought to, give rise to discussion. Indeed, the quality and usefulness of any ABM are hidden in the choices made here, and we are proud that all chapters make a clear statement on what they did. We would love to get the reactions of our readers exactly on these points, just as we have reacted to these issues among ourselves, while discussing earlier concepts. When presenting ABM research, audiences often react by suggesting complexification of the model, e.g., "you could build in separate female and male offenders." Perhaps we could, indeed we are sure we can, but generally that is not the most useful type of reaction *as yet*. Before pondering on extensions of a model, authors and readers should agree that it makes sense how the author in the presented model has implemented certain elements of the theory. Is the way Steenbeek and Elffers (Chapter 5) implemented a *near repeat* mechanism compatible with the criminological literature discussing this phenomenon? And is the way Groff and Bradham (Chapter 4) model *guardianship* in their simulation sufficiently watertight? If not, why not? What elements of a given ABM raise doubts about whether the model adequately represents the theory under test? Questions like these should be discussed and answered prior to planning any next steps in which more complex ABMs may be constructed. We believe that it is one of the contributions of an ABM approach that it makes such a discussion possible, exactly because an ABM is by its very nature completely explicit about how the various agents in a model are supposed to act and react in given circumstances. Being explicit on all concepts in a theory, and how they are interrelated, is a true contribution of the ABM approach for theory testing and development.

The authors in this volume have at least convinced each other (among them the editors), as well as the anonymous outside peer reviewers, that the presented ABMs have a leg to stand on. We would love to get critical reactions from our readers, as we believe that the field of simulation research should try not only to baffle the audience with fancy computer models, but to build on earlier simulation research in order to make progress (Townsley and Johnson, 2008).

Third criterion: stylized facts

Following Birks et al. (2012), we argue that simulation research, though artificial, can nevertheless contribute to empirical testing of theories. The key concept is the use of stylized facts, through which the empirical cycle changes in what we have called in Chapter 1 the *stylized empirical cycle*. If, in almost all applications of a certain theory, certain regularities have been observed, we propose to abstract from differences and distill such regularities as stylized facts. The argument is here: as we have seen that in (almost) all earlier applications based on a certain theory (usually not having used simulation), the stylized facts have been observed, we infer that such stylized facts should occur in all applications of a theory, in particular also in an application using an ABM implementation of that theory. The stylized fact approach overcomes the problem that we cannot find an empirical real-world parallel for the necessary abstractions the ABM must make in depicting a real-world system. In this approach we now investigate whether an ABM indeed generates the stylized facts as having been distilled from earlier research. Of course, first and likely foremost, authors must convince readers that a given phenomenon is indeed commonly and ubiquitously observed in the real world, in order to qualify as a stylized fact.

Now how did the six studies do in using this approach? Well, it did not turn out to be a very smooth ride.

In Chapter 7, Van Doormaal and colleagues report on problems concerning the identification of stylized facts, as corruption research about repeatedly cooperating actors is rather scarce, or sometimes not quite adequate, and they had to revert to a rather general-level stylized fact from deterrence theory. Their analysis is that, while deterrence theory as such is clear on an abstract level, it becomes problematic to apply it in a rather new and unexplored concrete setting.

Araújo and Gerritsen (Chapter 6) went a step further. In fact, they rejected the stylized fact approach and attempted to validate their ABM with real data. That is, their ABM was not situated in an abstract environment, but in a real one, a representation of part of the city of Lavras in Brazil. They use registered crime data from the Lavras police for comparison with their ABM-generated data. In that way, they circumvent the problem that no parallel between ABM environment and real-life environment can be found; on the contrary they make the environment identical in ABM and real life. Their yardstick of success of the ABM is whether the distribution of time of the day of crimes in their ABM and in their police data is equivalent. We notice that the distribution over time of day as found in the police data in Lavras is compatible with time of day of research elsewhere, hence we may, after all, call this a stylized fact as well.

Tether and colleagues (Chapter 3) pointed out that there is not much around in their field that can be qualified as stylized facts. They had to rely on a theory-based extension of "half of a stylized fact." Available stylized facts are rather qualitative in kind, such as "around edges, crime concentration takes place," but no clues are given about what strength, in a quantitative sense, of that concentration would count as a sign of sufficiently strong concentration, compatible with findings in the literature.

This problem of wanting a quantitative standard for the degree to which a stylized fact is present has been felt in the remaining three chapters (2, 4, and 5) as well. Notice that this is just what Axtell and Epstein (1994) had formulated as a level 2 quality standard for the congruence of ABM outcomes with theory or empirical real-life macro-observations, viz., quantitative agreement with macro-structures. While none of the sets of authors in Chapters 2, 4, and 5 had difficulties in identifying a qualitatively formulated stylized fact, they felt, just like Tether and colleagues (Chapter 3), the necessity of quantifying its strength and each of them then proposed a measure for the degree to which a stylized fact holds in their simulation. Such a yardstick then makes it possible to compare the strength of a phenomenon in a simulation to the strength of that phenomenon as found through traditional empirical observation. Axtell and Epstein did express in their 1994 paper the hope that the field of ABM by and large had passed from level 0 and 1 (*sketch of or qualitative congruence*) to the higher levels 2 and 3 (*quantitative congruence on a macro- or micro-scale*). We see here that, even over a quarter-century later, that hope was, at least for the field of criminology, rather too optimistic.

Davies and Birks (Chapter 2) demonstrated that their ABM did indeed produce concentrations of crime as had been identified by them as a relevant stylized fact. They propose the *location quotient* as the yardstick for comparison of simulated results with what has been found with traditional empirical observation. Recognizing that the literature has not yet suggested what level such a location quotient should reach in order to speak of sufficiently strong concentration, they at least have a quantitative measure of concentration now, which makes comparison over cases possible.

Groff and Badham (Chapter 4) had no problem in identifying stylized facts (called stylistic facts by them), which in their case is, again, concentration of crime, both with respect to places and with respect to offenders. They then introduce a global measure of concentration in the vein of *Lorentz curves and Gini indices*, in all cases checking what percentage of places, or offenders, is responsible for 5% of all crimes. This measure is then used to compare simulated findings with what has been found in the literature.

Steenbeek and Elffers (Chapter 5) could quote an avalanche of literature that has suggested the existence of near repeat patterns (in burglary) as the stylized fact to be used in checking their theories. They did, however, observe that no satisfactory and commonly used measure of degree of near-repeatedness exists, and they introduce one, the *Knox Sloping-down Index,* ξ, again for comparative use, recognizing that as yet no standard for a minimally to be obtained ξ exists.

Taking stock of these experiences regarding identification and use of stylized facts, the conclusion is inevitably that our introductory chapter was rather too optimistic: in many cases there were no, or no clearly recognizable, stylized facts available in the literature. Moreover, even when stylized facts could be found, the literature often just states that some phenomenon is the case, where no indication is given about the strengths of the phenomenon. This last issue was clearly the case when the stylized case was existence of "spatial concentration." In reality this challenge relates to the degree to which we require our stylized facts to be "stylized" and the degree to which we also wish them to be specific, and the tradeoff that comes between these two viewpoints. While we acknowledge that this question remains unanswered, we do notice that all chapters managed to proceed despite this challenge, providing a stylized fact or at least something that is close to a stylized fact, with which they set out for theory testing and development.

We must learn from these observations: we cannot take it for granted that stylized facts are easily available in previous studies, and as they are crucial for using ABM as an instrument, this is worrisome. It seems advisable to investigate whether stylized facts can be found in each setting, and to work on setting quantitative standards for qualitatively specified phenomena. For the science of criminology, it is again a call to concentrate on more specific theories. Indeed, if studies using the same theory nevertheless do not show results that can be put together under the heading of a stylized fact or facts, what has empirical research on these theories then produced? We tend to interpret such a state of the art as calling more for theory development than for theory testing. In that sense we might, in hindsight, conclude that we were slightly too optimistic about where criminology stands now. With that said, again this volume demonstrates how engaging with ABM, while not solving these problems, serves well to make them explicit, such that we may develop better and more rigorous means to address them as our discipline progresses.

The last three criteria for ABMforCTT

The last three criteria concern a clear plan of which parametrized set of ABMs will be run, a clear statement whether for what parameter choices stylized facts do and don't occur, and an exploration about which set of rules is sufficient to produce stylized facts, and which rules are superfluous. We refrain here from a detailed comparison of how this has turned out in the six content chapters, as these aspects really need a deep dive into the individual simulations.

We satisfy ourselves by observing that in all models authors identified some parameter settings that did produce the desired stylized fact(s) as well as parameter settings that did not result in the hoped-for stylized facts. Thus, all of the theories tested (or, more specifically, the components of them formalised) get support in some circumstances, and are rejected in others. In the strictest sense, this means that these theories are not *universal* and hence are rejected. But on the other hand, circumstances have been identified under which the theories do hold. In this respect we can conclude that the ABM approach indeed qualifies as very fruitful, making it possible to explore the bounds under which theoretical propositions produce plausible outcomes, and, in turn, refine those broader theories from which those propositions are derived.

While it could have been the case that some authors had to conclude that the theory under investigation is beyond saving, this has not occurred in the six simulation studies presented here. Indeed, all chapters continue by attempting to understand the conditions under which stylized facts do or do not emerge from theoretically derived micro-mechanisms, and come with cautious suggestions on how to amend, improve, or change the theory they test, in other to remedy its failing to generate stylized facts. Consequently, we may perhaps qualify the chapters more as theory development rather than testing enterprises.

We may interpret these mixed results, sometimes as corroboration, sometimes as rejection, as one of the strengths of our ABM for theory testing and development, as it shows the analytic capacity of the method to find out what is tenable, and what not in a theory, directing where to look for specification of theories that is so urgently wanted.

Summing up

Our enterprise of using ABM, in six different investigations, as a means for testing and developing criminological theories has resulted in the following reflections.

1. Existing criminological theories tend not to be specific; they are incompletely specified, and formulated at a too great level of abstraction to support formal testing. While this could have been observed anyway, it is exactly when building an ABM – which requires this utmost explicitness – that we realize that theories tend to be too vague, too abstract, leaving room for too many specifications. We urge the criminological community to work toward fully specified theories.
2. Building ABMs forces authors to make explicit (and hopefully transparent) choices, fully specifying how actors act and react in what circumstances. It is exactly this explicitness that invites others to try and test whether the formulated model indeed is a fair and correct representation of a theory; we do invite criminologists to criticize our efforts.
3. We had sailed on the assumption that it would generally be possible to identify in previous published research so-called "stylized facts," i.e., regularities that occur in many, if not all, previous investigations of a certain theory – against which to validate our formalized models. This turned out to be an overrating of where criminology as a science stands

currently. Quite often, it was hard or almost impossible to find stylized facts, or it was necessary to base the idea of a stylized fact on just one or a few relevant publications. We interpret this as another sign that criminology needs to work on better specified and better investigated theories. Moreover, *rebus sic stantibus*, "ABM for theory *development*" seems more to the point than "ABM for theory *testing.*"
4. There is a need for quantitative standards for the degree to which a stylized fact holds, i.e., we need to proceed to Axtell and Epstein's level 2.
5. In all chapters, authors identified parameter settings in their ABMs that produced the relevant stylized fact, as well as parameter settings in which the stylized facts did not occur. Theories, therefore, are sometimes rejected, sometimes corroborated. While this shows again that the theories under scrutiny need further elaborations and qualifications under which circumstances they hold, it also demonstrates that ABMs are helpful in exploring why and under what circumstances theories are holding and failing, and provides the means to explore how they might be refined.

Our question, "are ABMs fruitful instruments for testing and developing criminological theories?" may be answered affirmatively, but this "yes" is a much stronger "yes" for developing theories than for testing theories.

We encourage researchers to try and apply this method for developing other theories than those that have been addressed in this book.

References

Andresen, M. A. (2019). *Environmental Criminology: Evolution, Theory, and Practice.* Abingdon, Oxon: Routledge.

Axtell, R., & Epstein, J. (1994). Agent-based modeling: understanding our creations. *Bulletin of the Santa Fe Institute, 9.*

Bernard, T. J., & Snipes, J. B. (1996). Theoretical integration in criminology. *Crime and Justice, 20*, 301–348.

Birks, D., Townsley, M., & Stewart, A. (2012). Generative explanations of crime: using simulation to test criminological theory. *Criminology, 50*(1), 221–254. https://doi.org/10.1111/j.1745-9125.2011.00258.x

Braithwaite, J. (1989). The state of criminology: theoretical decay or renaissance. *Australian & New Zealand Journal of Criminology, 22*(3), 129–135.

Bruinsma, G. (2016). Proliferation of crime causation theories in an era of fragmentation: reflections on the current state of criminological theory. *European Journal of Criminology, 13*(6), 659–676.

Opp, K.-D. (2020). *Analytical Criminology. Integrating Explanations of Crime and Deviant Behavior.* Abingdon, Oxon: Routledge.

Townsley, M., & Johnson, S. (2008). The need for systematic replication and tests of validity in simulation. In: L. Liu and J. Eck (eds.) *Artificial Crime Analysis Systems: Using Computer Simulations and Geographic Information Systems* (pp. 1–18). Hershey, PA: IGI Global.

Index

anchor point 105, 113, 121–2, 127, 140
attractiveness: Crime Boosts Attractiveness CBA 116–7, 128–41; target 4–5, 23, 37, 76, 83, 105, 113–20, 127–41, 147, 164; vertex 157–9
awareness 83, 159–61; Crime-affected Awareness Space CAS 114–42; Dynamical Awareness Space DAS 114–42; space 77, 113–142, 189; of victims 160

betweenness 31–39
boost 114–7; 124–42; *see also* Attractiveness: Crime Boosts Attractiveness CBA
bounded rationality 76, 83, 174
bribes 167, 184
burglary 4–9, 49, 74–7, 104–10, 115, 119–20, 148, 188–9, 193

close to the equator 158
commuting 79–81, 93, 98; to other activities 81; to work 25, 81
comparative parameter space exploration 8
corruption 167–85, 188–9, 192, 194; collusive 173, 176, 184; drivers of 168; emergence of 169
crime attractors 13–16, 45–70, 189
crime concentration 13–4, 29, 37–9, 45, 58–9, 63–5, 85–90, 106, 188–9, 193; *see also* spatial concentration
crime generators 13–41, 45–70, 189–90
crime pattern theory (CPT) 13–19, 28, 31, 37–40, 47, 49, 72–6, 79, 82–4, 88, 113–7, 121–2, 127, 147, 188–90

density: commercial 79–84, 92–4; of people 157–60, 164; population 90; residential 79–84, 92–4
deriving expectations 4–5, 9
deterrence 74, 82–95, 98–9, 167–186; general 168–86; specific 168
distance decay 20, 50–1, 63, 66, 140

edge effects 45–67, 190
effect size 18
empirical cycle 3–6, 9, 105, 190, 192; *see also* stylized empirical cycle
endogenous transition 169

flag 114–5, 119, 141, 189

game theory 169
generative sufficiency 18
Gini coefficient 85, 193
gradient-like decay pattern 110–1
guardians 4–7, 13–21, 28, 35–41, 46, 48, 50, 65, 71–100, 113, 119–20, 147, 156–7, 189, 191; guardianship in action (GIA) 72–100, 189; guardianship intensity 71–100

Hammond model of corruption 167–185

interaction: one-shot 169–185; repeated 167–185

Knox Sloping-down Index Ksi 108, 111–2; significance corrected Ksi-sc 112, 129, 141
Knox test 107–9, 117, 141

Larceny 77–8, 167
Lavras 146–63

Index

law of crime concentration *see* crime concentration
lighting 157–8
location quotient (LQ) 18, 30

memory: decay 125–42; length/weight 172–82
mobility 41; offender mobility 149
mode of transportation 80
morality 171–184
motivated offender 20, 23, 27, 37, 45, 48, 55, 59, 71, 76, 92, 100, 113, 119, 147, 150, 159–61, 171
mugging *see* street robbery

near repeat: pattern 104–142, 189, 193; theory 189; victimization 104–142
node: activity node 14–42, 120, 149; navigational node 53, 55–6, 59; shared activity node (SAN) 15–42
null model 7, 130

observation 2–6, 39, 74, 105, 164, 168, 193
opportunity 4, 7, 45, 49, 52–6, 72–93, 99–100, 146, 160, 164

parameter: tuning 146, 160–4; sweeping 161
practical predictions 2

rational choice perspective (RCP) 72–9, 83–8; *see also* bounded rationality
rational deterrence 167
reciprocity 169
repeat victimisation 20, 104–8, 114–5, 119
requirements for theory testing 8

robbery 50, 72, 104, 109, 188–9; *see also* street robbery
routine activity (RA): 4, 6, 17, 20–8, 37–8, 42, 48, 71–89, 93, 113, 120–2, 147–150, 155–6, 162–4, 189
runs *see* spates of crime

shared activity node (SAN) *see* node
sensitivity 59, 77, 85, 88, 141, 181; *see also* comparative parameter space exploration
spates of crime 116–7, 128–139
spatial concentration 20, 58, 194; *see also* crime concentration
spatio-temporal: data 149; distribution 105; heterogeneity 115, 141; interaction 106; pattern 73, 93, 109, 120, 149
specification 4–8, 15, 21, 47, 51, 55, 80–3, 140, 188–190, 195
spree *see* spate of crime
street robbery 76, 146–65
street segments 13–42, 85, 104
structure of a theory 3
stylistic fact 84–9, 98–100, 193; *see also* stylized fact
stylized: stylized empirical cycle: 7, 192; stylized fact 6–11, 18–9, 38–40, 47, 51, 58, 108, 120, 123, 129, 138–41, 146–7, 162–4, 170, 182, 185, 187–96; stylized reality 6
suspension 167–185

temporal pattern 146–165; *see also* spatio-temporal pattern
theft 71–100, 104, 188–9
transition 167–185; time to transition 178–81; transition probability 24–27, 41
trip scheduling 24–28